EARTH
SPIRIT
LIVING

EARTH SPIRIT LIVING

BRINGING HEAVEN AND NATURE INTO YOUR HOME

Ann Marie Holmes

ATRIA BOOKS
New York London Toronto Sydney

BEYOND WORDS
PUBLISHING

ATRIA BOOKS
1230 Avenue of the Americas
New York, NY 10020

BEYOND WORDS
PUBLISHING
20827 N.W. Cornell Road, Suite 500
Hillsboro, OR 97124-9808
503-531-8700
503-531-8773 fax
www.beyondword.com

Copyright © 2006 by Ann Marie Holmes with the assistance of Adelia Kehoe

The information contained in this book is intended to be educational.
The author and publisher are in no way liable for any misuse of the information.

Editors: Jenefer Angell and Laura O. Foster
Managing editor: Henry Covi
Copy editor/proofreader: Jade Chan
Cover, interior design, and illustrations: Carol Sibley
Composition: William H. Brunson Typography Services

Library of Congress Cataloging-in-Publication Data

Holmes, Ann Marie.
    Earth spirit living: bringing heaven and nature into your home / by Ann Marie Holmes.
        p.   cm.
    Includes bibliographical references and index.
    1. Interior decoration—Psychological aspects.   I. Title.
NK2115.H514 2006
747—dc22

2006023907

ISBN-13: 978-1-58270-150-9
ISBN-10:   1-58270-150-4

First Atria Books/Beyond Words trade paperback edition January 2007

10 9 8 7 6 5 4 3 2 1

For more information about special discounts for bulk purchases, please contact Simon & Schuster Special Sales at 1-800-456-6798 or business@simonandschuster.com.

The corporate mission of Beyond Words Publishing, Inc.: *Inspire to Integrity*

To Fir Haven,
always our home in the earth

CONTENTS

PREFACE

SOME YEARS AGO, upon moving to our nature sanctuary, a vivid dream touched me deeply and opened a new path for me. In my dream, an old Native American woman leaned over a broken ceramic bowl on the ground in front of her. Tears ran down her wrinkled brown face and her hand shook as she reached out to touch the fragments of the bowl. I could sense her memories and see that the clay bowl had been lovingly shaped from the red earth and painted with age-old sacred earth designs.

Suddenly I realized that I was the old woman, inhabiting her being as my own. As I rocked back and forth, I felt her deep wails rising up from my own belly.

I had been the caretaker of this sacred bowl for my tribe, a tribe that had always lived in a covenant with the earth spirit. It was the context we lived in, like fish in water. All our actions, decisions, plans, and knowledge sprang from this relationship. And in return, the earth and the energies of nature gave us comfort, security, and wisdom. Living in this way had brought us harmony and balance for generations.

And now this broken bowl on the ground before me was the final signal that the old ways were gone, that the tribe was disintegrating and the pact with the earth was broken. I was overcome by a grief almost too deep to bear. Engulfed in a numbing despair, I suddenly heard these words:

PREFACE

"These times are different.
People are coming back together as caretakers for the earth.
The sacred bowl of life is filling again.
A new cycle is beginning."

In that moment I understood that my grief for the earth was holding me back from developing an intimate relationship with our land. I knew from these hopeful words that it was time to release the grief, to move forward, and to open once again to dwelling *in* the land—not just on it—and feeling her rhythms and sensing her daily messages.

I saw in my mind's eye that many are gathering again; a quickening, an awakening is stirring our hearts. Throughout the world, people are feeling the call to be caretakers of the sacred bowl of life, to reverently care for the life in their own bodies, in other beings, and in Earth herself.

My years of paying attention to and working with the earth have brought me a certainty that we can heal the earth—or rather, partner with the earth to heal herself and us—by paying loving attention to our own surroundings and our own properties. This book is an offering for all who long to live in ways that are healthy and harmonious, joyfully connected to Self, to others, and to our planetary home.

ACKNOWLEDGMENTS

MANY THANKS GO to Cynthia Black, editor in chief of Beyond Words Publishing, for her mentoring, her empowering counsel, and the level of engagement she encouraged.

I also want to thank the wonderful staff affiliated with Beyond Words Publishing, especially Laura O. Foster and Jenefer Angell, editors who lovingly brought more strength to the manuscript, as well as Henry Covi, Carol Sibley, and Rachel Perry.

An important acknowledgment goes to Adelia Kehoe for her commitment and belief in this book. Through her interviews with me and research sessions, she created a structure for my early text. This book could not have been done without her. I extend my gratitude and respect for all she brought to the project.

Special thanks to Quest Books, imprint of the Theosophical Publishing House, for granting permission to reprint quoted selections from *The Power of Place: Sacred Ground in Natural and Human Environments*, edited by James A. Swan.

I also want to thank my friends and colleagues Dianne Brause, Sandra Jeffs, Bob Theiss, Koka Laws, Nancy Moss, Bette Steflik, Mackenzie Petersen, Courie Hill, and New Renaissance Bookshop for their insights and help along the way. I especially want to thank Carolyn Wayland for her help in reading the manuscript at various stages. Also thanks to the many students and clients I have had the privilege of working with for their insights, stories, and commitment to their own wisdom about the earth.

ACKNOWLEDGMENTS

Many thanks to Kathleen Welsh Luiten, a gifted intuitive and mentor who has helped me root myself in the deep earth of my own being, and find my own way to express my gifts, insights, and knowledge. She embodies and mirrors a way of "physical enlightenment," a phrase she developed that reflects a way to live exquisitely and naturally with this earth we inhabit.

Many thanks to H. H. Grandmaster Professor Lin Yun Rinpoche, a man attuned deeply to his own sensitivity and a great scholar as well. At times, his presence alone would encourage me to go deeper and wider with my work. I also want to thank Khadro Crystal Chu Rinpoche for her support over the years, and thanks to all affiliated with the Yun Lin Temple.

And finally to my husband, Ray, who is part of my ground, I extend a deep gratitude for his encouragement, love, and humor, no matter what.

INTRODUCTION
How I Discovered the Invisible Side of Nature

If there is harmony in the house, there is order in the nation.
If there is order in the nation, there will be peace in the world.
—**Chinese proverb**

IN MY WORK as an earth intuitive I help people capture a quality of aliveness and beauty in their living or working environments, and create environments that are as healthy, enjoyable, and sustainable as possible. An earth intuitive is someone who is able to sense and interpret certain influences and factors on a site, similar to the way a medical intuitive senses and diagnoses medical conditions in the human body. In eighteen years of consulting, I have been called by contractors, designers, homeowners, and renters to help them with predicaments such as homes that aren't selling, a family room that the family never visits, a need for greater productivity or harmony in a work environment, the poor health of a household member, or a construction project that is inexplicably bogged down. Sometimes I'm summoned by a builder or designer looking to create something special to enliven an anonymous building or to create an environment that makes good use of beautiful or unique features. It is a particular joy to find and liberate the extraordinary in what had looked bland and uninviting.

I use my training in various arts to produce the results, but I also frequently receive practical insights from nature. In my mind's eye, I hear a voice or see pictures that give me useful background about the site and the particular challenges or potentials there. These insights from nature came as a surprise in the beginning of my practice, but I've come to realize that they are core messages for a site and now initiate consultations based on this added input.

All humans have an innate ability to pick up subtle clues from the natural world. Living in industrialized societies, we have become less attuned to nature than animals or the aboriginal human societies that still rely on this awareness for daily survival, but the potential remains within each of us.

Even now, while we may not be aware of the sensory information we gather, we often pick up more than we realize. Many times when I make a suggestion in a consultation, a client will say that he or she has always wanted to try a particular idea but dismissed it since it did not seem to have a logical reason. People are delighted to find that these hunches, feelings, and observations from the natural world are real, and that acting on them leads to more successful and satisfying results.

Nature is a powerful and willing ally. This alliance makes it possible and, with practice, even easy to create human environments that look and feel wonderful, environments that contribute simultaneously to the health and happiness of the people who use them and to the natural world around them. The focus of this book is to help you achieve these results by becoming more adept at sensing or reading the subtle energy levels around you.

Reach back into your own life and think about times you may have made some illogical changes in your environment, acting on a feeling you couldn't explain. Sally, a student, moves flower arrangements around a room until she finds the place that feels right. She has noticed that it makes a difference, creating an "ahhh" feeling when she walks into the room, and increasing the time her family spends there. Another client, Nancy, remembered moving some flowering plants in her family's backyard when she was a child because the feeling was not right where they were. (Fortunately her mother did not mind.) Many of us have had the experience of making such changes and then noticing an increased sense of satisfaction or enjoyment in that area, a greater sense of flow or balance.

INTRODUCTION

SHARING MY PASSION

This book began with a desire to share my research on the possibility of two-way communication with nature as a means of improving our living environments. Over the years I have found many ways to help my students and clients awaken their innate ability to discern and interact with the natural elements present on a site, increasing their sense of connection and alignment with the earth and allowing them to create their own unique solutions. I have also included more extensive background information to make this book accessible for the broadest range of readers.

Whether you are a professional designer or builder, urban apartment dweller, or rural homeowner, *Earth Spirit Living* contains insight that will help strengthen your connection to the natural energies in our physical space. This book will not teach you feng shui, geomancy, interior design, construction, architecture, or landscaping, but by helping you wake up your own ways of interacting with your environment, it is likely to enhance your practice of those arts. Throughout the book you will find specific tools, tips, and exercises to hone your instincts and sharpen your ability to work with the energies in your home, office, and backyard and in the world around you. In part 1, you will find an overview of the way that earth energy operates, and how and where it is found on the earth and in your neighborhood. Part 2 contains practical applications for specific situations in homes. Part 3 presents ways to include tips from the nature's energy when looking for your next home or building or remodeling a home. Lastly, part 4 comprises exercises, visualizations, and ceremonies collected together for easy access, and at the back of the book is a list of resources for those who wish to explore a topic more deeply.

Throughout this book you will find many examples from my practice and personal experience that illustrate various points. Many of the tips and examples will expand your understanding in ways that will deepen and enliven the benefits of partnership for you, no matter where you live or work. With practice, you too will learn to read the subtle influences and energy currents of the earth and to respond in ways that create healthy, sustainable buildings and landscapes. But the most important benefit you will receive from this book is simply a new awareness. If this book does its job, your life—at home and at work—will feel different. You will walk around with a new relationship to the world, a heightened awareness that need not rely on outside expertise but knows how to receive information directly from the interactive world around you.

THREE KEY PRINCIPLES FOR INTUITIVE ENVIRONMENTAL LIVING

1. **The solutions to every dilemma are inherent in each site and the humans who occupy it.** Whether the problem is a need for more comfort or productivity in the home or office or an aesthetic question of design, the most profound and satisfying answers will emerge from paying attention to the space itself, the energies present in and around it, and the needs of the people who occupy it.

2. **Using your senses (all of them!) as well as your knowledge and thinking allows you to access those solutions.** While it is useful to know good design principles and techniques, it's equally important to develop your sensitivity to the energies present on the site, regardless of whether it's a home, office, or lot. In this way, you can access the solutions that are already present along with, and sometimes within, the challenges.

    The rational and nonrational ways of knowing balance each other. The more knowledge you have, the more finely tuned your intuitive insights can be. It's a bit like playing the harp: the best results come from the blend of natural talent, complemented by knowledge (or training) and practice.

3. **Everyone can do this.** Your brain and body are already wired with the necessary equipment and ability. This sensitivity is natural to all humans. It is retrievable with information and practice, along with open-minded curiosity and a willingness to pay attention.

HOW MY KINSHIP WITH THE EARTH EVOLVED

As an introspective child growing up in a strongly intellectual, acquisition-oriented environment, I yearned to immerse myself in the physical world of nature. Though I didn't have words for it at the time, I wanted to find some way to integrate my two worlds.

My childhood home was part of a 1950s tableau, with my parents focused on creating the American Dream for our family after the tumultuous years of World War II. "Educate and develop the mind" and "create financial security" were our family's mottoes. My father, a small business owner, joined all the business associations and clubs in town and was on the city council. Our house slowly grew into a domestic jewel, the setting for many social occasions where Dad worked and schmoozed with local business owners and politicians, and a showplace to reflect the fruits of his hard labor.

Nature was an accessory to this agenda, an adornment like the furniture in the house, nicely tamed and appointed. The lawn was perfect and the bushes trimmed just so. We were the spectators in the yard, witnesses to the creative efforts of the professional gardener; I was encouraged not to interfere until, in my early twenties, our picture-perfect lifestyle ended abruptly with my parents' divorce. Along with the economic and emotional hardship came a gift: with the departure of the gardener, I assumed the role of interim garden caretaker for my mother. I thoroughly enjoyed the opportunity to be outdoors while possessions and feelings were being sifted into a new family arrangement. The split in the family fabric had dropped me with a thud to the ground. Sitting on the calming earth, weeding or digging, was my best way of coping; I felt a level of support coming from the earth that was more profound than any I had ever known.

My recently earned sociology degree and full-time job were set on the back burner as I joyfully plunged into the physical world I could grasp with my heart, senses, and now muddy hands. I started a gardening business with a friend, and for the next five years, most of my time was spent outdoors in clients' backyards, planting and tending flowers, shrubs, and trees. I talked to the plants and instinctively knew which ones to use. The business was remarkably successful almost from the beginning—a result, I believe, of the overall joy I felt in nature.

EARTH'S ETERNAL ENERGY

During this same period, I took early morning walks in our suburban neighborhood with my dog. One morning, while trekking around an old estate being developed into home sites, we discovered some loose fencing and slipped onto the grounds. Wandering through the overgrown bushes, I stumbled across an old-fashioned wooden arbor, still covered with a gnarled wisteria vine. Beneath it, a curved stone bench stood in a patch of daffodils and tulips. Tiny violets grew between the worn stepping-stones underfoot, and the sound of birdsong rang through the surrounding thickets. I began to linger in this hidden urban nature sanctuary for a blissful half hour each morning, listening to the birds and marveling at how different it was from the surrounding city streets and the rectangles of lots being drawn all around it.

In those early morning moments there were no owners or boundaries, just a sense of the oneness of all life. I never felt alone there; I had an impression of visitors, a subtle presence there with me. I imagined nature spirits still present, tending this small spot. Here was an old order still alive, a stream of vitality that seemed to fill me, body and soul, stirring up a resonance with an echo of long ago.

In the following weeks, as the new lots came closer to my oasis, I was saddened by the thought of losing this lovely little place—not just the physical beauty, but the sense of peacefulness and joy I felt there and the strong positive impact it had on my day. I longed to somehow preserve the presence in this place, to transfer its delightful energy somewhere else so that it would not be lost. I vowed that as soon as the blooms had faded I would transplant some of the bulbs to our garden. I knew that this presence inhabited more than just the flowers, but I felt that this energy—whatever it was—would recognize and respond to the invitation in my gesture.

Alas, on my next visit, a foundation for the next house had been staked out on my special spot. The newly leveled ground was a clean brown slate. All the past was gone, with no trace of a bulb or bench or pattern; a new order was imminent.

As I stood in the pale spring sunlight, a slight breeze came up, encircling me with a caress that seemed to say, "I'm still here." I sighed, relaxing as I sensed this gentle reassurance, an invitation to hold this connection inside me. The earth spirit does not go away, even when buildings cover these vital, thriving areas so abruptly.

In a flash of understanding, I knew that there are cycles and phases that return again and again, like the brass ring on the merry-go-round. The ring doesn't disappear. We can relax and trust the turning. The vitality in the earth is irrepressible, and will continue to pulse in and out of visibility like a star winking in the night sky.

NATURE BECKONS FROM FINDHORN

The next revelation came when a fellow gardener handed me a book on the Findhorn Garden in northern Scotland, and I realized that there were people who experienced nature the way I was learning to. This remarkable forty-acre garden, growing in the sands of the Findhorn Bay on the out-skirts of a small village, had been started in 1962 by a trio who believed nature, as an expression of its Creator, possessed an innate intelligence that humans could interact with to the benefit of both parties. They experi-mented, using meditation along with their gardening skills, to increase their intuitive ability to communicate with plants and other nature energies in the garden. And despite the gardeners' inexperience and the rocky, arid cold of northern Scotland, their garden produced startling results, includ-ing roses that bloomed in the snow and cabbages that weighed up to forty pounds. So remarkable were the results of this way of gardening in coopera-tion with the plant energies that people came from around the world to learn about it.

I read the book on Findhorn in one sitting, so excited to discover other people who shared my understanding of nature presence. It fulfilled the promise I had sensed: the idea that I would feel the vitality of my secret gar-den again in another place. I quickly made arrangements to visit Scotland. Seeming impossibilities melted away in a series of wonderful coincidences, and soon I was working, living, and studying with this remarkable group of people, which at the time numbered about three hundred, plus a steady stream of visitors from around the world.

During my first few months at Findhorn, a community member began telling me about the presence of life force within buildings and the effect of consciously interacting with it. For example, when she walked through a building imagining a golden breath of life circulating in the halls and rooms, she found that the moods and vitality of the people in the building visibly improved. As she said these words, I felt a shiver down to my toes and knew it was important for me to investigate the idea.

My eagerness to explore this concept led me to become the focalizer (manager) of cleaning for the Cluny Hill Hotel, a one-hundred-year-old, five-star hotel the community had recently acquired to house staff and guests. This job and department was the least favorite in the community, and the focalizer often had to beg for helpers. At first I was reluctant to become a focalizer, but Findhorn was based on the idea that every task relating to the environment is significant; therefore, approach and outlook were important. So I decided to explore the premise of cleaning with a positive attitude and to practice sprinkling a cleansing liveliness throughout the building. Another new community member joined me, initially as reluctant as I was, but with her group skills and my leadership role, we dove in. To my great surprise, I ended up learning exactly what I had hoped to and more. Our Cluny Hill cleaning team became one of the star attractions of the weekly tours. We even had a waiting list of new members wanting to join our team. International visitors and staff alike were drawn to my Saturday morning cleansing meditations, in which we prepared for the rigorous physical work by greeting and appreciating the local energies and beings, and then visualizing ourselves clearing grimy energies from the hotel with their help. People often had profound experiences during this meditation, and cleaning certainly felt easier, less draining, and more fulfilling.

Cleaning became a charismatic and popular activity at Cluny Hill. Many visitors stayed after the meditation each week to help clean the hotel, partly drawn by curiosity about the unusual accounts they were hearing from people who had practiced cleaning our way. One visitor, who insisted on working in his three-piece suit, came back to delightedly report that cleaning the men's loo (bathroom) had given him a major insight for his next big step in life. Apparently interacting with the life energy he encountered there had led to an epiphany that his health challenges would resolve and his new business would thrive if he simplified his busy life by reducing his workload and taking more time to connect with nature.

The attitude and intention with which we approached our materials and our work elicited a response from what most consider to be inanimate matter. Many of us experienced matter as alive, discovering that when approached and cleaned with a feeling of love, respect, and cooperation, everything—vacuums, beds, floors, and walls—responds in ways that many people are able to feel. An energy grime lifts in the process, and many experience vitality, better moods, and a clarity of mind.

Today Findhorn welcomes more than 14,000 visitors every year from more than seventy countries. It's a major destination worldwide for leading-edge conferences and classes on many subjects and an organizational heart of a widely diversified community, spanning dozens of holistic businesses and initiatives, all linked by a shared positive vision for humanity and the earth. The Findhorn Foundation is recognized as an official United Nations Non-Governmental Organization and has participated in UN events such as Earth Summit and Habitat 2. One major project, the Findhorn Foundation Ecovillage, received the Best Practice designation from the United Nations Centre for Human Settlements in 1998. In addition, Findhorn is now one of twelve CIFAL training centers in the world whose main focus is sustainable urbanization.

At Findhorn I found the language to describe the presence that I had instinctively felt in places like my secret garden. Concepts like devas, ley lines, and power points, which we will explore in the next chapter, gave me a more concrete understanding of the impressions my senses had picked up. I learned that this type of energy is part of a vast network that circulates the life force of the planet both inside and outside. I was able to consciously practice receiving these pulses and then strengthen and support their beneficial influence on human well-being and the well-being of the land.

Back in the United States, I began to look for ways to continue these practices, particularly in working directly with the invisible energies that can be felt and observed by their effects on the visible world. I began a cleaning business and hired people who were also interested in researching the effects of working with energy in buildings. My clients' homes were the laboratories where I conducted my research, amassing data from client feedback and our own observations. I observed the effects of my techniques on the places we cleaned or landscaped and those on my employees and me. We relaxed and blossomed in ways similar to what clients were reporting. Clients would ask, "What are you doing? When I come home after you've cleaned, it feels so good, I don't want to leave!" One client commented that he felt I'd saved his marriage. "After you leave, we can communicate so much better. It just affects the whole atmosphere of our home."

Slowly, I began to find a language to describe and explain what I was doing.

MEETING A MENTOR: FENG SHUI OPENS A DOOR

Then I discovered feng shui, an ancient form of knowledge that focuses on the balance between the logical and intangible aspects of life as a means to health and harmony. I enrolled in a class with Professor Lin Yun, leader of the Black Sect Tantric Buddhist School of Feng Shui. In a small room at San Francisco State College, I found a lively man in a black silk tunic with a crystal mala, or prayer necklace, radiating out on his chest, speaking in Chinese about the art and science of feng shui. An assistant painstakingly translated for the few Western students scattered among the Chinese students. The translator used a golf club for a pointer and lots of humor to get the different points across. My study with this master scholar who has developed, translated, and brought much of this sacred information to the West has spanned almost twenty years. The ancient wisdom that Tibetan monks and others passed to him, beginning when he was a boy in China, has brought me new ways to articulate and frame my own inclination for bringing a sense of the sacred to the walls and floors of homes and offices.

Western science recognizes that matter is 90 percent space. Feng shui and a number of other traditions—the latest being quantum physics—understand that this space between atomic particles is not empty but filled with a creative, interactive energy. This is the field of all possibility described by Indian sages and the creative void according to Western mystics like St. John of the Cross and St. Hildegarde of Bingen. The surprising results that occur when using the methods in this book are simply, in part, an effect of interacting with this field of creative energy.

I have found many different approaches and traditions within the field of feng shui, and all have their place. The Black Sect Tantric Buddhist School, with its emphasis on the balance between the logical and intangible aspects of life as seen in the use of prayer, intention, and intuition, gave me a place and a reason to regularly practice my sensitivity to nature. In this book, I share what I've learned from many sources, integrating them with my own experience and observations.

HANDS-ON EXPERIENCE WITH THE EARTH— THE ULTIMATE TEACHER

For a decade, my husband and I lived in Fir Haven, a five-acre parcel nestled in a minivalley in western Oregon. The land itself had been my greatest teacher in a ten-year research project on cocreating with nature. We used many principles and practices from our prior experiences, but above all we followed our own inner promptings, letting the life-forms guide us in creating the retreat for ourselves, for nature, and for our guests and students.

It was a gradual process, but we experienced the land waking up and rising up to meet us as we continued to pay attention to the seemingly infinite layers of communication and cooperation that nature supplies. Using ceremonies, walking our boundaries with the intention of hearing nature's needs, regularly talking and listening to trees—all these activities became the tools of our craft.

YOUR TURN TO GET YOUR HANDS IN THE DIRT

So, dear reader, this book is meant to be a support for you, a boost for your own awareness and skills to integrate your land and buildings with each other and with the support available from the whole earth. I will show you new patterns and ways to unlock incomparable ways of living in this physical world. Some of the suggestions may seem unusual and illogical. They are. But as we will discuss in the next chapter, this does not make them invalid.

Remember that it was once considered crazy to believe that the earth is round. Science is a long story of amazing improbabilities suspected by some, ridiculed by many, and then eventually proven and widely accepted. I invite you to keep an open mind and take this adventure with me, trying out new ideas and exercises and judging the results for yourself.

Don't be discouraged if you find yourself skeptical of some of these principles. Modern socialization often conditions us to distrust ideas that depart from our education. However, I've seen many disbelievers have a change of heart with even small adjustments to their living environments.

When Mary hired me to help create more ease in the oddly angled rooms of her new home, her husband, a builder, was skeptical and wary. "It was tough for me in a couple of ways," he told me later. "Those rooms were so uncomfortable that I couldn't stand being in them for more than a couple of minutes. But to me, 'intuitive consultant' meant airy-fairy stuff, and I knew this was a serious problem. So on one hand, I was afraid you couldn't help, and on the other hand, I dreaded the more expensive, conventional alternative." He observed our consultation behind folded arms from the corner of their sofa, but his frown faded as he heard the practical nature of the solutions I proposed. We balanced the energy with easy changes like moving furniture and adding certain color touches, and he was so delighted with the results that he asked me to help him with his office.

For renters and homeowners, the benefits of attuning to the energies that surround us may include

- a more comfortable experience in your home;
- more harmonious relationships;
- better health;
- improved prosperity.

For business owners, benefits may include

- more effectiveness in your work;
- a more productive and enjoyable experience for employees;
- a better ability to attract and maintain satisfied customers.

For building professionals, designing and building cooperatively with these energies may result in

◈ a mutually beneficial symbiosis with the natural environment;

◈ expansion of your beliefs about the role of nature;

◈ the ability to create healthy, sustainable homes and offices that are cost-effective to build and maintain;

◈ a smoother (less costly, less frustrating, less injury-prone) construction process;

◈ reduced stress and more fun;

◈ a better reputation as creators of healthy, desirable homes and offices;

◈ increased income due partly to delighted clients.

In my experience, many people may sense a connection with earth energies but aren't necessarily aware of what they're picking up. Since we weren't taught in modern culture to recognize this right-brained information as valid, it often goes unnoticed. We fail to give credibility to these passing fancies or illogical bits of information until we are trained to recognize them. My focus in this book is to give you the background information along with the practical tips and exercises that will allow you to recognize and retrieve these impressions and to use them in your life in tangible ways.

Some of the potential benefits of using your sensitivity may include

◈ making better decisions because of the broader range of information you are taking in;

◈ gaining more clarity about your fondest wishes and deepest aspirations, and thus a better chance to fulfill them;

◈ creating better results by tapping into the subtler aspects and patterns of the site as you build or remodel;

◈ healthier, calmer living conditions in your home;

◈ enhancing work situations and personal relationships;

living more fully and tapping into a level of joy and vitality that can foster better results and a new awareness of the invisible aspects of nature in your life.

Perhaps the biggest payoff is that Earth herself benefits. As more people create buildings in resonance with their surroundings, or reweave the energy of existing structures and landscaping, the world benefits. A wiser, more creative use of natural resources is one result, along with actual cooperation from the nature energies themselves. Small acts of acknowledgment and connection—growing a garden, paying attention to how we reroute water and how we place structures on the land, talking to and appreciating the trees, rocks, and flowers—contribute to a healthy earth and bring health and abundance to humans as well. As we tend and love our patches of earth at home, the earth spirit thrives, responding to our attention and care. The ripple effect radiates throughout the web of life, extending even to the improvement of the world's climate. Recognizing the earth spirit as a partner in our dwellings is a practical way of supporting world peace for the human community.

PART ONE
The Big Picture: Getting the Lay of the Land

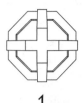

1

EARTH PARTNERSHIP

So do you not feel that, buried deep within each and every one of us, there is an instinctive, heartfelt awareness that provides—if we allow it—the most reliable guide as to whether or not our awareness, this wisdom of the heart, may be no more than a faint memory of a distant harmony rustling like a breeze through the leaves, yet sufficient to remind us that the earth is unique and that we have a duty to care for it?

—Charles, HRH The Prince of Wales

THE EARTH IS ALIVE AND INTERACTING WITH US EVERY DAY

AT ITS CORE, this is a book about relationship. You and I are in constant relationship with earth elements and energies that are alive, intelligent, and interactive. Throughout each day, we are affected by (and have an effect on) a relationship that many don't even realize exists. There are tremendous benefits to be gained, by us and by life on our planet, when we are aware of this relationship and participate in it with awareness and intention.

Remember how the world changed when you learned to read? Suddenly you could look at a page covered with black marks and know a story. To remember what life was like before you could read, just look at a Chinese or Greek newspaper. A whole new world of information and emotion opens up when you know the language.

When an Australian Aborigine finds water in the desert without the help of technology or visual clues, he or she is reading the landscape in a way that our modern culture has largely forgotten. Aboriginal trackers can successfully locate people by following tracks that are many months old. They do this partly by using instinctual, intuitive senses to follow subtle clues in the environment. It is less obvious but equally important to look for these clues in everyday activities like buying land, site planning, construction, and creating healthy living environments in our homes and apartments.

When you are building, purchasing land, or moving into a new apartment, house, or office, there are so many issues to consider. Finances, timelines, color choices and other design preferences, and local codes and regulations tend to dominate our attention, but so much can be gained by recognizing that you are also entering into a relationship with the earth on and around your lot. In the complex web of influences already in place, your plans, ideas, actions, and energy are now part of this interactive mix. Like all good relationships, this one requires attentiveness and respect, time for bonding, and good dialogue.

(RE)LEARNING EARTH'S LANGUAGE: A QUESTION OF BALANCE

Experienced farmers and sailors develop an instinctive feel for the elements. They learn to decipher subtle nuances of the weather, the soil, and the sea. Informed by years of experience, veteran fishermen read the water using acutely developed senses and reflexes. Our ancestors lived more closely with nature, and children have that connection until they unlearn it through socialization.

Our orientation in this culture has been strongly weighted toward logical, linear ways of knowing the world, but as anyone who follows sports can tell you, in the heat of a play you cannot rely on strategy alone. Feelings and intuition are as important as knowledge and equipment. When the chips are down, it's often instinct that carries the day.

In the wake of the December 2004 tsunami, we saw dramatic examples of the effectiveness of this blend of sensory knowledge, alert observation, and intuition. Observers noted that although there were tens of thousands of human victims, very few animals seemed to have perished, even in the waterfront game reserves. The animals had somehow sensed the coming catastrophe and headed for high ground. There were stories of elephants trumpeting and restless for days, growing increasingly distressed when their alarm was unheeded, and finally breaking their chains and heading for safe territory hours before disaster struck. People noticed dogs running toward the hills before the giant waves arrived.[2]

While some concluded that animals have acute sensitivities that humans lack, others recognized that humans also have the capacity to register some of the same information. CBS News observed that during the tsunami's mass destruction, some of the most astonishing stories of survival were among those of descendents of ancient tribes. The Moken tribe on Thailand's South Surin Island lost only one of its two hundred members because several elders had detected unusual movements in the Bay of Bengal and warned villagers to evacuate immediately to a nearby hilltop.[3]

In the Bay of Bengal, authorities feared the worst for the nearly extinct tribes on the hard-hit Nicobar and Andaman group of islands that took days for relief workers to penetrate. But the *India Daily* reported in amazement, "While there is massive devastation, the primitive tribes are relatively unaffected, even though most of them lived close by the ocean. The Nicobarese [the most modernized tribe] have lost the most. Very few of them sensed the incoming tsunami. But the more primitive tribes moved out to the higher grounds days before the catastrophe. According to some of the tribal leaders, [the] earth communicates to them. And this time they could view and hear the tsunami coming and they moved to higher grounds way before the tsunami came and earthquake shattered the islands."

Narumon Arunothai, a social scientist at Chulalongkorn University in Bangkok who has long studied the Moken, hopes the younger generation will be inspired by their elders' survival skills. "People are safe from tsunamis because these elders know the sea. We should encourage the young to have pride in their wisdom before these skills are lost," she said.[4]

We have much to learn from the cultures in which these ways of knowing the world have been continuously practiced for thousands of years. Eons of handed-down training and practice, combined with a worldview that recognizes such knowledge is possible, counts for a lot.

At the same time, this way of knowing the world is natural to us. Our brains contain the same kind of magnetic particles found in the brains of homing pigeons, bees, salmon, and many migrating species. Scientists speculate that these particles allow these species to orient themselves on the planet.[5] Elizabeth Rauscher is a research physicist who, along with her colleagues, has been able to accurately predict a number of volcanic eruptions and earthquakes by measuring oscillations in earth's electromagnetic field. She has found that some of the frequencies associated with the earth are very similar to human brain wave frequencies. In fact, she and her colleagues have noted changes in human brain wave patterns corresponding to local seismic activity and solar winds. "So when people say they 'feel' an impending quake or weather change," she said, "they may be at least partly reacting to actual physical signals, as well as parapsychological perception."[6]

There is so much untapped potential available even to those of us in the modern world who choose to pay attention, open our minds, and develop our capabilities. Partnering with nature is an investment that can yield the seemingly miraculous results that students, clients, colleagues, and I see on a regular basis. Symantha, a longtime client, is a partner in a real estate investment firm. Her role in the business is to utilize her "intuitive tool bag," as she calls it, to assess each site. She reported that sometimes she is able to locate areas of concern, such those with as moisture or dryness, more quickly than her contractor partner, who uses logical, technical methods. She and her partner find that by integrating both sides of their awareness (intuitive-sensory and intellectual-technological), better results are accomplished.

This is the inner game of building and design. Your gut feelings, the subtle sensations, images, or knowings that arise in you as you walk onto a site, are as essential as any tool. The most successful projects are the ones that incorporate this balance.

The Great Wall of China stands as a splendid example of the partnership approach to design and building. Still intact after thousands of years, this huge, ancient construction meanders with the earth's curves. It aims to fit in rather than stamp an artificial boundary on top of the earth. Its age and beauty make it a compelling argument for the enduring success of building methods that include awareness of and conscious cooperation with the energies of nature.

SENSITIVITY IS NORMAL—AND MUCH NEEDED

Neuroscientists estimate that we currently use 8 to 12 percent of our brain's capacity. They speculate that what we consider "normal" is a hazy state of semiconsciousness, compared to what we are capable of. Dramatic or seemingly miraculous achievements like aboriginal tracking abilities are examples of how we use more of our capacity by tapping into heightened sensory awareness and other modes of knowing.

Why does this matter to you and me? Because everything in the natural world holds information for us—information that can help us live healthier, happier, more successful lives. And a great way to access this information is through the partnership of our physical senses and our intuition.

In various ways, life seems to be urging us to be more aware of this partner, to open to new ways of living with the earth now. For instance, storms seem to be increasing in intensity and strength, and extreme changes in natural phenomena tend to attract our attention. A key to living successfully through these changes is to continually open to our sensory, intuitive experience with the earth. Elders from many indigenous and other spiritual traditions have been sharing with the world messages treasured in their cultural archives for hundreds of years to provide encouragement and guidance about being on the earth at this particularly challenging point in history. Tribal leaders of earth-savvy indigenous groups and ancient spiritual traditions around the world, including the Hopi, Tibetans, Mayans, the Lakota, Africans, and Australians, have expressed a common theme in recent decades: the earth is at a turning point where we may see tremendous changes in our physical and social reality. Across the board, in their own various ways, they are urging the people of the world to develop their sensitivity to the life force in plants, animals, water, rocks, soil, and other earth energies around them. These elements are alive and interactive, say the elders, and by relating to them with appreciation, curiosity, and respect, we can gain powerful allies. They are urging us to recognize that our lives depend on them, and that human attitudes and actions do affect the earth in intangible, energetic ways as well as on the physical level. Ancients from many cultures used to read the weather as an indication of human affairs, which is an interesting thought that some research in quantum physics appears to support.[7,8,9]

The good news is that these abilities can be reclaimed and cultivated even in the modern world. We do not have to be born in the Australian outback or into a remote tribe to hear and respond to the information in our environment. We can begin right where we are and learn directly from nature by paying loving attention to our own surroundings. As we take small steps to connect and cooperate with nature on our land, there is a corresponding calming of the intensity around us. The microcosm of balance affects the macrocosm.

When you feel the wind brushing across your face, consider that it may be a message, a subtle nuance that is still real in the language of nature. Or notice birds, with their songs and movements, as messengers from the subtle energies around you. In each case, to decode the message, notice the feelings that arise in you. Do you feel welcomed? Warned? Alerted to pay attention to something else?

Dan Kehoe is a Washington, DC, builder with no special training in environmental sensitivity, a former high school football player, and a World War II veteran. His previous exposure to nature had been occasional picnics and a week at the shore each summer. But he found that the same instincts that had kept him safe during the war and on the tough streets of his childhood gave him a competitive edge in his construction business. From job estimates to sizing up prospective partners, clients, and locations, his success has been based on a combination of careful research and following his hunches.

In the 1960s, when he embarked on a boldly speculative venture to build large apartment complexes in rural areas around metropolitan DC, he based his decisions on a combination of intuition and rational homework. "I watched the population trends, studying where the Beltway was going to be built and then logically looking for attractive land in those areas," he said. "But when it came down to several different parcels, I slowly walked around on each one, looking and listening with my instinct as well as my mind. In the end, I had a good gut feeling on one particular piece of property which also met all the rational criteria. But it was such a huge risk that I felt hesitant until I noticed this little chickadee following me around the property chirping in this really friendly way. Somehow I knew it was nature's sign that this piece of land was a winner."

He and his partners purchased the property and went on to build an extremely successful 230-unit garden apartment complex, innovatively designed to keep the peaceful, natural feel of the surrounding area. Several of his projects have won design awards for the quality of life the projects provide for tenants.

Having recognized and acknowledged the importance of nature as a partner in his ventures, Dan often finds a chickadee flitting near him as he inspects land for future projects. He looks for this messenger from nature each time he considers developing a major piece of property.

Tuning in to the language of nature can change the quality of your life and work at least as profoundly as learning to read. By increasing our awareness and sensitivity to the world around us, we begin to make more informed choices, thus creating more satisfying outcomes.

CLEARING THE DECKS AND TUNING IN TO THE LANGUAGE OF NATURE

Developing greater sensitivity requires openness to life and to new information. Many of us have old concepts that cause rigidity in our thinking, diminishing our receptivity to new data. Let's sweep out a few common misconceptions that may get in the way of a vibrant, living relationship with nature.

MYTH

The earth spirit is gone when the natural forms and patterns are replaced by human development and activity. This often feels true when, for example, a new shopping center replaces a favorite woodland or meadow.

FACT

Concrete-covered nature needs love too. The natural patterns on the surface are gone, but the earth's chi is still present. While it is often slumbering deeper in the earth in these areas, nevertheless, the embers are still there and, given attention, nature will respond with balance. It's important to recognize and connect with the life force that remains in the areas that have been paved or otherwise repatterned with human development. The earth, even in those paved-over places, still communicates with us and is still ready and capable of partnering with us to restore balance.

As you work with your home, property, or neighborhood, you will often find that you experience healing right along with your environment. Any gardener can tell you about the therapeutic value of working in a garden.

Despite any appearances to the contrary, life is communicating with us everywhere all the time. What will you notice when you approach life with this view?

MYTH

It takes massive action and money to create a healthy world—way beyond what you or I can do. When we focus on the huge problems in the environment caused by pollution, they can seem overwhelming.

FACT

The only Earth you need to—or truly can—save is the one in your own yard or neighborhood. Touching any part of the web of life affects the entire web. Suzy restored her garden to an oasis of color with sensuous curves, lush plants, and whimsy. Her loving touch encouraged the embers of the life force to reignite in her yard. Neighbors on their walks began to stop to observe and feel the beauty and life force beaming from it. After some months, Suzy noticed new gardens sprouting in her neighborhood with the same attention to beauty as that in her own. The embers of life force were igniting and spreading bit by bit.

MYTH

Bigger is better. It's easy to believe that the larger a project or organization is, the more impact it has.

FACT

Every small act with nature counts. The richness and full power of the earth exists everywhere. The fullness of a giant oak or sequoia is completely contained within a small seed. The boisterous dandelions springing up through a city sidewalk or the few plants lovingly placed in the soil between the curb and sidewalk embody a strong spot of life force. Like concentrated drops of liquid fertilizer, these small spots are potent sources of healthy growth that have an effect on their surroundings. Small touches made with awareness and intention have a surprising and mysterious effect on human life and on the natural world, supporting human needs such as prosperity, health, and thriving relationships.

It is often more powerful to work on the microcosmic level, the tiny worlds within worlds. What we do in a smaller, finite, clear pattern may often have a greater effect than a larger, more diffuse effort. And this change does ripple out. In my experience, a single building on a single lot, when designed and built with awareness, intuition, and goodwill, can have a positive effect on an entire neighborhood. A pattern of balance with the life force on one lot radiates out to others, attracting more balance for the area, improving neighbor relations, and opening doors for abundance on many levels for land and humans.

And who knows how far those reverberations continue? After all, Mahatma Gandhi helped his country win freedom from a world power in a startlingly short time by starting with small, practical, local actions.

MYTH

It's may be impossible for modern humans to understand nature. If we only focus on the noise and hubbub of modern life, it can feel like nature is so suppressed that we can never truly connect.

FACT

The more intention you have to learn nature's language, the more she will communicate with you. The necessary instincts are natural to us. The expert instructors at Tom Brown, Jr.'s wilderness programs regularly turn average city dwellers into skilled trackers who can find food and shelter without any help from modern civilization. Just having a clear intention is enough most of the time. Nature generally responds with the eagerness of a puppy, often surprising us with how easy it is to see the immediate results of our efforts. There are exceptions to this in areas where real trauma has occurred in nature, but even there a common-sense approach is useful. We will discuss this in more detail in chapter 3.

Generally speaking, the lighter your approach, the more you are likely to pick up nature's messages. Have fun with this! Follow what feels good. Mark, a former student, discovered that he didn't have to go out and hike in a wilderness area to get in touch with nature. He was amazed to find a similar effect just from sitting on his deck in the city. "When you first talked about it I thought, 'No way. I can't feel a thing out here with all the traffic noise and my work waiting at my desk,'" he said. "But then I started to notice that when I just go and sit there, without another agenda, the birds seem to come around more and the answers I've been seeking just pop into my mind. Sometimes it takes a while, even an hour or so, but I do get there."

One architect accustomed to using her intuition with nature reported that when she is drawing up a blueprint, she holds a clear intention to connect with the larger nature patterns on the site, and to create a design conducive to balance for both building and land. After she feels connected, she then imagines her pen is like a wand, feeling and responding to the flows of energy on the site, and finds that her inspirations for drawing and design seem to "fly off the paper."

The hard part for most of us is stepping away from our busy schedules and taking time to breathe slowly and just notice the natural world around us—animals, plants, rocks, and sky. It may feel like wasting time, but it's one of the most powerful and productive things we can do.

I invite you to open up to new ways of knowing, and to consider the possibility that life/nature has healing capacities beyond anything your linear mind can conceive.

RENEWING THE PARTNERSHIP

The basic principles, like the patterns of nature, are interconnected and overlapping. In the first issue of her newsletter *Building with Nature*, architect Carol Venolia put it this way:

Though we are trained in compartmentalized thinking, we all have within us the spark of life, which embodies tremendous wisdom. Life knows what it needs; it knows what feels good and nourishing . . . That pulse connects us with all of life and the planet; it knows better than any experts or books what kind of places we need to create in order to flourish. [To begin, we can simply] take a deep breath, tune in to our physical senses, listen to our instincts, say hello to the vitality within [and learn to] recognize vitality when it occurs around us.[10]

While these earth energies are subtle, especially compared to the sensory bombardment of our fast-paced, industrialized culture, humans still retain the potential for sensing life energies. They can be restored and developed, like the ability to ride a bike or learn foreign languages. Real mastery takes time, but you can develop a surprising level of proficiency fairly easily with the power of your intention and persistent practice. As you begin to recognize the language of nature, you will make the startling discovery that it is always communicating with you.

2

THE EARTH ENERGY WEB

Geomancy operates within a worldview that regards the earth as a conscious living being . . .
The earth's body is perceived of as more than a hunk of inanimate matter—it is interlaced
with flowing veins of biomagnetic energy.[1]

—Richard Feather Anderson

NATURE LOVES A PATTERN, and it is through patterns that she accomplishes everything she does. Whether it's the ordered dance of stars, the migration of birds, the mysteries of DNA, or the intricacies of fractals, nature is endlessly patterning.

One of earth's important patterns is the grid of invisible energy currents. Often detectable by their faint electromagnetic fields, these energy streams form a web of power points, ley lines, and vortexes that encircle the planet.

Ancients all around the world were aware of these patterns; megalithic monuments on several continents stand as testaments to the knowledge of these energies and their effects on harvest and health. The large stones of many sacred sites, still standing after thousands of years, are specifically placed to gather and strengthen the life force in these powerful earth energy zones. In *The New View over Atlantis*, John Michell wrote that these sites were often determined by signals and portents from nature—including dreams and other sensory indications of the increased energy movement—and then marked with stone constructions to maximize the positive effects on humans and land.[2]

James Swan noted in *The Power of Place* that power points, or areas of increased life force, "have been the central focus of cultural values and meaning, as well as the physical anchors for myths, ceremonies, and rituals."[3] Stonehenge and the Egyptian pyramids are well-known examples. Stonehenge is believed to date from 2,000 BC, and scientists have discovered that its four circles of erect sandstone blocks are arranged in carefully calibrated alignment with our sun and moon as well as the earth energies beneath them.

Many of the great cathedrals of Europe are also located on power points. In *The Mysteries of Chartres Cathedral*, Louis Charpentier asserted that the Gothic cathedral locations were strategically chosen to make use of these areas of strong natural energy, and engineered to accumulate and amplify the positive effects of these energy currents. Chartres Cathedral, for example, is located above the intersection of two strong subterranean energy streams, and for centuries had been a site of pilgrimage and reverence even for Christians. Charpentier wrote that "the earth there has a particular quality" that enables people to achieve an unusual state of inspiration and spiritual connection.[4]

Like other cathedrals built under the direction of the mysterious Knights Templar, Chartres has precise mathematical proportions found in ancient pyramids and temples. Features like flying buttresses greatly improve the energy-amplifying qualities of the structure, creating a dynamic tension in the stone so resonant and balanced that the whole building has been compared to a well-tuned musical instrument. To this day, visitors feel the effect, describing palpable feelings of deep peace, inspiration, and well-being gained there.

Geomancy is the science of sensing these energies and designing and building in harmony with them. Feng shui, which has gained popularity over the past decade, is but one form. The science itself has been used all over the world for centuries. Tribal customs throughout the Americas and Africa include traditional ways of choosing construction sites, orienting buildings, and placing various rooms and functions within the home. James Swan, again in *The Power of Place*, mentioned that "the Salish tribe has a term, *skalaltitude*, which refers to a sacred state of mind when all things are in balance and the spiritual dimensions of life seem to predominate consciousness, which results in 'magic and beauty being everywhere.'"[5]

WHAT IS THIS ENERGY WEB?

To understand earth's energy grid, it is useful to think of electricity. We talk about the electrical power grid, a pattern that connects us to light and power. In England, the electrical outlets in the house are called power points, which is precisely what those who study earth energy call areas of strong energy concentration. The wiring in the house connects the power points to promote good circulation and an even balance of light and energy.

Nature, too, has an invisible system of energy that flows within and around Earth in a huge and complex pattern (Fig. 1).[6] Like the electricity pulsing through our structures, we cannot see or touch the vitality and power in the earth energy, but we do feel the effects of its movement. There are two primary reasons that it is important to become aware of this energetic grid:

◈ **It affects us physically and emotionally:** Knowledge and an ability to recognize Earth's energy allows us to function in harmony with it, which brings better health, clearer thinking, more tranquil emotions, and a sense of well-being. It also contributes to more cost-effective and successful living, construction, and landscaping experiences.

◈ **It affects the health and productivity of humans and of nature as well:** When we interact with the energy grid, we are affecting the health of our planet on a number of levels. It is important to preserve these lines, swirls, and spots whenever possible for best circulation of the life force on the planet.

In *Surfing the Himalayas* Frederick Lenz tells a fascinating account of his adventures in the mountains of Nepal. Like a real-life Karate Kid, his quest to become a master snowboarder led him to a monk who taught him much more than just snowboarding techniques. In the following passage, his teacher, Master Fwap, has brought him to a special cave high on the mountain

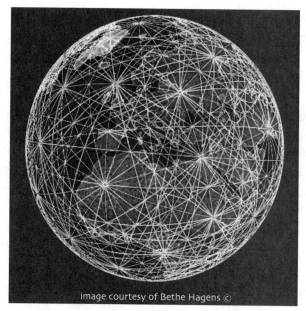

image courtesy of Bethe Hagens ©

Figure 1

to discuss certain spiritual principles. Master Fwap explains why he has brought Lenz to this particular place for their talk:

> There are physical locations on the earth where it is easier to meditate, to study, to learn, to make corporate decisions, to fight battles, and to see into other worlds. What gives a physical location a particular type of power are the dimensional lines that run through it . . .
>
> Think of the earth as being superimposed on a grid of horizontal lines. Dimensional space and locations are superimposed over horizontal grids of light and energy. These grids are points of egress-points that open into other dimensional realities in which there is much more prana (life force or energy) available . . .
>
> There are specific energy lines running through the earth that open up to artistic and musical dimensions. If a composer or an artist lives and works in a place that has those

types of lines running through it, then it will be easier for him to create great works of art or music.

While most people may not consciously know about energy lines, grid planes, interdimensional vortexes, and how all this works, they unconsciously use their intuition, which I call the second attention, to find and use "just right" locations where they need them to achieve success.[7]

Upon walking into a spacious home for sale, Russ and Barbara knew in the first few minutes that it was the house for them. When they moved in, Russ, a longtime fine-oil painter, found that he had tapped into a strong creative field that pushed his work in a totally new direction. However, after a few months, Barbara called for a consult because she found that he never wanted to leave his studio and she worried about his health. When I walked onto the site, I could sense that his studio was directly on top of one of these points of egress; the room seemed brighter, clearer, and extremely stimulating. I experienced many images of swirls and colors in the studio. After suggesting a lot of ways to anchor the energy with rugs, plants, and stones to balance the magnificent earth energy streaming through the place, I also recommended that Russ take regular breaks. Now Russ and Barbara are learning to coexist with the power point in their home.

MAJOR COMPONENTS OF THE ENERGY WEB

POWER POINTS

Power points are concentrated areas where strong earth or cosmic energy comes to the surface. In these spots, vegetation grows better, animals prosper, weather patterns are more diverse, and humans have better health or find inspiration. These centers act as nodes or hubs for the currents of electromagnetic energy—ley lines—that crisscross our planet. Mounds or mountains often mark power points, as do sacred groves of trees or natural springs. Many are familiar to us: Stonehenge, Lourdes, Niagara Falls, Mount Fuji, the great pyramids of Egypt, Easter Island, and the Grand Canyon. (On the Internet, www.SacredSites.com has extensive list of sites around the world.) Strong power points are often preserved in parks such as Yellowstone and Yosemite and other nature reserves as well as in ancient temples and cathedrals around the world.

Many report that after visiting these sites they have a greater sense of calm and relaxation. The vitality of these places interacts with the body's nervous system, supporting clarity of mind and sweeping away tensions. One can come back to face life with a new perspective, ready to tackle life's next challenge.

Power spots can also be small and not necessarily famous. Jim, a student, found this out for himself. He reported,

> After taking Ann Marie's training, I decided to find a special spot in nature, a power spot for me. I sat and opened an attunement with nature, asking to be shown such a spot nearby. Soon after, on a walk I take regularly in our big city park, I noticed a small parking area and an almost hidden path down to the creek. As I made my way down the crude steps, the leaves from the trees rustled as a gentle wind moved through the branches. It felt like a welcome. I felt drawn to sit on an earthen wall by the creek and close my eyes. After a bit of time, a sense of safety and relaxation washed over me, almost like I was sitting in a favorite cathedral. This was my spot. I return to the creek area regularly to get recharged by nature.

I first heard of the web of earth energy while residing at the Findhorn Community. During that time, many people mentioned that this place was on a power point in the earth's grid. With the concentration of life force in this spot, people often experience accelerated growth. Findhorn was well known for the unusual health, size, and vigor of its vegetables and flowers. In my instance, the growth was soul growth—a deepening of perception and understanding. I found the blueprint for my life's work while living on a power point; my life since has been a gathering of the tools to bring this blueprint to life.

LEY LINES

Ley lines are circuits, or energy pathways, that connect these concentrated energy centers, similar to the way the nervous system of the human body is interconnected. In their natural state, ley lines flow in curves following the contours of the landscape. Like high-voltage electrical lines, ley lines connect power points around the globe in the original worldwide web. These lines have a magnetic quality, and some believe birds, mammals, and bacteria use them to migrate across long distances.

Traditional knowledge about the nature or shape of ley lines, confirmed by modern measurement, typically shows these underground magnetic currents flowing in gently curving lines, like the line traced by China's Great Wall. Yet in some places, including the English countryside and the plains of South America, the ley lines are arrow-straight, connecting a series of standing stones, churches, and other ancient earthworks. Both types of lines—straight and curving—have been confirmed by devices like the Squid Magnetometer, two superconductors separated by thin insulating layers that may be configured to detect even very small magnetic fields, or the more portable magnetic field detector patented by Elizabeth Rauscher and William Van Bise.[8]

So how can earth energies be flowing in wavy lines in some areas and in straight lines in other places? John Michell speculates that the prehistoric engineers who built the monuments along the straight paths had a profound knowledge of how to work with the magnetic energies of the ley lines. They used their stone circles and other sacred sites like an acupuncturist uses needles to affect human energy flows, thus altering the naturally wavy underground currents to run in straight courses along the route of their constructions.[9]

In our modern living today, you can benefit from more awareness of this invisible web in your homes and offices. One Western geomancer was startled when a retired engineer called for a consultation on his property in the Rocky Mountains. He wanted to site his new home to take advantage of the breathtaking mountain views, but also have it in alignment with the local energy currents and ley lines. "You look surprised that I know about these energies," he said with a laugh. "Well, I know about the earth's energy grid from working on missiles. We couldn't figure out what was pulling the long-range missiles a few degrees off course until we discovered that it was happening when they crossed a ley line. So we started accounting for the ley lines in our calculations. In my research I saw data about the effects on humans. It makes sense to me to align my home with the existing pattern here."

Below is an illustration of three renowned power spots in England linked by ley lines. Glastonbury and Iona, in particular, have attracted flocks of pilgrims and visitors for centuries. Both play central roles in the Arthurian legend—Iona as the Isle of Avalon and Glastonbury as the site of Camelot. Each location was sacred to the Druids and later gained further fame as a Christian site of learning and spirituality. Much has been written about the dragon line or Rose line that connects these and other ancient sacred sites in the British Isles, including Dan Brown's fictionalized references in his novel *The Da Vinci Code*. Sources for further reading on ley lines are listed in the Resources section at the back of this book.

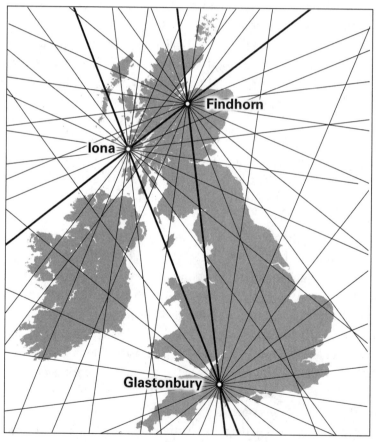

Figure 2

VORTEXES

Vortexes are concentrated swirls of earth energy that act like invisible vol-canic spouts for the earth. They move energy in circular patterns, similar to the chakras in the human energy system. These openings bring energy from a source in the earth, generating feminine-receptive energy when they swirl clockwise and masculine-active energy when they spin in a counterclockwise direction. They are sometimes connected to the grid of ley lines and power points, and are sometimes in areas with features like subterranean water flows or strong mineral deposits.

While power points radiate energy along a horizontal plane (carried along by ley lines that fan out from it like spokes on a wheel), vortexes tend to swirl energy in a more vertical direction, like an invisible tornado or waterspout. This combination promotes good circulation and an even bal-ance of light and energy in the earth body.

There are different types of vortexes with different functions. Sometimes two vortexes are located near each other, with one spinning clockwise and the other spinning counterclockwise, creating a more balanced polarity. While they are characterized by whirling motion, the vortexes themselves stay in one location. Think of an engine with two pistons that move up and down alternately. It is the up-and-down movement coupled with the alternating pat-tern that generates the energy in the engine; vortexes unfold in the same way.

Vortexes are the least common earth energies to detect, but they come in all sizes and intensities. They may be found in a backyard or at well-publicized sites like Sedona, Arizona. It is said that these earth energy sites can stimulate the right side of the brain and help quiet the mind. The effect varies with the electrical polarity of the vortex. Vortexes with a positive polarity have a magnetizing effect while those with a negative polarity have a repelling effect.

A NOTE ABOUT TERMINOLOGY

From its earliest definition, Western geomancy is simply used to observe and analyze patterns with the earth. Over time, tools and techniques developed, and today, like quantum physics, it is a combination of hard science and intuition. Because of this, different researchers use different terminology. Here is a simple overview of the terms I use in this book:

⊕ *Earth energy, terrestrial energy telluric currents, subterranean currents:* The energy currents generated from deep within the earth—mainly (or at least partly) electromagnetic in nature

⊕ *Chi:* The life force present in all life—the earth, the heavens, animals, and humans

⊕ *Cosmic currents:* The energy currents that come from above—some or all originating in our sun. Some of these are also electromagnetic in nature, arriving in the form of radiation generated by solar storms and other solar radiation.

⊕ *Solutions, cures:* Symbolic, intentional gestures that enliven, rebalance, or calm down the life force on the site. These are usually made from items that stimulate the senses, such as light, color, stones, a trickling water feature, mirrors, and bird feeders. Intention is important as well in the application of the cure.

⊕ *Site:* Wherever you are located. It could be an apartment, an office, a room in a house, or an outdoor area, developed or undeveloped.

Earth's energy grid apparently operates with a combination of magnetizing and repelling currents, and some of the hubs that we call power points or vortexes have the job of regulating and balancing these energies as well as distributing them around the planet. The following creation myth, retold by James Swan, describes the same powerful energy grid from the Hopi perspective and experience:

> *In the beginning, it is told, Tiowa, the Creator, saw a need to have a guardian for the earth, and so he assigned the task to Spider grandmother. Descending to the earth's surface, Spider grandmother saw she would need help, and so she reached down and picked up two handfuls of earth. She spit into her hands, and instantly two handsome young men appeared, one named Poqanghoya and the other named Palongwhoya, who became her helpers.*

Spider grandmother and the twins sat in meditation for a time to link their minds, and then Poqangboya journeyed north to the North Pole, where he began his special magic, the power which gives structure and form to life.

Then Palongwhoya went to the South Pole. He made his prayers, and in the stillness he heard a distant, slow rhythm, which he began to beat out on his magical drum. The distant sound was the heartbeat of Tiowa, and when the two beats were in perfect harmony, a surge of life force energy came shooting down to the earth. It struck the navel of the earth, the South Pole, and went down and down until it came to the crystal at the very center of the earth.

Striking this crystal, the energy then shot out in all directions, channeled by the structural magic of Poqangboya. The reflected life energy then popped from the earth's crust, bringing the planet to life. At some places this life energy is more abundant, sacred places (power points), the Hopi say. They call them the "spots of the fawn."[10]

This poetic retelling of the creation of the earth energy web demonstrates how information about the web was common knowledge in indigenous cultures, and how important it is to pass it on to future generations.

DETECTING THE WEB: EVERYDAY GEOMANCY

In order to build in harmony with the natural energy flows of earth's energy grid, you must first be able to detect them, which can be done a number of ways. Because these energies have electrical polarity, magnetic qualities, and sometimes a temperature difference, modern technologies are being used to detect and track them. While some research facilities have devices like the Squid Magnetometer for measuring the biomagnetic radiation from ley lines or power points, such devices tend to be very costly. The Rauscher/Van Bise magnetic field detector is more available, but the most popular and effective method of detecting these fields is a low-tech method called dowsing.

Dowsing is most commonly used to detect water flows for well digging. Dowsing rods can be a forked stick with the dowser holding the forked end of the stick, or they may be two metal rods with the dowser holding one in each hand. The stick or rods are pulled downwards or upwards (or the rods may cross) as the dowser nears the different energy areas.

A 1967 *New York Times* article reported that Marine Corps engineers were using divining rods to detect tunnels, mines, and booby traps in Vietnam.[11] Small farmers in Florida used dowsing to determine the sex of avocado trees (it takes a male and a female to produce fruit). A ten-penny nail on a string suspended over the young tree will indicate the gender of the plant by the direction of spin. One old farmer even used this method to correctly predict the sex of both of his grandchildren by suspending the nail over their mother's pregnant belly.

In many parts of the world, it is common to employ a dowser before drilling for water. Good dowsers have remarkable accuracy, and many can even sense at what depth and flow rate the water can be found. Some skilled practitioners use this technology to locate veins of oil or gold or other minerals. The Resources section at the back of the book lists some dowsing associations that can provide classes and practitioners.

BEYOND TECHNOLOGY: YOUR BUILT-IN SENSING SYSTEM

When I consult, I receive impressions from nature as I walk around a client's home. I note the birdsong as I ring the doorbell or the puff of wind calling my attention to a certain area of the yard or building. Solutions begin to reveal themselves as I pay attention to the energies and beings on the site; many of the client's problems are revealed and solved even before I employ other methods or make physical changes to the site.

The use of tools such as rods, pendulums, or other devices may help you become more aware of what you are sensing, and thus help you develop confidence and sensitivity. But humans have interacted with this web for thousands of years, and everyone has an innate ability to sense and respond to energy. Too much reliance on technology may overshadow your own sensitivity, so take time to notice your own sensory and intuitive input and continue to develop this vital asset. With practice, willingness, and openness you can begin to feel more, know more, and have a bigger sense of how much you can perceive on your own. If you persist, every bit of time and energy you invest will eventually result in rich rewards. The following tips will give you a starting point.

CLUES FOR DETECTING THE ENERGY WEB

Energy is reflected in forms in nature. Human history gives excellent clues, and your own amazing instrument—your body—is communicating with energy all the time using sensory data.

1. *Forms in nature*
Nature will often mirror the subterranean flows of earth energy. Ley lines and power points sometimes show in the landscape. This is most easily seen in winter, as the shapes and patterns of the land appear best without foliage to hide them. Look for physical representations such as

- *unusual shapes or patterns in the landscape* that may mark areas of strong biomagnetic energy (ley lines, for example, are sometimes visible in a forest as trees often curl or bend in unusual shapes to accommodate the strong invisible flow coming through the area);
- *mounds or concave indentations in the earth* that may indicate power points or other areas of concentrated energy;
- *actual lines in the earth*, like swales, animal tracks, or plants naturally growing along a line, that may denote a ley line.

Students Don and Niki, a building-design team, asked me to help them read a potential building site for strong indications of earth energy. Standing in a sunny meadow, I was aware of a rather buzzy, turbulent energy—a surprising experience in this former cow pasture. As I paid more attention, I could feel that we were standing at the hub of some strong energy lines coming from the four surrounding mountains and meeting in the middle of this meadow. It was as if many high-voltage lines were converging and creating a concave hub into the earth at the spot. I sensed that the purpose of this particular center was to ground, anchor, and blend the strong energies of the mountains and beyond, which in turn were like power stations for the larger lines of force in the earth's grid. This piece of property was a minor power spot, a hub for many lines coming around the planet. Knowing that these ley lines are often reflected by physical indications, we looked around and found a slight concave area where the center of the hub seemed to be. It even had small swales radiating from it, indicating the ley lines that converged there.

2. *Human history*

Human activity can give a clue to the presence of strong energy flows. Think of the ancient temples or worship sites that have lasted through the ages, often with subsequent layers of religious buildings on the same site. Locations with strong earth and cosmic energy currents seem to produce more inspiration or spiritual quickening in humans, who flock to these areas for worship, contemplation, learning, and creativity. Scenic areas that are often painted, photographed, and visited—those that seem to attract and inspire humans—are usually areas with strong telluric currents.

In her book *The Camino*, Shirley MacLaine describes her pilgrimage, a grueling trip for a woman in her sixties, completed in a remarkable thirty days along the Santiago di Compostela Camino, an ancient trail for spiritual seekers in Spain that may follow a far more ancient track. "People from Saint Francis and Charlemagne to Ferdinand and Isabella to Dante and Chaucer have taken the journey, which comprises a five-hundred-mile trek. It is suggested that the Camino is directly under the Milky Way and follows ley lines that reflect energy from those star systems," she wrote. This trail has been continuously used for many centuries, with ancient pilgrims' inns still located a day's walking journey apart. MacLaine wrote that taking time to walk on such an energized area of the earth gave her tremendous insights about her next step in life.[12]

Closer to home, I found an example of creative human activity linked with an earth energy site at Charlene's home in Oregon's Cascade Mountains. Impressions of an increased magnetic field came easily without much concentration on my part—a signal for strong earth energy. A jittery feeling in my spine, my body's signal for a ley line, was my final clue that a major ley line runs from the mountain through the middle of her property. Energies this strong are often difficult to live near, but Charlene is a teacher and healer who holds seminars and classes at her home. Since she recognizes and honors these energies, they actually feed her work. Her students experience a high level of inspiration and healing.

It is interesting to note that this home also had a history of being a hub for creative and interesting events. In the 1930s it had been a favorite summer gathering place for an artist colony and a site for stimulating political forums. In this case, the energy from nature nourishes both humans and nature, enhancing the creative purposes for which this home has been used for decades.

3. *Sensory clues: Your body's radar*
One way to retrieve some of the vital information being offered by your partner, the land, is to use your five senses and the many subtle senses beyond that. Set your intention to receive input from the environment and assume that your reactions are being stimulated by the environment. Notice your body sensations and first impressions as you approach a site. Then notice any others that arise after you have been standing there quietly. When you begin to walk around, continue to pay attention to your body.

Chapter 5 will give you specific exercises on picking up this kind of information. Meanwhile, the list below will give you an idea of what you might experience.

INDICATIONS OF STRONG EARTH ENERGY

Below are sensory responses I detect in strong earth energy areas such as power points, ley lines, and vortexes. Remember that many sensory reactions are due to the natural environment around you.

Near a power point, you may notice

- lots of insights or impressions flooding the mind and feelings;
- a shift in your breathing as if you are standing in high wind;
- an expansive spacious feeling as if you are standing in a large room;
- a sense of deep restfulness, peace, or well-being.

Near a ley line, you may notice

❀ a sense of strong movement nearby as though you're standing by an invisible freeway, river, or creek;

❀ a sense of jitteriness or an urge to keep moving, the way you might feel when standing by a busy road;

❀ a heightened sense of clarity if the ley line is intact and undisturbed;

❀ a sense of confusion or lack of clarity if the ley line is disrupted.

Near a vortex, you may notice

❀ a sense of a whirling motion that is almost dizzying, like you are standing next to a merry-go-round;

❀ a sense of standing next to a fire;

❀ an unwelcome feeling in certain areas, especially if the vortex is in or near a structure;

❀ a quickened heartbeat (remember, this is an electromagnetic field, and your cardiac rhythms are regulated by electricity).

TANGIBLE BENEFITS

The ability to sense the energies present in and around a building or a piece of property is a natural skill that is useful when checking out a new apartment or office; looking to buy, build, or develop land; or just paying more attention to your current living arrangement.

Designing in harmony with the earth energies not only diminishes potentially harmful effects but actually enhances both nature and humans in the area. I have seen this many times when people understand and care for the patterns of life around them. A favorite grade school science experiment is to stroke a steel nail repeatedly with a magnet, causing the atoms to line up in such a way that the nail becomes a magnet. In that same way, thinking and acting in harmony with the life force around us creates resonance. After ten years of consciously integrating their designs and lifestyle with the earth energy in their area, Warren and Suzanne helped form their own particular energetic field in their area, thus attracting neighbors who shared their interest in harmonious relationships with nature.

Preserving the health of the web in this way is important for both the earth and humans. Since ley lines, power points, and vortexes are very active on their own, they tend to bring delays and problems to the construction process and distress to subsequent inhabitants if not handled carefully.

Construction and landscaping establish new patterns that are different from those already in place on the site. When this is done with a spirit of cooperation by allowing the important elements of the old invisible pattern to stay in place while respectfully introducing the new pattern, a harmonious integration takes place. This harmony will be experienced as a smoother construction process and as better well-being and satisfaction for the new occupants. Otherwise, the disturbance created by conflicting patterns can slow things down and introduce an element of agitation to the process. This agitation or disturbance lingers on the site and affects the new inhabitants and visitors as well as the earth.

In general, the more room you can leave around such an active energetic site and the more respectful attention you give it, the more harmonious and beneficial are the experiences of the humans nearby. Too little space or too little attention to the energetic patterns tends to lead to agitated experiences. Divorces, illness, financial woes, depression, and other troubles increase in areas with disrupted energy patterns.

In addition, people respond differently to certain types of energy. People who are highly creative and self-directed can live more easily in a highly charged area, while others feel disturbed and agitated in the presence of such strong energy.

A growing number of builders, architects, engineers, and other professionals have discovered how much their work is impacted by the energetic grid of the earth. While many residential and office sites are not directly impacted by these larger energy patterns, there are subtler layers of the network at play on every piece of land.

3
NATURE BEINGS: EARTH'S ENERGY MANAGERS

Heaven is under our feet as well as over our heads.
—Henry David Thoreau

VERY FEW OF US live or work near major ley lines or power points, just as very few of us have major electrical generating plants or substations in our neighborhood. In the same way that electricity is stepped down—from power stations to transformers to individual streets and houses—nature's energy web steps down into continually smaller webs or weavings. Most of us actually contact the electrical grid in the form of lamps, refrigerators, and computers. In the same way that these appliances carry electrical energy in our homes, the elements listed in this chapter and the next—nature beings, trees, earth, water, stones, and fire—carry earth's life force into our homes and environments.

In any given field, yard, or city block, intricate lines of energy run between each plant and structure on a site so that all are interconnected and interacting. On our land, I have a sense of a golden web, an impression that each tree, building, bush, and flower, from the smallest weed to the largest tree, is held together in one web. This layer-on-layer patterning of nature is like a computer fractal program; the macrocosm is reflected in infinitely smaller microcosms.

R. J. Stewart, Celtic bard, mystic, and author, speaks of "beings within beings" on the land acting together as allies, helping to maintain the complex, interconnected web of life.[2] The art and stories of most indigenous cultures also describe various forms of energetic beings with an unseen but real influence on the well-being of humans and the rest of the world we depend on.

Whether we live in a busy urban center or rural backwoods, our lives are inextricably involved with these basic elements of the web. They are woven into and around our buildings, roads, parks, cities, and countrysides.

How we live in relationship to these elements actually affects the patterns of balance significantly. In order to have balance and health in our home or office, or in our larger geopolitical regions, it is extremely useful to understand the role played by each of these elements in circulating life force throughout the planet. This chapter and the next will focus on the intangible or energetic aspects of each of these elements.

A WORD ABOUT IMAGINATION

Imagination, like sensitivity, is often trivialized. Both imagination and sensitivity connect you with internal sources of wisdom and knowledge, which tends to make you less dependent on external sources of information, including suggestions about what you should wear, drive, join, or buy in order to have meaning or happiness in life.

Modern notions about imagination, particularly the idea of making things up, amuse many indigenous elders. To them, the ideas and imaginings that come to us do not come from our own mind or ego but are gifts shared with us by the invisible world.

Because of this, many people waste a lot of time with questions like "Am I just imagining things?" which distracts them from the information they could be receiving. If this happens to you, try considering imagination as one of the faculties you use to pull in or translate information from the environment. You will feel progress in time.

NATURE BEINGS

To understand the role of nature beings, remember two important principles discussed in previous chapters: first, nature always operates according to patterns, and second, every aspect of life has an energy blueprint. Nature beings, which are living energy patterns charged with holding the energetic templates for every aspect of life, are part of the way that nature creates and maintains the complex, intricate order of life on our planet.

Just as a mountain, with its heights and crags, has different physical characteristics from a softer and shorter hill, the invisible patterns around these physical forms also vary. A particular type of nature intelligence or energy form holds the invisible pattern or blueprint for each physical form, from mountains to individual blades of grass. These living energy forms that hold the energetic patterns for the physical world are collectively known as nature beings, or devas.

Although nature beings are known by many names in many cultures, Dorothy Maclean, a founding member of the Findhorn Community and a pioneer in communicating with this aspect of nature, first used the ancient Sanskrit word *deva* to capture the essence of this role of energy manager. In the early days of the community, Dorothy first heard the message in her mind from a being or energy identifying itself as a cabbage essence and offering concrete suggestions on how to grow robust cabbages, even in Findhorn's rugged northern garden. As Dorothy and her colleagues followed these instructions and the additional messages that came from this being and others on the property, they not only obtained the startling gardening results that brought international attention, but they also began to understand the role of these architects or guiding angels of the nature kingdom.[3]

A deva can be likened to a caretaker, a nature architect. Magnetic in nature, its role is to attract physical matter to the energetic blueprint, manifesting the perfection of the pattern in form. Devas can be large, holding or tending the pattern for an entire region, or tiny, holding the pattern for the smallest of plants. The term "overlighting deva" refers to a being that holds the pattern for a whole species or region (or project or group).

Throughout this book, I use the terms "muse," "nature energy," "deva," "nature spirit," and "nature being" interchangeably. It is challenging to capture nonlinear reality in linear terms, so I find it useful to approach the subject from various angles. If you pursue this subject in more depth, you may discover that some authors use certain terms in highly specific ways, but my purpose here is to introduce a general concept and allow you to become aware of your own sensations and experience.

Many names and traditions describe different types of devas or nature beings. From the leprechauns, faeries, and elves of the British Isles to the menehune of Hawaii, the kontomble of West Africa, the kachinas of the American Southwest, and the household spirits greeted daily throughout Asia, it is nearly impossible to find a locale on our planet without stories of local nature spirits or deities that are usually involved with harvest, hunting, weather, and fertility.

In earlier times, those who could commune with such beings were valuable to their communities. Even today, individuals who are particularly attuned to the language of nature can make the difference between life and death for their group by picking up vital information about the location of water or game, the approach of a distant tsunami, or the best way to save a failing crop.

Unfortunately, as human lifestyles shifted from close contact with nature, superstition and misunderstanding began to distort our instinctive understanding and interaction. With Newtonian science, we began to define the world only in terms of what was physically measurable and observable. While this filtered out a good deal of distortion, it also dismissed some deep truths that have only begun to reemerge with quantum physics and the leading edge of science.

William Bloom, a leading researcher and teacher in the field of energetic beings, suggests that perhaps devas are in fact the mysterious "attractor" force recognized in modern chaos theory. As he wrote in *Working with Angels, Fairies and Nature Spirits*:

> There is an essence of religious folklore which is true, beautiful, and creative—even if it cannot be scientifically proved. Elves, muses, angels, and similar beings, known collectively as devas or devic beings, belong to this essence ... And whether we invite them in or not, whether we acknowledge their presence or not, they exist and they are everywhere.[4]

Discovering that nature is alive and communicative in ways we had not imagined (at least not since we stopped believing in the Tooth Fairy) definitely stretches our modern notions of reality. But we can count on this: the universe continues to operate according to its own laws, regardless of our human perception or beliefs. As Albert Einstein said, "The most beautiful thing we can experience is the mysterious. It is the source of all true art and science." Since the laws of the universe are more vast and mysterious than a human brain is likely to comprehend, it is rewarding to follow Einstein's lead, keeping an open mind, a lively curiosity, and a good sense of humor.

THE ESSENTIAL ROLE OF NATURE BEINGS

Devas, in addition to holding the energetic blueprint for a plant, animal, species, or area, are always weaving energy—reinforcing any weak points and responding to changes in their area by attempting to weave or integrate these new patterns into the established pattern. The new patterns may be generated by humans, for example, by cutting trees, bulldozing earth, straightening water flows, or erecting buildings, or by nature, by storms, fires, and grazing animals. The job of these nature intelligences is not to prevent change nor to react to it with distress, but rather to maintain health and harmony by adapting to changes in ways that stay true to the blueprint, keeping the patterns of life force clear and flowing.

Understanding this, we can ease our own experience by communicating more consciously with nature before making physical changes. In the same way that human team members communicate well in order to create a successful project or a winning game, we can signal our intentions to nature and open our minds to the impressions and suggestions that come back to us.

It can be challenging for us to conceive of these energies, which are so different from humans. It is not surprising that we tend to project familiar characteristics in order to picture them. It's also possible that as these nature beings attempt to connect with our human consciousness, they utilize forms that already exist in our minds, such as archetypal images of fairies or elves. Different types of beings become associated with different characteristics. Fairies are associated with flowers or small, delicate plants while gnomes are more often associated with earthy objects like mushrooms. Often, thoughts or impressions like these come from our body's radar, which registers subtle data from the energy patterns around plants, trees, and all life.

These images of fairies, gnomes, or angelic beings may even be useful, as long as we don't limit our understanding to storybook stereotypes. Keeping in mind that we are using these images for convenience, they can serve as a kind of symbolic language that may help us recognize the type of energy we are encountering.

It's important to remember that while nature beings operate according to natural laws on their own plane of existence, they do not have physical forms and thus are not bound by the physical limitations that we are accustomed to. They do not, for example, have size in any conventional way that we would imagine. We tend to imagine a green pea fairy as small and a tree spirit as huge, but I remember tuning in to some small sugar ants and being amazed at the large size of the energy pattern.

Since nature beings operate in a sphere beyond the comprehension of physics, the results of working with them often seem miraculous to us. Machaelle Small Wright recounts eye-popping experiences in her book *Behaving as If the God in All Life Mattered*. Since 1976 Wright, a true pioneer, has dedicated herself to the science of working cocreatively with nature intelligences. The dramatic results have made Perelandra, her forty-five-acre research facility in Virginia, famous around the world. Once as she was transplanting seedlings, she became frustrated when she found herself chopping up the earthworms she had so carefully invited to soften her hard clay soil. Exasperated, she stomped out of the garden, announcing that she would like the worms to leave the area by the time she returned from her tea break. Returning, she was pleased to encounter not a single worm in the rest of the row. When she was done, she decided to continue the experiment by sitting back and quietly requesting them to return. Ten minutes later, she picked up a handful of soil to find it once again filled with the little soil doctors.

Inspired by this miracle, she walked over to her ravaged lawn, sat down quietly, and sent an experimental request to the Mole Deva, the nature intelligence overseeing moles. She acknowledged the importance of moles in the overall life cycle on her property but requested that they relocate from the lawn to a large field two hundred feet away. When she returned to her work in the garden a half hour later, she heard leaves rustling and stood up to see about a hundred moles scuttling along the edge of the woods to the distant field, under the stunned eyes of her two dogs and three cats who had run over to watch the spectacle.[5]

TUNING IN TO NATURE BEINGS

The good news is that we do not have to master quantum physics in order to communicate with these potential partners. All humans already possess the instinctive ability to register information at this level and to communicate simply and directly with our heart and intention.

Some nature beings have a lot to say when you come into an area ready to change the natural patterns there. Listening to this input from nature can save time, speed things up, and sometimes save money on a project by avoiding problems in the same way that consulting an architect or engineer saves time and trouble. Connecting with nature's energy can also add a sparkle to the more routine aspects of daily living and working. Contact with devic energies generally leaves humans feeling refreshed, inspired, uplifted, and peaceful. Carolyn, a student, noted her experience after attuning with a deva of her favorite island: "I get in touch with the absolute loveliness of this magical place, and I feel the strong earth energy and that there is a guiding, helpful, benign spirit close by. I always feel more calm and peaceful afterwards, and my doubts and concerns disappear."

Contact with nature beings is generally subtle, sometimes signaled by an unexpected change in emotions, similar to the way that you can feel someone's mood just by sitting near him or her. Have you ever turned your head to discover someone staring at you across a room? The same silent contact that got your attention in that case is the way we connect with devas. It's in the world of thought and emotion. Sometimes I experience it physically as a humming, buzzy sensation.

Terry and Jane called me for a consultation because their lives and land felt different to them, as if things were on hold. Growth in their large garden, the source of their business, seemed more sluggish and troubled than usual, and money was not flowing well in their life. Intuitively, they felt it was related to their lot; a neighbor had cut a substantial stand of trees near their property.

Standing near their property line on a crisp fall day, I felt a strong presence, the sense of an old tree gnome, a sort of gnome king, whose job was caring for the large trees of this area. Although I had been to this property numerous times, I had never felt him before. Surprised, I walked away and returned several times, but each time I continued to sense this strong energy.

In my experience, many of these ancient nature beings don't need contact with humans. They just want to do their nature work and be left alone. Most likely, their experiences have caused them not to expect a beneficial partnership with humans, so they go about their tasks mostly ignoring the human world. When you do make contact with them, you may pick up an irritated or seemingly hostile energy, particularly if the cause of your contact is a human-generated disturbance to the local patterns.

This one did seem aggravated, so I extended my respect and backed away so I could take some time to consider the situation. Back at home, I went into a meditative state and brought Terry and Jane's property to mind, and the gnome king came right in. I could immediately feel his energy and realized that he was merely upset, not hostile. He sensed our sincerity and was reaching out for help. I was deeply touched. He asked that we humans cocreate with him and join him in reweaving the patterns with the small forest that had been disrupted by the neighbor's tree cutting. He was particularly concerned with the remaining stand of trees on Terry and Jane's land. Everything was on hold until the new pattern could be set.

I felt a bit cautious because of the intensity of his emotion. (Imagine an invitation to partner with a mountain lion.) But Terry and Jane were open to reaching out, so I had them begin by bringing offerings to the spot. They chose pink quartz rocks that were special to them, to convey their love and appreciation to nature. They spoke of their willingness to cooperate with nature and promised to preserve the remaining trees.

They then anchored this intention with action. They replaced the old fence that had fallen down between their property and the neighbor's land where the trees had been cut. This symbolic gesture helped create an energetic boundary around the space that they now designated for wild nature.

They continued to use the attunement process (described in part 4) and to carry out the suggestions inspired by nature. They found large stones at a local landscape business and set them in their tree grove to physically anchor the new pattern. Every few days they took time to send gratitude and appreciation to the nature spirits for the reweaving that was underway.

Within weeks, they felt harmony restored. As money began to flow again for them, their garden recovered, and they experienced a smoother and more settled feeling in their lives. Terry commented, "Our garden produce business seemed to pick up immediately after we spent the time with our small forest, bringing in the rocks and replacing the fence. They were such simple acts, but so worthwhile."

THE BEST TIMES TO CONNECT WITH NATURE BEINGS

Tara, a student, sat in her tiny urban backyard asking the nature allies where to place a wild area for them to have all for themselves. She knew from my classes that having such an area is like a homeopathic dose of nature, a small spot that can invigorate the life force of a large area, and she wanted a place where nature beings would feel welcome. But no clear impressions or thoughts emerged. Frustrated, Tara resettled herself and tried the attunement again, but she still did not receive the answer she sought.

A friend called her a few days later in great excitement to tell her about a house that had gone on the market. Though Tara and her family had only had vague ideas of moving in the next year or so, when she walked into this house and then saw its glorious garden, she knew it was meant for them.

Things fell into place, and within several months, Tara found herself sitting in the garden of her new home, asking again about the placement of a wild area. This time, she got a clear impression right away. She realized that she hadn't received an answer at her old house because the move was imminent.

Much can be learned from a connection or even a lack of it. Furthermore, certain events or circumstances lend themselves to connecting with nature beings. Connect with nature beings when

- you are curious or want more awareness of their presence;
- you are moving into a new apartment, home, or office;
- you travel;
  (It's a good idea to introduce yourself to the nature beings and energies of the area. I know African and Asian people who

still do this whenever they visit a new place. It's a lovely way to take time to notice where you are, to really arrive.)

- there is an upcoming change in your environment;
  (One such change is if you (or your landlord or property management) plan to remove vegetation, plants, or trees, or add new construction or landscaping. This includes changes like the city cutting a tree out front, a phone company trimming limbs, or new bleachers being installed on your local baseball field. Nature doesn't care who "owns" property in the human world. All these alterations are a change in the existing patterns, and thus they are great opportunities to practice partnering with nature.)

- you would like to ask about their role on your land or on your surroundings;

- you wish to inquire if the nature beings have any suggestions for your project or present living environment;

- your life or a project is feeling stuck or frenetic.

For exercises for attuning to nature beings, go to page 181.

TYPES OF NATURE BEINGS

Attunement happens on many levels and with many elements. You can attune to the devas of plants, wildlife, and the nature being of your lot or neighborhood, as well as to water, trees, fire, and stones, which are discussed in the next chapter.

PLANTS

Use the Attuning to Nature Beings exercise described in part 4 to follow your curiosity and to get to know unusual species you encounter, or to ask for the best location for a compost pile, find solutions to problems with your houseplants, or ask about soil amendments or other suggestions for growing better flowers or vegetables. Gene, a landscape designer and fellow Findhorn Community member, always takes time for an attunement with the deva of plants just transplanted in clients' gardens. Standing above each plant with outstretched hands and eyes closed, he asks the deva to assist the plant in adjusting to the new location. He also visualizes an image of a healthy plant with lots of blooms for the client and the earth. Gene said, "I was sold on the technique for a couple of reasons. It really works and I love working with the invisible side of nature, but it also yields more job bids. Two neighbors watching my attunement routine over time hired me for their yard, commenting that even though they didn't understand what I was doing, it unquestionably made the plants grow."

ANIMALS AND WILDLIFE

You can ask to connect with the deva of any animals you encounter. Birds, for example, are harbingers or messengers. Hawks can give warnings of danger. Eagles can be a reminder of flying high to gain perspective, and waterbirds can remind us of flow. Birdsong around you can serve the purpose of reminding and connecting you to the energy of joy.

When you are aware of birds on your land, pause and listen to their song and, more importantly, breathe it in. Birds sing in rhythms. Breathe in as they sing, and when they rest their song, breathe out and feel the energy or vibration of joy in their song settling into your body. This process can be a great energizer and a mood raiser. Call on the deva of birds to bring their gift of song to your land.

Gena, a client, spoke of a long walk on the beach where she had a strong realization and a resolution to an ongoing problem. A weight lifted off her shoulders as she realized the shift for herself, and in that instant, seagulls and other smaller seabirds flew around her, serenading her with great sounds and songs. She felt the birds celebrating and adding to her joy.

When my husband and I moved to Fir Haven, we discovered a family of pheasants living where we had planned to construct our house. It was a large extended family, since pheasants return to the same area for life. We began by greeting them and appreciating their beauty. We let them know that we respected their life and their right to be there, and told them that we were interested in sharing the space. For ten years we maintained our attitude of honoring them and ourselves, and we observed their patterns, taking care to leave their favorite spots undisturbed. Preserving what we could of their habitat and setting aside certain areas for them, we integrated their needs with our human use of the land. We peacefully coexisted, and I was often rewarded by the sight of the large, beautiful birds strolling across the nearby meadow, even as I wrote this book.

Observe the wildlife that appears on your site. An unexpected encounter can be a message or a gift from nature. Such was the case when Dianne, a student, created a time-out for herself while house-sitting for us. She announced to nature and all that she was taking a retreat to sort her busy life. She brought a chair up to her favorite wooded area on the land, sat down, and attuned with the wildlife, asking for an ally to guide her. She closed her eyes, took some deep breaths, and heartily connected to the devic level. Enjoying the silence, she soon noted a rustling sound nearby in the brush and opened her eyes to see an old cougar walking by her some hundred yards away. The cougar went on her way, but Dianne was aware of the incredible timing, realizing that her wish for an ally had come true. In many traditions, the lion or cougar represents fierce, strong leadership, and she, a manager in her work, was grateful for the reminder to be fierce at times in her leadership role at work.

Like us, wildlife may just want to connect. Notice if an animal stops its usual habits for a bit and watches you. One summer night while walking down our long driveway, I noticed a red blur of fur coming out from a nearby stand of trees and running in a frenetic zigzag pattern. Suddenly I realized a small red fox was making her way toward me. She actually brushed my leg and then continued on, seemingly unaware of my presence. I watched in amazement and extended my hands to send healing energy to the disturbed animal as her zigzag pattern continued around me. In that moment, the fox stopped and turned to face me, blinking and gazing up at me. For two or three minutes, we basked in each other's presence, and I felt the fox receive the healing energy. I also heard, "Thank you. I need your calming support. It is difficult for me right now with the summertime and humans." I understood; it was midsummer, with lots of human noises, music playing, lawn mowers chugging along, phones ringing, children cavorting—a cacophony of human sounds drowning out nature sounds. When I brought my hands down, the small animal moved in a calmer fashion, looking back once more before scurrying back into the woods. It was a true gift to connect with a wild one in a way that felt like a partnership.

LANDSCAPE

You can use the attunement process to contact the devas that hold the larger patterns for your property, block, or neighborhood. Ask for insight into problems that involve a larger area, or request information to support more balance or overall health for your site.

As part of her design process, Joyce Ward, an architect, goes on a shamanic journey. Shamans are a type of medicine man or woman especially distinguished by the use of inner journeys to hidden worlds otherwise mainly known through myth, dream, and near-death experiences. They typically do this by entering an altered state of consciousness using monotonous percussion sound and meditation.[6] Joyce uses these skills to connect with the being of the land on her projects. She asks for any insight or feedback and uses the time to bond and connect to this being as another partner on the project. She spoke of one being that was pleased and surprised when she made contact. Right away the being mentioned that it had been two hundred years since anyone had bothered to say hello. He thanked her for contacting the area and was grateful to connect with humans again.

Some beings, however, are not so happy because of an area's neglect or abuse. These cases require patient, regular expression of your love, respect, appreciation, and willingness to help in healing. The nature beings themselves may need some healing time as well.

If there has been a recent fire, serious illness, or death in the area you are tuning in to, I recommend that you begin by doing your attunement off-site. Your results will be as effective because your physical presence at the site is not necessary to connect with the energies there. But adding some distance will diminish the intensity of your exposure to the troubled energies that linger in such locations.

Remember that nature has many invisible layers, facets, and fine weavings of interconnectedness. Explore your nature-being neighbors. Develop and expand on these ideas and exercises and be open to practical insights you may receive from your exchanges.

4

WATER, TREES, FIRE, AND STONES

Nature is not a place to visit; it is home.
—Gary Snyder

IN THIS CHAPTER, you will notice that a lot of space is devoted to water and trees. Over the years in my practice, water and tree nature beings have made the importance of their roles in bonding building to land particularly clear. This chapter and the exercises at the back of this book are designed to awaken and deepen your perception of the role of water, trees, and fire on your sites. Fire, for example, is mostly regarded as a disaster, but I will show you other ways to view and interact with this lively muse. History of the area, emotional connections, and even health issues are aspects impacted by how we view and use these particular elements.

WATER: THE VOICE OF FLOW

Whether you live in an urban high-rise, a five-hundred-acre farm, or somewhere in between, water has a strong invisible influence on your surroundings and your life. Even without the obvious presence of a stream, lake, irrigation ditch, or seasonal creek on your land or in your neighborhood, water is often present in underground streams or springs. There is also an energy imprint from ancient glacial modifications that shaped the landscape. We are aware of the power of water in floods, tsunamis, tides, and rainfall, but the intangible qualities of water wield just as powerful an influence. Victor Schauberger, an Austrian naturalist-forester, put it this way: "Scientists must be made to realize that water is not something to be handled carelessly, like an inanimate object. Water is not merely H_2O, but a living organism with its own laws commanding respect from mankind."[2]

Familiarity with the energetic aspect of water and its effects is an important factor in creating a harmonious, productive experience in your living spaces. As with all other earth energies, the process of landscape, building design, and construction is much smoother and more cost effective when you are aware of these aspects and able to work in harmony with them.

Bob, a client, is a landscape designer whose project to restore a severely abused creekside property with native plants had been hampered for six months by a seemingly endless string of frustrations. His friend, who had taken my classes, suggested that he consider the creek itself as a living entity and a potential partner in the project. Bob was frustrated enough at that point to consider anything, so he sat quietly by the creek after work one day, listening to the water and expressing his respect and appreciation to the life present there. He placed an offering for the creek deva and promised to respect the water's needs as a living organism, spending more time quietly attuning to the creek itself and paying attention to ideas and impressions that might come to him. Within the week, machines began to work again, crew members began showing up for work more regularly, and his money began flowing. He told me that listening and acknowledging the presence of life in the water had a dramatic effect on his stalled project.

WATER'S HISTORICAL INFLUENCE

Water has a history, a lineage that leaves an energetic imprint on your land. Did glaciers scour your area? Did an inland sea once occupy your currently landlocked region? In sensitizing yourself to the energy in your building or your land, being aware of this kind of background information allows your perceptions to be more complete and accurate.

In the Pacific Northwest, many epochal floods and events in the last ice age sculpted the beautiful Columbia River Gorge, with its towering basalt spires, broad river, and abundant waterfalls. They have been described as per-haps the largest floods ever to take place on the face of the earth. Water came from a thousand miles away, from today's western Montana, and there were many floods over the course of about seven thousand years, as the ice dam was breached, re-created, and then breached again. A four-hundred-foot body of water roared through the Gorge and filled the Willamette Valley like a bathtub. You can almost feel and hear a thundering echo today. The water spirit from long ago is still felt on the land, its imprint or energy band linger-ing like an old invisible map revealing the layers of history in the area.

You might be surprised by the influence such ancient history can have on your own experience of living or working in an area. When Theresa purchased a second home in the Columbia River Gorge area after living in an urban set-ting for many years, she found that her own life changed in an epochal manner. She felt that visiting in this dramatic region helped her by giving her strength, clarity, and courage to endure the dramatic changes in her life. She related, "I feel the ancient teachers, the nature spirits, the ancestors, the wise ones. They call to me and I respond, taking time out to travel there. Often I am only able to be there for less than twenty-four hours. It is always enough and never enough. My heart sings as we head out. The layers of work, worry, and mental focus are shed like a snakeskin. I am cleansed and renewed by just being there. Grounded, empowered, and energized, I am able to see my next steps more clearly and ready to venture back into the civilized world. It's reassuring in a funny way. The earth is so powerful, and I am like a child who sees it all for the first time and laughs with joy."

WATER'S SUBTLE INFLUENCES

While trees and earth offer us a quality of grounding, stability, and consis-tency, water is a voice of flow, change, and transition. Growing up near the coast, I learned to visit the ocean when I felt stuck in life. To this day, being near the ocean reminds me that flow is normal, that life waxes and wanes like the tides. Walking near water and feeling my bond with it restores my per-spective and gives me the courage to let go and move on.

When I needed to loosen up or restore a flow in my life at Fir Haven, I often sat by the creek near my house. Sometimes a blue heron would make a rare appearance, or the sudden splash of a nearby fish or frog was water's way of making contact, a kind of "Hello. I'm here." My husband used to notice that the water energy signaled him with scent. When he smelled a damp, earthy, musty smell on a dry day, he knew our creek deva was saying hello.

Theodor Schwenck observed in *Sensitive Chaos*, "A prerequisite for an effective, practical course of action is the rediscovery in a modern form of the forgotten spiritual nature of those elements whose nature it is to flow."[3] Indeed, the way that we interact with water in the environment has more far-reaching effects on both humans and the environment than most people realize. A number of traditions connect the water element with the flow of energy in human lives, specifically material abundance and health. Prosperity rituals and healing rituals in the West African Dagara tribe, for example, are always water rituals.

We create problems for ourselves by changing water patterns without awareness of the existing pattern and of the life force carried by the water and our relationship with it. When we reroute water without paying attention to these things, we can unknowingly go against natural laws that allow life to function in its wonderfully complex web of interaction. This is why the experience of those who live or work on the site tends to be healthier and more harmonious, joyful, and prosperous when these subtle aspects are handled with awareness and in cooperation with nature.

WATER'S ENERGY

Like the earth itself, water is alive and constantly communicating with us. Masaru Emoto, a Japanese researcher and educator, has discovered a way to record and display some of water's communication by photographing the crystals that form (or don't form) in various types of water under different conditions. He began by studying the differences in tap water and water from unpolluted natural sources. Astonished at the regular crystal formations in "natural" water and the malformed or missing crystalline structure in tap water from many sources, he went on to test water's response to various types of music and even to thoughts and emotions projected into bottles of water. His fascinating photographs and observations have received worldwide attention and connected him with other researchers around the world who explore water's ability to reflect human thought, intention, and emotion as well as the energy of nature, and the effect of these influences on human and plant health. In his book *The Hidden Messages in Water*, Emoto observed, "Water records information, and then while circulating throughout the earth distributes information. This water sent from the universe is full of the information of life, and one way to decipher this information is through the observation of ice crystals."[4]

Emoto's research confirms my own work with clients. In my clients' cases, building or gardening projects get bogged down and work stops because the water's pattern has been dislodged. From Emoto's perspective, the patterns from his water crystal photographs of polluted or disturbed water portray a crystal with little or no pattern; the image looks almost like an oily blob. Life is not thriving here, the crystal suggests. Furthermore, his photographs of crystals reflecting a beautiful thought such as love display a beautiful pattern, whereas a crystal reflecting a negative thought such as anger displays a malformed pattern.

Similarly, abruptly changing the flow of water, burying water in pipes for long periods of time, or covering natural water springs weakens the waters' energetic patterns as well. And the weakened energetic water patterns affects our human patterns.

The water crystal images give excellent visual clues about the human impact on water's vitality. When we treat water and all aspects of nature as partners, we thrive. When we don't, life can get bogged down.

For an exercise to sense water's energy, go to page 185.

WATER AND THE FLOW OF PROSPERITY

When we introduce a new pattern for water on a site by installing or altering sewers, water pipes, or dams and diverting existing water flow, for example, the balance and flow of energy in the area may stop or grow sluggish until nature readjusts to the new pattern. This rebalancing and integration can take a long time when the change is not undertaken with awareness or connection with nature.

Jerry, a client, called for help with a puzzle: in an area that was growing rapidly, sales in his development of sixty lots were stagnant. Walking around the site, I sensed a disturbed energy that felt watery to me, so I asked him about water flow on his site. Sure enough, they had rerouted an irrigation canal into a straight pipe with a ninety-degree angle to channel the water along the edge of the development.

It was a logical move, but they had changed the water flow too much and too quickly without communicating the change and giving nature a chance to adapt. When you come along with heavy machinery and remodel an entire landscape in a few days and transform a meandering creek into a straight canal, patterns can be disrupted for both humans and nature. With the character of the water so abruptly dislodged, a general malaise had descended over the project and affected many pocketbooks. Jerry was puzzled but intrigued by my assessment since, in fact, they had gone way over budget in the process of rerouting the water.

To reset the patterns, we began by making an offering at the canal's original site and acknowledging the living organism of the waters. Then I suggested that Jerry create a water feature on the lot that had been most difficult to sell—one that had had several potential sales fall through and that no one had even looked at it in weeks. This water feature would be a miniature version of the original water flow, echoing the old pattern and adding stones and large trees to help anchor and integrate a healthy new pattern for the area. I told Jerry that he should look for a buyer with a lot of feminine, creative energy, the type of person who would be attracted to and thrive in this kind of watery energy.

Jerry agreed to implement these changes and called two days later to report that lots were already starting to sell. Almost incredibly, the lot where we had planned the yet unbuilt water feature had sold while Jerry was out of the office—to a female artist who mentioned that she planned to create a water feature in her front yard!

Nature sometimes responds eagerly to our intentions to cocreate. Often just the shift in our awareness is enough to initiate positive change. Nature is automatically drawn toward renewal, and the very character of water is to easily return to a solution when given the opportunity. Everyone wins when we think of nature's needs both practically and spiritually. In Jerry's case, this small step opened up the new pattern for the whole development and its future residents to prosper. It is important to note that while the new pattern was inaugurated by the intention to connect with and honor the water spirit, it was also important to follow through by taking the required actions and continuing to relate to nature from this new level of awareness. The spontaneous changes won't last without the context of a continuing relationship. Like human relationships, our relationship with nature thrives when we are not taking her for granted and when we stay aware and appreciative of her.

Other clients, Joe and Evelyn, decided to install a water feature outside their house to honor this element and increase the flow of abundance in their lives. When the pond and waterfall were complete, they invited friends and family to dedicate this new addition to their home. As the guests made good wishes for the water and the couple, some placed special gifts of stones or other items in the water to symbolize their hopes and intentions. Soon after the dedication, Joe and Evelyn added a mirror in the room closest to the water so that they had a view of the water every time they walked into that room. This reminder of flow in the water encouraged a sense of personal flow in their lives, and they reported that their incomes doubled in a year's time. Evelyn remarked, "The water view and sounds and the intentions and good times connected with the water feature contributed to the increase in our good fortune."

WATER AND THE FLOW OF HEALTH

As mentioned earlier, water's energy and patterns are intimately connected with human health. Our bodies are 90 percent water when we are born, diminishing to about 70 percent in old age, and we all know the debilitating effects of dehydration or drinking impure water. But our health is also directly linked to the healthy or unhealthy energetic patterns of the water around us.

Mary called me after she developed cancer because she felt that her environment was affecting her health. At her home, I went directly to her bedroom. Bedrooms are often an influential spot when health is involved; in addition, it was the room in which Mary spent a lot of her time. Not only was there a mildewy dampness in the room, which was surprising in her Southern California location, but I also got an image of standing water and a feeling of being near a big puddle. When I asked about water, Mary told me that they had a big problem with water seeping in during the rainy season. This is a classic situation that can cause problems with both health and money flow, both of which were affected in Mary's life. Mary moved to another bedroom and immediately began to show improvement. She is planning to move to a drier location.

Remember that both humans and water operate within certain natural laws that regulate the complex interactions of life. These laws must be followed for life and water to continue to flow. Computers provide an example of this concept: As much as people may want to skip steps to accomplish a certain task with a computer program, they need to follow the format (pattern) set up by the program or they won't get the results they want. Computers function by following patterns that people don't understand or see but that they agree to follow. With nature we also do not see the large patterns, but now after a couple of centuries of skipping steps, the nature program is starting to freeze up.

TREES: GROUNDING THE CURRENT

My favorite childhood haunt was a huge old buckeye tree whose branches spread out over one-third of our yard. The whole garden was designed around her majesty. With her gnarled trunk resembling a wise, kindly old face, this tree was a refuge for me in challenging times, a friend, and a teacher.

According to Findhorn founder Dorothy Maclean, a leyland cypress deva once communicated to her, "Your need for trees must become as much a part of your consciousness as your need for water."[5] Though the developed world tends to forget, trees are an integral part of the human experience and are essential to life on this planet. We instinctively turn to trees and woodlands for comfort, healing, peace, and insight. On the physical level, they are the planet's lungs, taking in carbon dioxide and returning it as life-giving oxygen. Other tangible benefits include shade, soil retention, wildlife habitat, building materials, and firewood—all of which are essential to the complex interactions that maintain life on earth.

But perhaps the greatest value of trees (and the least understood) is intangible: Within the planetary grid, trees anchor a strong energy that is vital to the well-being of humans and the rest of the natural world. See page 186 for an exercise to connect to tree energy.

TREES AND ENERGY

While power points, ley lines, and vortexes characterize the web at a macro level, each individual lot and neighborhood functions as a microcosm, a small-scale version with its own force field in which trees serve a number of important purposes. A landscape deva once described it this way to Dorothy Maclean: "Large trees are conductors of energy . . . channeling the universal forces that surround and are a part of this planet. They are carriers of especially potent vibrations, sentinels of cosmic energy, transforming the power in an aura of peace. Large trees are essential for the well-being of the earth. No other can do the job they do. It is no accident that the Buddha is said to have found enlightenment under a tree. Let your love go forth to the trees. Give thanks for their creation."[6]

Understanding the energetic roles a tree may serve on your property is important when designing or siting buildings and landscapes, but it is also useful for city dwellers to understand how trees function on their city block and in their neighborhood. What happens to one tree can affect the energetic and physical framework of an entire area.

Recall the smaller, local patterns described in chapter 2, where the web looks like interactive lines of energy connecting each plant and structure on a site. At this level, trees are integral to the pattern. Most pieces of property do not contain vortexes or power points. Within these local networks, trees serve as stabilizers and junction points, anchoring the energy in the local grid. Professor Lin Yun suggests that trees are the bones, the framework for the life force on the land. They are the main component of the vertical energy lines at this finer level of the web.

When large trees are present, their branches act as a webbing at the top of the framework, a protective mantle keeping the energetic pattern intact on the site. In addition, trees take on different roles and energies depending on where they are located. Trees along a property boundary may serve as sentinels, or buffers, while others are more central, anchoring a calm and steady foundation for the activity around it.

Arriving at Susan's five-acre parcel some years ago, I caught a glimpse of the distant ocean as I got out of my car. Her modest, single-story home was nestled into a hill, its view opened up by decades of logging and farming of the rambling hill country around it. Unfortunately there was a very disorienting feeling on her land, which made it difficult to concentrate. When we stood very close to one tree on her land, I could feel a sense of grounding and finally get some clarity and cures for the client. Standing on top of the old tree's deep roots anchored us, and the session went smoothly with this help.

Along the same lines, Sandy, a student, learned about the sentinel function of the trees around her home. She and her husband had always enjoyed privacy in their home of thirty-five years, even with neighbors on all sides. With their own children raised and gone, they were pleased to see a couple with young children move in next door, bringing new life to the established neighborhood. However, after these new neighbors cut down some mature trees to make room for their children's play equipment, my client's view—both literally and internally—changed radically. Those trees had formed a boundary between the properties. When they were gone, this couple not only lost a privacy screen between the two families, but they now found themselves living with a close-up view of power poles across the way. The trees had also provided energy protection from the electromagnetic properties of the power lines.

Sandy had never realized how valuable the trees had been to her. The visible and invisible framework was changed in a way that devastated her and her husband. They have replanted young trees, but she has a whole new awareness and appreciation of the subtle ways that trees provide a buffer.

TREES AND EMOTIONS

Sandy and her husband became painfully aware of the fact that any change to trees tends to affect emotions, health, and well-being for both land and humans. I see this again and again in my work. The good news is that when these changes are handled with awareness, it's quite possible to mitigate and even avoid the distress that humans and trees experience when changes are made unconsciously.

Our first summer at Fir Haven brought this lesson home to me. The five-acre woodland parcel is ringed with mature fir trees, and younger trees surround the two small meadows outside the home and yurt. Trees were the first thing we saw each morning and our most constant neighbors.

One morning during that first summer, I was awakened with a jolt by a sound that came through the open bedroom window, just as the first traces of dawn lightened the sky. Shaken and feeling that someone was hurt, I listened intently for another distress call to show me where the sound had come from. There were no human cries, but after a moment a creaking, caving sound rang out, followed by a resounding thud that shook my bed. A falling tree! I realized that they were logging part of the Federal Bureau of Land Management land behind us.

I tried to understand the source of my distress. Had the cry that woke me actually come from the tree as it was being cut? My day was busy, but an unsettled, sad feeling stayed with me. That night, unable to sleep, I was still feeling the change in the forest so strongly that I sat down to connect with the fallen trees.

I acknowledged the tree spirit and felt a connection, followed by a swift thought. The sense I got from the trees was as if they were saying, "OK, we're cut, and it's distressing because patterns have been disturbed. Please just recognize that our essence is still here. This energy is eternal, and you can reweave it into the new pattern. It's the energy that's important. Our forms were an expression of our life force. The life force is still here and still wants to serve the purposes of life in this area. We can be partners in these changes."

I was pleased to discover that the life force from the trees was not destroyed after being cut. They also communicated the understanding that the feelings of distress came from the pattern in the forest being disrupted so quickly, without warning or preparation.

So I invited the essence of the falling trees into our forest and asked the life force of the falling trees to interweave a new pattern with the one on our land. Connecting to the essence in nature brought a way to cope with the disruption to the bones of our surrounding area. I could sense that the pattern was not lost but was indeed being integrated into the existing one on our adjoining land. With that awareness, my sleep pattern returned as well.

Change is an integral part of nature's pattern, and when a change is inevitable, we can prepare to make the transition smooth. Please remember that while these tips and guidelines are quite useful, using your own well-honed intuition as you evaluate and respond to the unique situations you encounter is your greatest asset. Simply noticing your own emotional and energetic responses to trees can really help enhance your sensitivity to this life form. Another way to strengthen your intuition with trees is to read books like those by Dorothy Maclean, who has been an articulate proponent for the life force in trees, giving them a voice by sharing the communications she has experienced. My intention is to help you feel and relate to all aspects of trees, and thus to create homes and offices that resonate with the feelings of contentment, inspiration, and beauty that you have experienced in the arbors of your childhood or the wilderness areas you enjoy today.

FIRE: CLEANSING AND RENEWAL

We are familiar with the physical presence of fire, warming our evenings in fireplaces and campfires and striking awe in volcanoes, forest fires, and lightning. Fire is a quick-moving energy that transforms matter and energy. Wood, for example, is transformed by fire into heat, light, and gases.

Most of us are instinctively aware of fire's transformative quality, consigning old letters or photos to the fire to release ourselves from burdensome memories or constricting emotional patterns. We have mortgage-burning parties to celebrate a passage from debt into a new financial freedom. Many cultures celebrate important historical victories with fireworks, symbolizing a new beginning and honoring the major commitment of the culture to reclaim sovereignty. New Year celebrations around the world often feature some kind of fire ritual to release the energies of the old year and declare our dreams and intentions for the year ahead.

Native Americans, like some contemporary forest managers, used fire to bring renewal to the land, clearing underbrush and opening up food sources like the meadows where camas roots and other wild foods were gathered each year. It's good to consider the biological role of fire for a moment, for it reflects the invisible or energetic function of this element. Wildfires help maintain forest health by preventing the fuel buildup that leads to catastrophic fires, which kill everything in the landscape. A normal wildfire moves through quickly, with lower temperatures that mature trees survive, naturally thinning overgrowth and providing the catalyst for certain seeds to open. There are, in fact, some seeds that will only open and mature after fire has passed through.

Many humans have a certain dread of fire. We know how quickly it can claim our homes, possessions, or even our lives. Some of us have seen beloved landscapes radically altered, and have worried for the safety of the intrepid men and women who risk their lives to fight the fires. It is indeed important to respect the tremendous power and potential of fire, and to continue to restore the balance of nature and to interact more consciously in order to reduce the occurrence of catastrophic fires.

One way to restore balance is to respect and appreciate the tremendous gift that fire brings, as well as its capacity for destruction. In the cyclical nature of life, fire is often a promotion or graduation, nature's way of saying, "Congratulations. You're ready to move on. You're graduating to the next level in your life path." Like other graduations, it can be a bittersweet experience. Growth is generally a mixed bag: pain at what we're leaving behind, joy at what we're gaining. Experiencing a fire in our life can be like a shamanistic dismembering, clearing away the familiar that is now in our way and opening the way for the new life situation that's possible for us.

People whose homes have burned down often talk of a surprising sense of liberation. Sylvia and Theo came home from a weekend getaway to discover a blackened hulk where their beloved family home had been. An electrical problem had sparked a conflagration that swept through their home, fortunately sparing the trees and neighboring homes in their wooded suburban neighborhood. Along with the shock, the mourning of irreplaceable mementos, and the stress of replacing lost possessions and relocating, they were surprised to notice a sense of freedom. It was as if some of their possessions had also carried an energy that was weighing them down, miring them in old ways of thinking and behavior that were now swept away by the fire.

Theo had dreamed of creating an innovative center for integrative medicine that would address the energetic, emotional, and physical components of health for clients with a dynamic, multidisciplinary staff in an uplifting environment. But he had been unable to get traction with the idea because the momentum of his busy life kept him occupied. A well-respected expert in his field, his responsibilities kept his days humming along at a dizzying pace. How could he find time to even think about starting something so new?

Somehow the shock of the fire caused a reorganization of his priorities. When he realized that the fire had destroyed the data for his presentations, Theo took this as a sign that it was time to let them go for the moment. He took time to slow down, step back, look at his life, and notice his feelings. Realizing how much his dream meant to him, he committed time and attention out of his busy schedule to think about it and talk to some people. Within months, he discovered unexpected support even within his old world and serendipitously made connections that moved his dream rapidly toward fulfillment.

At the same time, Sylvia had been longing to develop the intuitive gifts she sensed in herself and find a way to use them. But pursuing an intuitive career path had seemed too far from the down-to-earth, professional world she shared with Theo and their friends. At first she was devastated by the fire, shocked by the loss, burdened with thoughts that they had somehow caused the fire, and worried that it was a bad sign.

I explained that fire is better understood as an agent of transformation, a cleansing gift offered by nature as preparation for new blessings. With this support, Sylvia opened to the potential that the fire had brought her. She had dreamed of a new career using her intuitive gifts, but instead had been planning to return to teaching now that her children were older. But the fire had consumed all her teaching materials, and while she could have replaced them, their loss also seemed like a clear message to let go of the familiar and risk reaching for her dreams. She had held back partly because it seemed as if her new path might create too much upset in their domestic routine and social life. "One morning I realized that the fire had created that upset for me!" She laughed. "So now there wasn't as much to lose. It's so amazing to see that the fire, which had seemed so awful at the time, actually made it easier for me to risk going for what I really wanted." Sylvia enrolled in one of my yearlong trainings and is rapidly developing her intuitive gifts and enriching the lives of her family, clients, and friends.

Fire provides the spark to overcome inertia and allows the breathing space to see more clearly. Fire energy helps open the way for choices and actions to be more aligned with our authentic nature and deeper dreams.

When someone has been injured in a fire, a cleanse is needed to clear the energetic or emotional residue and allow the gifts of the fire to emerge from the pain. Fires are truly a sign of rebirth, although, like the process of birth, they are rarely comfortable at the time.

STONES: EARTH'S RECORD KEEPERS

Rocks are among the oldest substances on earth, and in many indigenous cultures they are recognized as those who hold stories. To know the history of a place, African elders say, sit or sleep with a stone from that place and it will give you impressions or stories. The mineral tribe, stones, and bones, they say, are the storytellers, the record keepers. Stones are the bones of the earth, like power points or concentrated areas of energy in the soil. They convey calm, helping us ground ourselves and feel our deep and ancient connection with this planet of ours.

Joan S. Davis, who spent decades doing water research at the Zurich Technical University, coined the phrase "wise water" for the water that has taken decades or centuries percolating down through earth and rock to become groundwater, absorbing information from minerals along the way and thus becoming wise or seasoned.[7]

We instinctively pick up stones on hikes or along the beach or roadside, often carrying favorite stones in our pockets or our cars, or placing them on our desks or windowsills to remind us of a special time or place or feeling. Stones retain their original structure and energy more than other elements, even when moved or subjected to changed environments. They bring us a sense of continuity, a feeling that all will be well. Placed in patterns on the earth, in a flowerbed, or in a hearth, they can help anchor a desired energy and bring stability to an area.

Jason and Sam encountered many obstacles at their new house, including a mudslide and a flood. I recognized that the house and its stability were influenced by its close proximity to a big irrigation canal, the main source of water circulation in their city. They enjoyed the water view and the presence of birds and other wildlife there, but were suffering the effects of having too much of that strong flowing energy. To counteract it, we placed large stones in the landscaping on the opposite side to provide stability and balance. Several years later, they reported that improvement has lasted.

The intangible energetic aspects of nature are all around us, outside and in our buildings, offices, and gardens, impacting our lives every day. With more awareness about the different facets of nature intelligences and ways to key into your own energetic radar system, you gain a wider range of choices to improve your indoor environment. It is deeply satisfying to cocreate solutions with nature and feel her do more than rise up to meet you. In many cases you discover a greater result, more than you had thought possible.

5

ACTIVATING YOUR PARTNERSHIP
WITH NATURE

Imagination is more important than knowledge. When I examine myself and my methods of thought, I come to the conclusion that the gift of imagination has meant more to me than my talent for abstract thinking.

—Albert Einstein

"YOU'RE JUST TOO SENSITIVE!" When I ask how many people have heard this phrase directed at them, the majority of my class usually nods in recognition. As a child, and even as an adult, sensitivity was like a disease I was supposed to get over, an annoying weakness to overcome. Over and over I heard, "Don't feel so much" or "Just get over it." Many of us have learned to disregard our illogical impressions as insignificant, a distraction from the "real" business at hand.

Fortunately I have learned that, far from being a distraction, these "insignificant" flashes are actually a great *help* to the business at hand, bringing added layers of insight and innovative solutions. In my work, my sensitivity is not only valid but it is also my major tool of analysis. With it, I download information that can resolve or avoid problems on a site by accessing creative ideas that otherwise would not have occurred to me.

In the bestseller *Blink*, Malcom Gladwell called this using our "adaptive unconscious" or "thin slicing," referring to "the ability of our unconscious to find patterns in situations and behavior based on very narrow slices of experience."

He suggested that while we can use the "thick slices of experience," which refers to all the logical reasons for doing something, it is often our intuitive flashes that give us the fullest information. He cited an example from the Getty Museum: In procuring a possibly rare marble Greek statue for the museum, rigorous authentication tests were conducted. Though the statue was passing these tests with flying colors, several prominent art historians had an intuitive repulsion to the statue without a logical reason. "It just didn't look right," they said. The museum could not find a reason to doubt the authenticity, but because of the hunches of the historians, they sought further expertise, which led them to a Greek historian who proved that this statue was indeed a fake.[2]

My clients and I are often amazed at the complex ingenuity of these solutions that arise in partnership with our sensitivity to nature. One student, a successful landscape designer, crowed delightedly, "It's so effective, I almost feel like I'm cheating! Nature is like this brilliant silent partner feeding me inside tips. I'm coming up with design solutions that wouldn't have occurred to me in the past. My customers are more satisfied, and so am I. The landscape is really alive for me now. It's always speaking to me." He added thoughtfully, "I realize it always has been, but now I've learned the language."

LEARNING THE LANGUAGE: BASIC RELATIONSHIP SKILLS

Now that you know about the interactive nature of the world around you, how do you get in on the conversation? As in any good relationship, a lively partnership with nature is based on your ability to listen and respond and to discover and develop a common means of communication. Communicating with nature is essentially a right-brained enterprise—freeform, intuitive, and nonlinear—that is best accessed by body radar and ceremony, two of the most effective tools in my intuitive toolkit.

Body radar is an instinctive system for detecting and deciphering subtle information. Ceremony or ritual gives us a system or format, a language for interacting with the unseen world. Broadly, you could say that body radar is a way of listening to or receiving data and ceremony is a way of responding to or transmitting it.

This chapter takes you through a deepening spiral of the experience and understanding of body radar. The exercises, which can be found in part 4 under Body Radar Workouts, build on one another. You could read through the chapter and begin with the workouts at the end of your reading, but your experience will be fuller, more nuanced, and more effective if you practice the body radar workouts while reading this chapter. They will mean more to you and prepare you for more advanced practice in later exercises and in real-life applications.

Finally, learning to communicate with nature, like learning any new language or skill, takes desire, instruction, and practice. Practice is essential. I can describe feelings and suggest ways of interaction, but this is no substitute for experience. You may find it helpful to refer to this chapter a number of times in between exercises, since you will understand more as you gain familiarity.

In *Blink* Gladwell pointed out that "educated snap judgments" take practice. While working with the Greek statue at the Getty Museum, art historian Thomas Hoving had honed his intuition to that degree because "he valued the fruits of spontaneous thinking so much that he took special steps to make sure his early impressions were as good as possible. He did not look at the power of his unconscious as a magical force. He looked at it as something he could protect and control and educate . . ."[3] While many of us have been conditioned to think that connecting with nature in this way is either frivolous or difficult, we need to have an open mind and let go of conditioning. It's a matter of educating as well as trusting ourselves.

BODY RADAR: EVERY BODY HAS IT

The combination of your sensory system and your intuition together compose your body radar. Body radar refers to your body's ability to function as an energy instrument that determines, detects, and responds to energy fields in your surroundings. I am continually amazed at the accuracy and speed of acquiring information in this subtle way.

HOW DOES BODY RADAR WORK?

Our bodies are transmitters and receivers, sending energy waves out and interpreting the energy echoes that come back. As the physical body sends out these waves, our antenna, or aura, scans the area to detect other energy fields. Once we have detected a field—a denser or more concentrated energy region—our next task is to define what it is, and then, if necessary, take action based on that knowledge.

For most of us, this is an automatic, unconscious process. You are already doing all this but are probably not aware of it. There is an advantage to becoming aware of our body radar because it becomes much more effective when used consciously. Like reading the manual or getting expert instructions for a new computer program, this knowledge expands the scope of what we can do with the tool.

We are constantly affecting and affected by the world around us, picking up thoughts and feelings from the earth, other humans, and events. Have you ever walked into a room and felt an unexplainable unease, an impulse to turn and leave? This is an example of body radar at work. There could be any number of explanations for a room's negative feeling: There may have been a recent argument, which may have left a lingering energy imprint of anger and distress. Or it may be located in the path of a ley line or an energy vortex, or near a disturbance in surrounding nature patterns.

Conversely, there are places we feel drawn to and would love to spend time in. Some people have felt this way in the homes of grandparents or other people who cultivate a tradition of faithfulness, joy, and peace. In earlier chapters, we also talked about the way that various types of earth energy—an ancient redwood, a power spot, or a cathedral—can have this effect on us.

The kind of energy field that you detect and respond to may be human or nonhuman. The impression may be coming from a nature being or element, or it may be an energetic imprint from a past human activity (a tragic battle or a wonderful concert) or from living humans or animals in the area (the agitated man beside you on the bus or the serene woman next to you in the theater).

With practice, you can begin to recognize how certain types of energy feel to you. This is one reason to keep a journal, as indicated in many of the exercises in part 4. The combination of experience and reflection helps you begin to recognize patterns on a number of levels. We all register energy in our own way, so your journal serves as a textbook or a scientific record, helping you begin to recognize how certain energies feel, sound, smell, and look to you.

It all starts with beginning to notice changes in your energy field. The following list may help you recognize some of your own physical sensations and emotional reactions, along with the type of information they may convey.

Physical sensations:

❁ Headaches or a feeling like you have a tight cap on your head: This may be an indication that you are on a highly charged site. It can be difficult to stay very long at this type of location. On the other hand, it may indicate that your energy circuits are being overused and your body is being pushed to a limit. Try taking a break. Change your activity, giving your body a rest to slow down the pace of the energy moving through it.

❁ Dizziness: This may be due to unstable energy at a site or to fast-moving energy such as a strong ley line. Walk away from the area for a few minutes and observe if the feeling dissipates. If so, it was probably a caused by the energy of the area you were in.

❁ Inability to make conclusions easily or to think clearly; a sense of ungroundedness: This is another indication of instability in the surrounding energy field. Visualize yourself grounding with the earth and watch for any changes in reactions. If you still experience instability, this is a clearer indication of an energy disturbance in the earth.

❁ A tightness or knot in your stomach: This can indicate an intense energy field or perhaps a negative emotional field or a distressed or agitated nature being. Try breathing deeply and visualizing breathing into your belly to relax the stomach area. If the deep breathing is only briefly effective, the environment may be causing the disturbance.

❁ An inability to breathe freely or feeling confined or constricted: This indicates a disordered energy pattern, usually a lack of flow, a constricted flow of life force, or possibly a disturbed or disruptive energy imprint. This reaction is usually an indication of an intense earth energy disturbance, and it is best to stay in these areas for brief periods to avoid too much stimulation for the body.

- A sense of space as you enter a site; an ability to walk easily from room to room and to breathe easily: this generally indicates vitality and life force flowing well.

- Seeing a small blue light or a dot of light blinking on and off around you: This may indicate that a helpful being has entered your space to support you. The blinking is very slight, so it is easy to miss these sweet messages.

- Personal signals from your own internal system: With practice, you will develop your own list of sensations and what they mean to you. Your journal will serve you well, as you can look back on other times you had that reaction and what you discovered.

    When I get to know a site I often see internally an elliptical cross. Like an architect taking measurements, I walk around a site gathering impressions until I know I've got a complete enough picture of the situation and am ready to move into the solutions phase. Over time, I realized that this symbol shows up as a sign that I've got all the impressions I need to orient myself, that I've gathered all the significant data and am now connected to the essence of the site and can move on to the solution phase. It's a bit like getting five bars on your cell phone; it's my own internal symbol by which nature lets me know that we've got a good connection and we're ready for the next step.

Emotional reactions:

- Nervousness or restlessness: This can be a result of fast-moving energy bumping and jostling your energy field. To give you another way to sense this, imagine the feeling of standing by a freeway. Even if you cannot see or hear the cars whizzing by, your subtle senses will register the movement.

❂ Lethargy, tiredness: This can be a result of subtle stagnant fields on a site where the life force is not flowing well. You may feel tired because it can be an effort to ground or maintain your awareness with energetic clutter around you.

❂ Calmness and clarity, a feeling of being able to step onto the site easily: This indicates a well-settled pattern of balance on a site.

❂ A sense of homecoming or welcome: Nature is welcoming you.

❂ Joy and ebullience upon coming to a site: This often indicates vitality and positive life force present.

For workouts to exercise your body radar, see page 189.

TIPS FOR DEVELOPING SENSITIVITY TO PLACE

1. *Let go of logic as your main source of information.*
Often when I make a recommendation for restoring flow or progress on a site, clients will say, "I've always wanted to do that, but it didn't make sense to me. I could not find a logical reason to do it." As it happens, the reason is not a logical one. It comes from intuition and senses picking up on subtle clues from the environment. In the words of an ancient Chinese proverb:

A side door is still a door.
A left path is still a path.
An irrational belief is still a belief, a way of knowing.

Intuition is like a side door—less visible, less obvious than a front door, and not used as often. It may have been ignored or forgotten, but it is still a threshold, an opening. Using a side door or left path means moving beyond the norm and beyond commonly accepted ideas. In order to acquire new information or abilities, we often have to use ways that are unfamiliar or not habitual to us.

Using your intuition is not so much a matter of *thinking* outside the box as *going outside* the box, outside the realm of logical thought. When you move beyond logical thinking, you become more aware of your other senses and the information they are providing. Like befriending a shy animal, it takes patience, an openness to new possibilities, and a willingness to pay attention. Intuition produces a knowing that resonates throughout the body. You may not be able to explain how you know, but you do.

2. *Trust your hunches, especially first impressions.*
Annalise often noticed an uncomfortable feeling when she approached her kitchen after being away from the house for a few hours. The room was barely used; people would leave the area as soon as a meal was finished. When she would come home, a warm intuitive image of yellow would flood her imagination and she would feel goose bumps. This impression would fade away the longer she was home, but she had learned that goose bumps were a signal from her own body radar, an affirmation or signal to pay attention. Experience had taught her that the ideas or impressions that gave her goose bumps tended to work out well for her.

So despite her family's preference for white walls and Scandinavian minimalism, Annalise followed her intuition and painted the kitchen yellow and added several other touches that gave her a sunny feeling. Her risk paid off in spades: the kitchen has now become a favorite spot for people to gather. Other family members have commented on feeling more warmth and togetherness there.

Many of us have learned to second-guess ourselves, growing up, as most of us have, in an educational system that taught us there is one right answer to any question—and that it is held by someone else and understood only by a lot of mental effort. We were trained to ignore and mistrust our own instinctive and intuitive answers.

To reverse that process and reconnect with your own wisdom and abilities, develop the habit of noticing that little voice inside and your subtle sensations and reactions. A sudden rush of happiness when entering an area can be an indication of healthy life force there. A sudden flush of goose bumps or the stomach tightening can be a warning, alerting you to something needing your attention. You probably know people who risked accepting a job or signing an apartment lease based on a good feeling that their logical mind couldn't justify, and found that their intuition was correct, or people who heeded their goose bumps or creepy feelings and didn't get on the plane that crashed or didn't invest in the great deal that turned out to be a financial bust. In a class, Nelson mentioned that he was sitting comfortably in his living room chair reading when suddenly he had an intuitive flash to go upstairs, where he found the candle he had forgotten to extinguish burning dangerously near a curtain.

It is easiest to recognize your body radar when you first come to a new place. Upon arriving, your energy field is like a fresh canvas ready to be painted with impressions. It is at this point, when the web of invisible data from the place has not yet begun to weave with your own, that you can receive the clearest data. Your human aura has not yet blended with the aura or energetic pattern of the place, and your mind has not begun to process the facts as you know them. So your first impressions tend to be a more instinctual—and more accurate—reading of the energy.

While special training and special sensitivity are helpful, please remember that the ability to receive and decipher energy is inherent in every human body. Trust yourself.

3. *Notice patterns, both visible and invisible.*
Nature is endlessly weaving and reweaving patterns, such as the seasons turning and spiders weaving webs to hold their nourishment, which is her way of getting things done. Builders or landscapers who can perceive and work with patterns such as the natural meander of water on a property tend to achieve better results than those who don't. Working with a pattern means respecting its integrity. This doesn't necessarily mean not touching or altering it, but it means doing so with awareness and in cooperation with nature.

When I walk onto a client's land or into a home or business, I pay attention to the patterns created by the water flows, trees, winds, breezes, and other elements in the landscape. I register them with my sight, hearing, skin, and smell, as well as with the more indistinct feelings or impressions.

Jane called me because her life had become more complicated after moving into a new house. As I drove onto her property, I saw that her house was located at the mouth of a river. The water flow was influenced by the ocean tides and the changing seasonal river flows. In addition, a natural spring cascading down a nearby shrubby hill produced a swampy wetland somewhat close to the house. These diverse patterns of water, ocean, river, and spring placed so close together created an earth energy dilemma, entangling it even more with a house on the site. A lot of clutter, such as piles of lumber, old tools, and magazines, had accumulated around the house, mirroring the chaos in the area. To illustrate this dilemma, imagine placing strong personalities—one talkative, another quiet, and another moody—in one room and asking them to live together without enough personal space to be themselves.

Bringing awareness to these diverse patterns helped focus our work, and over time we were able to remedy the situation with some cures, focusing on the largest area of concern: the swampy water closest to the house. For Jane, working directly with the water was the best way to balance things again. To pull the chaotically patterned watery energy away from the house, we created a line of nine buried crystals connected by copper wire. Pyroelectricity, practiced since at least the eighteenth century, is the ability of quartz crystals to generate electrical polarization when heated or connected with the mechanical stress of superconductive metal such as copper. In this case, electrical polarization occurred when combining the copper and quartz in the ground and was enough to draw the swampy water away from the house and direct it to a grove of trees and rocks—an area with a healthy pattern strong enough to contain and ground it. We added rocks and a few more trees to the grove and other areas on the lot to strengthen and contain the entire site.

Life became calmer for Jane and her family. Their communication improved along with their money situation. Whereas money had flowed in and right back out, they began to experience more financial stability as the pattern on their land stabilized.

Your body has the ability to detect the energy and form of these patterns. Many people actually see subtle energy fields, but even without that level of sensitivity, you can use the sensations of your body to pick up this kind of information. The ability to work with patterns such as many different water flows close together begins with recognizing them. For now, just pay attention and allow yourself to notice layers of patterns that may have escaped your attention.

4. *Remember to use your body radar.*
Using your body radar begins with paying attention to the information that your own body is giving you, noticing what feels good and what feels "off," and then taking action based on this awareness.

You will find that throughout your day, you have a choice: you can focus on these subtle cues or you can tune them out. Focusing means that you choose to filter out the distractions from within (doubts, ideas, to-do list items that seem more pressing) and from without (passing cars, ringing phones, people talking), choosing instead to focus on the subtle data coming from nature. By simply choosing to pay attention, you can pick up little blips on the body radar screen, subtle blips that momentarily flash across your awareness and are usually ignored, drowned out by the distractions of our busy lives.

This takes practice. But the more you practice, the stronger your antenna gets and the more awareness you develop. You will begin to notice more of what you had ignored or missed in the past. Fran, a participant in my training, reported, "After practicing with my body radar in nature and at home, I walked into my first client's house and was drawn to one room right away. The room did not feel right to me, and the client relayed that her depressed sister had been living in there. I knew that we needed to work in that room first."

5. *Have fun with it.*
Too much intensity will actually choke the flow. A light and playful attitude expands your scope and helps you take in information in new ways. It's like looking with your peripheral vision and softening and expanding your focus.

Going with the flow and allowing yourself to enjoy the process will give you more success and satisfaction than if you were to work hard at it. It's mostly a matter of taking time to pay attention, relax, let go of limiting ideas, and remember what is already part of you.

A WORD OF ENCOURAGEMENT

Each person registers energy fields in his or her own way. Partnership with nature is not an exact science; it is more of an art. You are surfing a wave and constantly monitoring and adjusting to many variables. But like surfing, it can be great fun.

Whether or not you think of yourself as sensitive, I assure you: this basic awareness and ability is intrinsic to all human beings. Like riding a bike or speaking another language, everyone can learn how to use it. In fact, you are learning another language: the language of nature and your natural self. What was meaningless background sight and sound will now give you information that is essential to your life.

Please take a moment to look at how far you've already come. A short time ago, you may have believed that all your thoughts and feelings were generated inside yourself. Now you are at least considering the idea that many of them may actually be in response to the world around you. Now you can have fun noticing the sensations and insights that will continue to unfold as nature joyfully responds to *you*.

CEREMONIES: ANOTHER WAY OF MAKING CONTACT

Ceremonies, or rituals, are a way of pausing to contact a deeper dimension of life. They tend to connect us more with ourselves, with others, and with something greater by tapping into resources beyond our everyday experience. In *Rituals and Devotion in Buddhism*, Sangharakshita noted that since ritual is a form of expression that brings something out "from the depths within . . . our whole being will be enriched and integrated. Tension between the conscious and the unconscious will be reduced. We will become more whole. In becoming more whole, we become more effective in our actions."[4]

Humans around the world mark life's transitions and achievements—births, deaths, weddings, a successful hunt, graduation, puberty, distinguished service to tribe or country, or commitment to a path of action—with formal or impromptu ceremonies. Most cultures and spiritual paths feature seasonal celebrations of the turning wheel of life. In our modern life, Carl Jung made the following observation: "We no longer need magical dances to make us 'strong' for whatever we want to do, at least not in ordinary cases. But when we have to do something that exceeds our powers, then we solemnly lay a foundation stone with the blessing of the church, or christen a ship as she slips from the dock . . . Through these ceremonies the deeper emotional forces are released."

A ritual or ceremony slows time down and focuses attention and intention enough to create a more graceful interweaving of the old pattern with the new, allowing for smoother and more auspicious transitions. It is a time-out to garner insight and support as we step over the threshold of change.

WHAT IS A CEREMONY?

In this book, I use the words "ceremony" and "ritual" interchangeably, though others may make a distinction, with ceremony meaning a more prescribed or formal type of ritual. For me, a ceremony is anything done with consciousness and intention. It can be simple or elaborate. You can perform a ritual or create one by yourself, with just a few others, or with a large group of people.

Cleaning is often a ritual for me. I enter into it with an intention to clean and transform not only my physical space, but also my consciousness and energy and the energy of the space I am cleaning. The results are very satisfying. I am transformed—my mood brightened, new energy released, inspiration and insights flowing—and the space is transformed. It is not only cleaner but lighter, brighter somehow, with a good feeling in the air that others notice upon entering. This kind of cleaning sends ripples of transformation out into the world.

Another very simple ceremony is to take a few moments to announce— to yourself and to nature—your intention for a project or change you are planning in your apartment, home, yard, or neighborhood. Don and Niki, the building-design team discussed in chapter 2 who developed and are building around the hub and ley lines in their urban mountain pastureland, perform little ceremonies at different stages of the building process. They

75

feel that there is more efficiency to the process if they set the patterns energetically first. Ground-breaking ceremonies and staking out the patterns of new lots and buildings, for example, are ceremonial ways of announcing the intended new pattern that allow the resident elements of nature to adjust and weave it into the existing pattern on the land.

Throughout the design and construction process in each of their jobs, Don and Niki take time to listen and feel for information from nature, and leave symbolic offerings as an expression of appreciation and partnership. This kind of ongoing conversation with the environment, they find, results in a more trouble-free construction process, easier sales, and more satisfied buyers.

I believe that ceremonies are effective partly because they increase our receptivity, enhancing our subtle bond with nature and life around us. The sounds, colors, scents, and movements help bring us to our senses and beyond. It's a way to get on the same wavelength with nature and increase our ability to communicate—and receive communication—in nature's language.

In looking for the roots and purposes of rituals, neurobiology researchers Andrew Newberg and Eugene d'Aquili of the University of Pennsylvania point to the elaborate butterfly courtship dance as an example of ritual "stripped down to its bare neurobiological essence."[5] The dance sets up a biological resonance between the butterflies' nervous systems. "Neurobiologically, the butterflies are 'vibrating' in harmony, like a pair of tuning forks. This sense of closeness and common purpose allows them to transcend the normal self-protective instincts that would usually compel them to avoid interaction with others, and reap survival benefits they could not have managed on their own." This, they infer, is a close parallel of how rituals work for humans and other species. In this case, we look at ceremony as a way to overcome the modern instincts that separate us from nature and patterns of life beyond our awareness. The new level of harmony and partnership thus achieved can yield seemingly miraculous results.

WHAT CAN CEREMONIES DO FOR YOU?

Let's look at some examples of how ceremonies can benefit you in working with your home, office, or land.

❦ *Ceremonies can be great focusing tools:* Building is a great production, with a lot of interlocking, sequenced activities, and actors that need to be closely coordinated. Performing a ceremony at each stage can bring in better concentration for each person involved in the project and sometimes helps facilitate completion of a stage right on schedule.

Joyce Ward, an architect with twenty-five years of experience, finds these intuitive practices an essential part of the design process. For instance, during the construction of a house she had designed, the ground-breaking ceremony had been postponed and then forgotten. After an unusual number of supply delays and other glitches in the building process, she remembered the ceremony that hadn't happened. Reflecting that one of the purposes of this simple ceremony was to facilitate a smooth interweaving between the old patterns and the proposed new ones, Joyce chose to hold the ceremony even at this late stage. On doing so, problems were resolved and the building process progressed.

With cleaning, I always do an attunement ceremony before I begin any project at home or at work. It brings me to the present and allows me to focus on the art of cleaning and polishing on many levels of the physical environment around me.

❦ *Ceremonies can reconnect us with a bigger picture:* It is an opportunity to pause before action and to reconnect with a deeper meaning and with our original purpose. In doing so, we reinvigorate ourselves and the work of construction, remodeling, redecorating, or just rearranging. June called me when she found herself frustrated and bogged down with the usual delays or setbacks that always seem to come during remodeling. Following my suggestion to do a little ceremony to reconnect with her hopes and dreams for this building, she called me excitedly to say that she had gone out to the beautiful willow tree on her property, which had been her reason for buying the lot. Taking time by the tree had brought her back to her original enthusiasm. Refocusing her attention on the beauty and joy of the project instead of on the struggles, the obstacles soon cleared away.

Ceremonies create bridges from one phase in life to another: Including a ceremony in transitional times can be a time to celebrate weaving the new invisible patterns coming together. As Victor Turner, professor of anthropology at the University of Virginia, put it, "The experience of sameness and continuity over the life span is deliberately destroyed by rites of passage, though one of their persistent functions is to symbolically state the fact of continuity despite the appearance of change and disruption. This is another of the paradoxes of the life course."[6]

This idea is poignantly illustrated by Pat and Larry, who organized a ceremony in their new garden as a memorial for a daughter who had died in an auto accident. This garden was a way to for them to celebrate and remember their daughter's joy for life and love of flowers. The backyard was transformed and filled with plants and flowers their daughter loved. A water feature by the entrance to the garden signaled the entrance to a special spot.

By conducting a simple private ritual before they began the garden, announcing their intentions, and inviting nature's support, they experienced deep healing while working on it. Now it was important for them to mark the occasion of garden's completion and affirm the intention that had created it. I conducted Master Lin's Exterior Chi Ceremony (described in part 4). It was a time for honoring and letting go, a time for moving forward with grace and honoring the gift that their daughter was to them by allowing her gifts to enrich their future. The ceremony gave them a way to celebrate this with their friends and, in the process, to receive the gifts more deeply. The ceremony with friends and family was a means for them to move forward. Larry told me that he noticed that after the ceremony he and Pat "just felt more settled somehow, more at peace, more able to enjoy the goodness in life again." Pat noted the way that the love, support, and prayers their friends had expressed in the ceremony seemed to linger in the garden afterwards. It had helped create a bridge of change for them from one phase in life to another, allowing them to relish the new invisible pattern arising from and interwoven with the old.

Another couple wanted to celebrate a job promotion that had allowed them to move to a larger, brand-new home. The ceremony they chose was just the activity needed to track the change on invisible larger patterns opening up, and to breathe in the feelings of this new expansion in their lives. Moving in seemed to go faster as well, they reported.

Ceremonies can breathe new life into large projects, giving respite from tedium or tension: The process of building or changing an environment is just as important as the result. Ceremonies can be a way to enjoy each stage of a project and to have a bit of fun in the process. Engaging the senses through sound, movement, and color, they provide a welcome break from routine. They create opportunities for workers, friends, and family members to get to know one another and allow feelings and thoughts to be a part of the mix. In this creative atmosphere, new ideas and better teamwork often result.

I learned this lesson well when working on the Great Hall at Findhorn. This building, now a major landmark used for most of the creative presentations and workshops, took seven years to build. Throughout construction, each phase was celebrated with simple attunements and feasts of good food. This added to the enjoyment and camaraderie of each worker and was also a means of renewal and commitment for this large project. I was a part of a group that sanded one of the major beam supports for the roof to fine smoothness. It was a small contribution but potent with our intentions.

Many of the regular workers said that these ceremonial work contributions from occasional workers were important for their individual perseverance on the project.

Ceremonies bring an inner transformation to complement and support the outward one: Think of your project as an invisible canvas that you as the celebrant can paint with all your wishes and hopes. Ceremonies are a premier way to transfer these intentions and dreams onto the blank canvas of time and space before you.

Recent science and business publications, such as the book *Blink* and *Fast Company* magazine, describe the power of our thoughts and intentions. Taking time for ceremonies is an important way to focus this power by allowing the strokes, whispers, and songs from your heart to register the tones and nuances of your thoughts onto the canvas. Rituals or ceremonies set more into motion than just the physical activity of building, remodeling, or redecorating. They are a way of attracting that extra something that can lend a deeper quality of satisfaction, peace, healing, and inspiration to life.

At the Great Hall at Findhorn, goodwill radiates within and from the building. The pauses that we took during construction to celebrate and renew our intentions created a lasting atmosphere that supports the building's purpose.

SOMETIMES OLD CEREMONIES ARE BEST

Like an old violin, centuries-old ceremonies carry a resonance, richness, and depth built from repetitive use and quality materials. My grandfather loved his old violin, which he had inherited from a family member. He always claimed that he learned to play so quickly because the old violin responded so easily to his beginner's touch. Conducting ceremonies with patterns enacted many times can transfer the power and resonance more easily to the participants and to the site.

R. J. Stewart says that an old, well-used, and respected ceremony attracts the gods or the creative forces because its familiarity draws them in. He uses the example of fish in a pond. If they suddenly swam in a pattern such as a figure eight, it would grab our attention because the pattern is familiar to us. It would stand out from the more random or unrecognizable patterns in which they normally move around the pond.

So it is when we enact an old ceremony. The pattern of the ceremony attracts bigger beings familiar with this old way and invites them to come and participate. It can be interesting to look into your own heritage. How did your distant ancestors celebrate the turning points in life? How did or do your grandparents mark these occasions? For some traditional and not-so-traditional ceremonies, see page 205.

BEGINNING YOUR EARTH PARTNERSHIP RITUALS

For your own rituals, you may want to use traditional ceremonies or you may prefer to spontaneously create ceremonies in relation to the present moment, reflecting your desired outcome. Traditional ceremonies can be like training wheels. You can follow them long enough to get the hang of it, and at some point you let go of the older forms to create your own rituals. Rituals are, after all, a statement of intention, dreams, hopes, and desires. They are as individual as the participants and the unique situation.

PART TWO

Living with Grace in Your Home or Office

6

VIBRANT DESIGN:
ANCIENT PRINCIPLES IN MODERN TIMES

We shape our dwellings, and afterwards our dwellings shape us.
—Sir Winston Churchill

As THE INNOVATIVE business magazine *Fast Company* frequently points out, design affects every aspect of our life and work. Whether you are rethinking a room that feels uncomfortable, addressing health challenges, launching a major construction project, or wanting a more productive office, this chapter has several novel ways to help you.

Good design principles are universal. Whether we refer to ancient practices from feng shui or look to European Renaissance architecture and its Greco-Roman roots, surprising similarities emerge. Ancient Western mathematicians discovered an irrational number, the golden ratio, that frequently occurs in geometry. They believed that physical existence is numerical and suggested that utilizing these expressions of ratios and proportions in buildings assured a structural and aesthetic resonance with all life. The classic proportions of great cathedrals and pyramids reflect the patterning of the natural world, where the same complex mathematical patterns govern the spirals of seashells and sunflowers, the distance between stars, a butterfly's wing markings, and the space between different parts of the human body. The golden ratio is still used frequently in art and design, which suggests a natural balance between symmetry and asymmetry.

Perhaps because they are an essential part of us, many of us create environments that harmonize and amplify natural patterns and energies, even without knowing the elegant mathematical formulas used by the pyramid builders. In fact, humans have been building sustainably around the world for thousands of years, using the same intuitive skills and sensitivity described in this book. Let's take a deeper look at some basic ways to work with the patterns in an indoor environment.

BREATHING LIFE FORCE INTO DESIGN

In my experience, a truly successful design for any room or building should allow a healthy flow of vitality or life force throughout the space. Think of a room where you feel good upon entering, a place where you feel at ease and uplifted. Those are signs of healthy flow of chi. People feel drawn to these rooms or buildings and tend to linger there when possible. On the other hand, in rooms that lack this vital energy, people may want to leave quickly or may experience a sense of constriction or oppression. They may feel less positive there and find it harder to think clearly or creatively. Some people actually develop health or other problems from living or working in a place with seriously depleted life force.

The best results come from a dynamic balance of the intangible, or mystical, and the linear, or logical, in an ongoing dance that the ancient Chinese poetically called the marriage of heaven and earth. The intangible presence of chi in an environment is influenced by the tangible objects and vice versa. Specifically, life force is affected by the shape and quality of physical objects like walls, windows, and furniture, and by how and where they are placed. When you can see or sense both the tangible and intangible aspects, you can create environments with healthy, balanced life force.

TWO PERSPECTIVES ON ENERGY CIRCULATION

There are several ways to view a structural design's energetic blueprint, which can make the interplay of forces more visible to you and help you create balance. One way is to use the proportions of the human body as a reference point, and the second is to consider the structure as a collection of energy centers. Both ways can help you assess and correct the way the energy circulates so that you can find the right recipe for a vibrant, well-loved environment.

PERSPECTIVE 1: A BUILD ING AS A BODY

Let us begin by viewing a building as a body, a living entity with breath and circulation. Hallways and other transitional spaces act as arteries and passages for the breath. The main entrance is a mouth, a portal for the life force to enter.

The building-as-a-body concept is not new in design. It has cropped up in various parts of the globe throughout history. Many temples and sacred buildings, east and west, were designed along human proportions. In Hindu culture, the body is exemplified in the design of the temple as a way to bring man to God. European cathedrals and the churches modeled on them reflect a human form with outstretched arms.

In 1 BC, Marcus Vitruvius Pollio, author of the first architectural-engineering handbook in Western culture, wrote that the parts of the body are related to one another in whole numbers and that these ratios should be used in architecture.[2] Sixteen centuries later, his ideas were extremely popular with Renaissance artists like Giorgio Vasari and Leonardo da Vinci.

Da Vinci's notebooks are filled with sketches reflecting principles he drew from Vitruvius and other sources, which he expanded with his own experiments and observations. Relentlessly curious about the mysteries of life, da Vinci discovered that the classical principles of the golden ratio also governed the growth of trees, the flight of birds, and the flow of water. As a result, he was the first to draw the human body in proportion and the first to apply these same principles to his architectural designs. His famous *Vitruvian Man* is a symbol of the essential symmetry of the human form and its relationship to the universe as a whole. It is a *cosmographia del minor mondo*, a miniature map of the cosmos showing the web or patterns of life as seen through the lens of mathematical proportion and symmetry.

WORKING WITH THE MYSTICAL BODY OF A BUILDING

Because it is created in the same cosmic proportions recurring constantly throughout our galaxy, the human body is a natural model we can use to mirror these patterns in our architectural designs. Black Sect Tantric Buddhist feng shui teaches the use of a body analogy to observe and correct patterns of vitality within a structure—an ancient cure for "sick building syndrome"— in order to optimize a building's energy and consequently help the health of those who live or work in it.

To use the approach, superimpose a human form onto the floor plan of a building to get a sense of where the life energy is flowing optimally and where it is not. The location of the building's entrance always determines the location of the figure's head. Usually, begin by visualizing a body lying flat on the floor plan with the top of the head in the front entrance and the feet at the back wall. You will see the body as evenly proportioned (Fig. 3) or as having one or more parts constricted, depending on where the entrance is located.

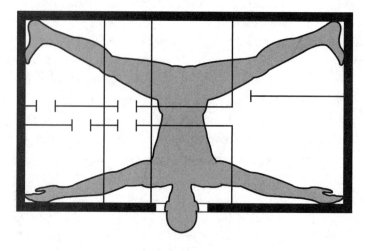

Figure 3

If the human form is cramped or contorted, it indicates an area in the design where life force will be constricted in the structure. For example, a stunted leg or arm in the symbolic body (Figs. 4 and 5) indicates that circulation in that part of the design is restricted.

Given the many factors involved in choices for design today, we may not often achieve classical proportion, but knowing these principles helps us make adjustments to keep the energy balanced. A cramped arm and leg in a

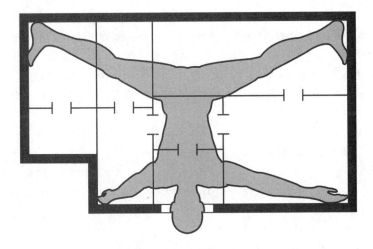

Figure 4

floor plan does not necessarily require a drastic design change, but it does signal a need to balance the flow by increasing an area's vitality. Joyce Ward often compensates for a stunted limb by including more windows in the area to encourage circulation of light and air (therefore chi or life force).

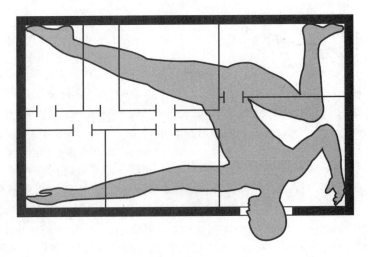

Figure 5

A stretched area also places stress on a house's energetic pattern, much like a person permanently standing on tiptoes or continually stretching to reach something on a high shelf. Just as a person could easily be pushed off balance in these positions because he or she is not standing strong, when the pattern is stretched in these ways, the energy can't circulate as reliably and the vitality isn't as strong.

A stretched area can be amended by placing heavier elements to bring balance. Heavier furniture or a heavy sculpture in the area, for example, can give a feeling of more strength or support, like a steadying hand. Flooring could be stone or wood with warmer, earthy colors on the walls.

VERTICAL APPLICATIONS

The imaginary body can also be superimposed on the design in a vertical position in the case of a multistoried structure. For one vertical application, the figure is head down, with the head in the doorway, facing into the structure (Fig. 6). The other vertical application places the head in the roof and the feet at the ground floor (Fig. 7).

Some consultants use both views to get more perspective on the design, especially if they are looking for the key to an occupant's health problem.

HEALTH APPLICATIONS

For persistent health issues, it is good to look at the work environment as well as at the home. Physical ailments often reflect a diminished vitality in the corresponding area of the home or office, so by locating the affected body parts in the building and raising the chi there, you can achieve corresponding results in the occupant's body. Remedies might include fixing broken furnishings, removing clutter, and increasing lighting or air circulation.

Sandra called me with respiratory problems. She was an artist who had let her work go, which was part of a pattern of tending to the needs of others and neglecting her own. As I applied the mystical body to her home, I noticed that the room in the lung area of the house had a window that didn't work and other problems with air circulation. The room wasn't used much and had a stagnant quality from lack of activity and attention. Vitality was escaping from the lung area of both her body and her home.

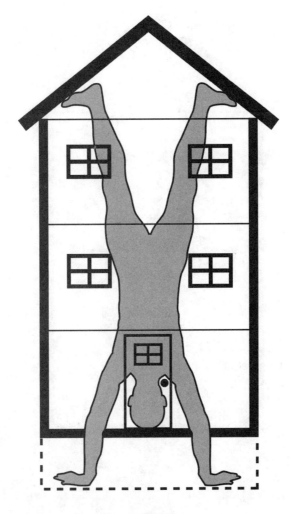

Figure 6

I noted with interest that the problem room was her art studio. Here was yet another level of mirroring: her failure to invest life energy in the creative pursuits that were important to her was reflected in the neglect and disrepair of the room, which in turn was reflected in her physical health.

Sandra fixed the window, installed a ceiling fan, and began using the room again. As she made the changes, she consciously held a mental picture

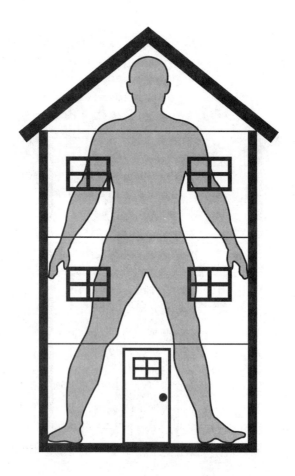

Figure 7

of creating health and harmony in her home. Recognizing that she had been spending too much time taking care of others and not enough time on herself and her art, she included an intention for a blossoming of her creative endeavors. Within several weeks her health had improved, and a month later she joyfully announced her first exhibit in an art gallery.

Doors, windows, and skylights are the openings in the mystical body, like the mouth, ears, and eyes in the human body. Designing, creating, and maintaining them can be important to the health and overall success of the occupants. Leaks in the plumbing can affect digestion; electrical outages can be reflected in nervous system problems. Broken windows, doors that stick, burners that don't work—all these problems can create stagnation in the body of the building and in the human body as well.

STEPPING BACK

Growing up with a mechanical understanding of the universe, many people are not interested in the science of energy and of working with patterns, symbolic language, and the power of intention. I imagine that someone from a "primitive" culture feels equally startled and perplexed when we light a dark house by touching a spot on the wall or when the sound of many people drumming blares from a small box.

The movie *What the (Bleep) Do We Know!?* makes the point that humans tend to be neurologically wired not to see anything we don't expect or anything that doesn't fit our current frame of reference. The movie dramatizes an incident reported by early European explorers to the Americas, where local people encountering these pale men on the shore of their island thought they must be gods appearing from nowhere. Even when the explorers pointed to their ships, the islanders were unable to see them because they had no concept of such ships.

But curiosity, observation, and intuition can open us to new awareness. In the movie, a wise old shaman stands patiently on the sand, studying the water until his body radar detects something different about the way it moves in the area. After continuing his observation, he is finally able to see the ships and point them out to others. I invite you to stand with me on the shore of this building-as-a-body concept and to experiment and observe, allowing yourself to gain a sense of the layers of interconnecting patterns involved.

PERSPECTIVE 2: A BUILDING AS ENERGY COLUMNS

Another way to ensure balanced chi flow through a building is to look at the structure in terms of energy columns. In the physical framing of a building, the upright two-by-fours are areas of concentrated physical strength and power supporting the structure. Whether they support crossbeams or curve inward to meet in an arch, the vertical beams are essential in a building, anchoring it solidly on the earth, carrying its weight, and allowing it to rise toward the sky.

Similarly, every structure has energy columns, power centers that act like generators and help evenly distribute the breath of life, sustaining the building and its occupants on a nonphysical level. In every building, there are nine columns—one in the center and eight around the perimeter—that are all interconnected and interacting in a regular pattern (Fig. 8). The nine columns expand and fill the whole shape of the structure. Figure 9 displays images of the expanded columns filling a balanced shape. Many of us live in irregular shapes, and the energy columns expand differently in these shapes. If the extended shape beyond the basic rectangle shape is less than half the width of the building, the extended section is considered an addition and its particular energy column is stronger or greater than the rest of the columns (Fig. 10a). If the extended section is more than half the width of the building, the shape is missing an energy column (Fig. 10b). In this case, a cure can be used to symbolically correct the shape. For example, placing a light or a tree in the area can complete the shape.

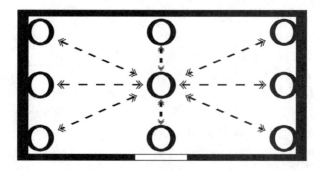

Figure 8

The configuration of energy hubs is echoed in many cultures. The feng shui tradition uses an eight-sided map, called a *ba-gua*, which includes the center as a hub. With the ba-gua, each section also has particular life attributes associated with each placement, noted here as Reputation, Joy,

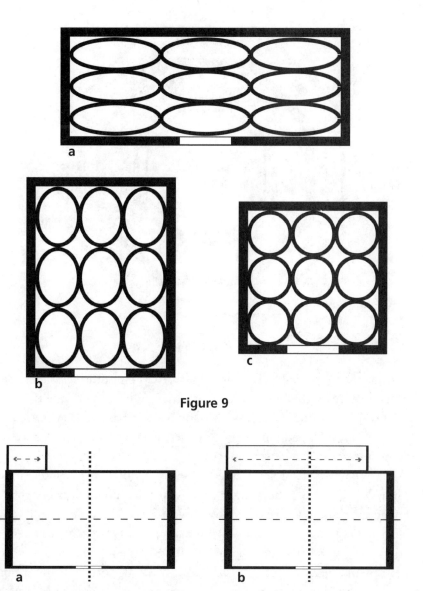

Figure 9

Figure 10

Children, Helpful People, Career, Knowledge, Family, and Flow, with overall Health in the center (Fig. 11).

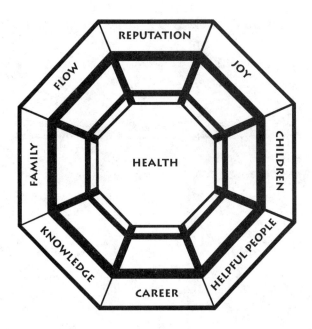

Figure 11

Author and architect A. T. Mann reports that in traditional Islamic design a mosque features eight angels or columns that support the divine throne that completes the nine energy columns. Many Middle Eastern homes are graced with octagonally shaped entrances or courtyards, and the octagon design is predominant in Middle Eastern motifs.

Ancient Taoist texts describe these nine energy columns as wise immortals or sentinels, noting that both the structure and its inhabitants benefit when these energy centers are acknowledged with a small activity like lighting a candle or simply thinking of one's intentions and hopes in each area.[3] Feng shui tradition also emphasizes the reinforcement and suggests placing an appropriate permanent object in an area to add power and support to the intention.

A cure is used to enhance, adjust, or strengthen an energy hub through the placement of a pleasant sensory reminder, such as good lighting, mirrors, sound, fragrance, water, heavy objects, color, or texture, in the area. The sensory liveliness awakens your body radar, reminding you of your intention and stimulating the intangible web of support to create balance. (See part 4 for a complete list of cures that can support and enhance the function of these energy centers.)

I combine the use of the life situations from the ba-gua with the energy columns. To determine the placement of the nine energy columns in your building, draw a floor plan of the building, highlighting the front door. Column placement is always determined in relation to the front door, the symbolic mouth or entry point for the building, even if you use another door more frequently. Imagine standing outside your apartment, office, house, or condo facing the front entrance. Place Knowledge on the left side of the front wall (the wall that contains the front door), place Career in the center, and place Helpful People to the right. Then distribute the rest of the columns evenly throughout the whole floor plan, as shown in Figure 11.

This same configuration of energy centers or columns exists on smaller and larger scales, which is another reflection of the universe's holographic nature. No matter how far you break it down, the totality is present in every tiny fragment or at every layer. All nine energy columns are present in each room in a structure's floor plan, and in the yard and on the grounds as well. Whether you go to the larger level or the smaller, the pattern is there.

Why does this matter? Let's say a homeowner has a serious drainage problem in her backyard or an apartment dweller has a drainage problem in one area of the playground outside his apartment building. One way to approach the problem would be to create a quick map of the property boundaries, using the driveway or parking lot entrance as the mouth of chi for the land. Once you have determined the front side of the lot in this way, position each column accordingly. In this example, let's say they notice the drainage problem is located in the Flow column area. They begin with the logical solution and call a plumber to look for leaks. They also place a symbolic cure such as a bowl of water in the home or in the apartment and see the water contained in the bowl as a symbol of containing the water, and visualize resolving the leak easily and inexpensively. This is a way of working with both the larger pattern of the land and the smaller pattern of the living space at the same time to facilitate a solution.

To use this approach with an individual room, use the largest or most-used door as the mouth of chi for the room and draw your map accordingly.

When you're unsure which footprint should get the most attention, begin with the structure and follow with the room on lot, depending on how it feels.

QUALITIES OF THE DIFFERENT ENERGY COLUMNS

The eight peripheral columns are divided into two groups, with four of them anchoring the earthy, stabilizing energy for the building and the remaining four anchoring the more expansive cosmic energy grid. The central hub is a point of stillness blending, renewing, and supporting the other eight.

There are fascinating correlations with da Vinci's *Vitruvian Man* (Fig. 12). The circle and square in his drawing have often been used for the interplay of heaven and earth and of cosmic and terrestrial forces. This is reflected in old Chinese coins, where the round shape of the coin represents mysterious energy, the circle symbolizes a whirling movement of heavenly inspiration, and the square or rectangle in the center represents the earthly and the tangible, which settles, organizes, and gives form to heavenly energy.

Framed in these shapes, *Vitruvian Man* alludes to the dynamic balance of these two elements and humans' potential to blend them. Feng shui tradition

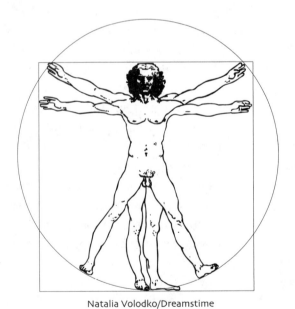

Natalia Volodko/Dreamstime
Figure 12

and other cultures suggest that anchoring the elements with intention and objects in our everyday living environment blends, reflects, and invites more of life's creative forces. Let's look more closely at the unique role each column plays within the larger patterns of the structure.

THE EARTH ENERGY GRID IN A BUILDING

The four earth energy columns in Figure 13 relate to the grounded pose of *Vitruvian Man*, the one bounded by the square. While the arms are not exactly at the midpoint of the vertical lines, there's such a kinetic feeling to this figure that one can imagine him representing the earth, symbolically anchoring the pattern in space.

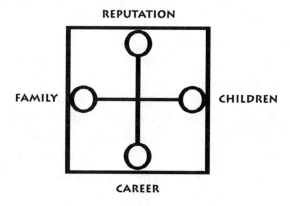

Figure 13

The labels in figure 13 describe the practical, mundane aspects of life associated with each energy hub, according to the feng shui ba-gua. These qualities relate to

- **Career**: Your work or occupation
- **Reputation**: Your image; your relationship or standing in the community
- **Family**: Extended family; friends you consider to be family
- **Children**: Your relationship with your own and others' children

When possible it is good to match the function of a room with the energy of the nearest hub. Placing a family room where Family energy is strongest or a home office in the Career area of the house can enhance the functions normally carried out in those rooms. Connecting your intention for an area with the energy naturally present in that part of the house is like going to a seafood restaurant when you want a good fish dinner. You could get fish at another restaurant, but you may have a more satisfying experience at a place that specializes in it.

Regardless, intention and cures can also be used to strengthen a hub's vitality if the room is not directly connected with its meaning. Longtime clients Sam and Agnes were familiar with the concept of energy columns, and went through big changes when their children grew up and moved away to pursue their own family lives and careers. Missing their children, they realized that they had a guest bedroom replacing their son's bedroom in the Children energy column for the house. Agnes suggested placing pictures of the children at different stages of childhood on the wall of that room. In our annual consultation, Sam admitted, "I didn't realize how much I would miss the kids when their jobs took them so far away. When she suggested placing the pictures as a cure, I thought, 'Why not? It makes me feel like I'm doing something.'"

As he placed the pictures, the couple used conscious intention as a cure, visualizing the children prospering in their new endeavors and keeping in touch with regular calls and e-mail messages. Sam reported enthusiastically, "We seem to keep more in touch now than before. Whenever I walk by those pictures, I think of them and often they call or send e-mail that same day. It's kind of fun."

When I needed to get the word out about my newly established consulting practice, I placed a small brass bell in the Reputation area of the house, a storage area that was awkward for placing a cure. Every day I would go by the area and reach up to the bell on a top shelf of a built-in bookcase to ring it, repeating my intention of finding help to get the word out about my work. A month later, a newspaper reporter asked to do a story about me. Remarkably, in taking pictures of different cures for the article on their visit to the house, the photographer focused on the small bell. Though I did not describe the intention with the bell, when the article came out, the bell was the center picture in the layout.

To support or adjust all the earthly areas of your life at once, select a cure such as a lush green plant, and place the same type of plant in each of the four earthly areas to reinforce the action with your intention, thereby amplifying the benefits fourfold.

THE HEAVENLY ENERGY GRID IN A BUILDING

As the circle in Eastern tradition relates to intangible, ideal qualities or divine perfection, in *Vitruvian Man*, the raised arms and spread feet touch the circle at the very points in a structure that embody the more intangible or spiritual qualities. Figure 14 illustrates the qualities traditionally associated with these points in feng shui.

Figure 14

The cosmic/less tangible qualities of these energy hubs are

- **Flow:** Wealth, abundance, success, plenty
- **Helpful People:** Mentors, allies, angels, guides, customers
- **Knowledge:** Self-cultivation toward embodiment of joy, spiritual practice, logic, and intuition
- **Joy:** Marriage/union, bliss, embracing the moment, allowing life to unfold, and living in good relationship to one another and to oneself

In rectangular, square, or even some irregular-shaped structures, these columns are in the corners, where they accumulate life force. Therefore, it is always a good idea to bolster corners by de-cluttering, cleaning, and using intention, especially after an energy adjustment has been placed. Toyoko Matsuzaki, a master of hado, a powerful Japanese energy healing modality, flicks a cloth in the corners of the room during healing sessions to coax life force out and to move any static energy, thus promoting circulation of healing energy in the person who resides there.[4] While good circulation is important in all areas, it is especially beneficial here since the corners hold energy more easily. The more life force you have circulating in an area, the more easily the desired or intended result can come through.

To support or adjust all the heavenly/intangible areas of your life at once, select a cure such as a lush green plant and place the same type of plant in each of the four heavenly areas, reinforcing the action with your intention, which quadruples the benefits.

THE CENTRAL ENERGY COLUMN

Arguably, the Center is the most important energy column. The Center is usually, though not always, located in the physical center of a building or room. The arrangement of rooms and traffic areas in a building often determines the Center. Imagine a home with a central transition area opening into four different rooms. Even if the area is a bit to one side of the physical center, the more frequent use of the transition area warrants the energetic center to be the energy hub rather than a closet or another feature located at the actual physical center of the house.

The other eight columns radiate energy toward the Center, which takes in this energy and refreshes and strengthens it and then radiates it back out to circulate through the rest of the columns. The Center is similar to the eye of the hurricane; it maintains its structure by the constant repetition of the cycling of winds around it. In the body metaphor, the Center is the heart and the nervous system of a structure. Notice that both are part of the autonomic nervous system, ticking along quietly without our conscious involvement. The Center, then, is for "being" rather than "doing."

The Center should be strong enough to renew itself and all the other energy hubs around it. This kind of strength is a quality of renewal, originality, and authenticity, not a strength in the active sense of force or power. Hestia, ancient Greek goddess of the hearth fire, embodies the quality of centeredness. Uninvolved in the turbulent politics around her, Hestia represents the middle ground, a quality of respite or refuge. The Center is a place to catch our breath and remember who we are before plunging back into activities refocused and refreshed.

An awareness of these energetic hubs makes a difference when designing or redesigning a space. There may be a connection between the frenetically busy life many people experience today and the fact that many homes are built with a lot of activity rooms in the center, such as a bathroom, kitchen, or staircase. On the other hand, these vital energy nodes tend to lose some potency when more passive applications, such as a rarely used closet, a garage, or a highly cluttered room, are placed there. As an exercise, try looking at the center of your home if you want to work with stress in your life. If you find yourself with an overly active or sluggishly passive feature in your home's center, try some of the helpful cures in part 4.

Ideally, the center of a home or building should be a serene spot, perhaps even a courtyard open to the sky. Create a place of rest at the center of your building, apartment, or office—a place for anchoring and grounding. This restful spot can be small—a small seating area, a beautiful light fixture, a small shelf with a favorite object, or just a serene painting on the wall. Plants are wonderful here and refresh the chi, as Marcus Vitruvius Pollio pointed out:

> The space in the middle, between the colonnades and open to
> the sky, ought to be embellished with green things; for walking
> in the open air is very healthy, particularly for the eyes, since
> the refined and rarefied air that comes from green things, find-
> ing its way in because of the physical exercise, gives a clean-cut
> image, and, by clearing away the gross humours from the eyes,
> leaves the sight keen and the image distinct.[5]

If plants aren't right for the area, cut flowers may do the trick. One busy friend placed a favorite picture and a small vase of flowers near her central energy hub. She often takes a moment to pause and enjoy the feeling in the picture—the sun slanting through lacy curtains on a cheery, peaceful domestic scene—and to remind herself that the feeling of being and serenity, rather than hectic activity, is the feeling she chooses in her home. Gathering fresh flowers for the vase each week has become a time to feel her gratitude for the beauty of nature and the beneficial life energies present in her home, and a way to affirm and appreciate their support for her family's dreams and goals.

THE POWER OF INTENTION

Intention is a vital factor in all design considerations. If the energy column is a highly active area such as a stairway, holding a clear, strong intention along with the cure for the area is what I call the "secret sauce." To cure your busy stairway, place a green plant on the landing and visualize the chi slowing down and being solidly rooted like the plant.

Intention is an important aspect of the creative process that helps focus your attention and attract a deeper level of support from the intangible level. Your intention alone, particularly if reinforced in a physical way such as placing a green plant in a space, can usually create the necessary energetic shift in a problem area without having to make huge design or structural changes.

Professor Lin puts it this way: "Making a change in the environment can have a 20 percent change for balance and success, but if you use intention, it can have a 120 percent effect." (His system for harnessing the power of intention, the Three Secret Reinforcements, is one of the ceremonies outlined in part 4.) Many other teachers have pointed out that the secret to real change is imaging your dream, hope, or prayer already fulfilled and engaging all the senses when picturing it so that we experience gratitude and excitement as if it has already happened. Among other things, gratitude opens our mind, heart, senses, and creativity to the good that we wish for. This combination of vivid, emotional imagery and gratitude has been part of indigenous interactions with nature and divinity for thousands of years on many continents.

In a radio interview, visionary scientist Gregg Braden, bestselling author of *The God Code*, described effective prayer by recounting his experience accompanying a Native American friend in the American Southwest to pray for much-needed rain. Braden, waiting for his shaman friend outside the centuries-old rounded adobe kiva that the Pueblo people use for prayer and ceremony, was startled when his friend emerged after a short time inside.

"You're done?" Gregg asked in curious surprise. "Can you tell me what you did in there?"

Laughing, the friend responded, "I imagined myself running through the cornfield after a soaking rain, hearing my footsteps splashing in the puddles, feeling the wetness of the leaves soaking my clothes and my skin as I passed. I heard the children laughing and shouting, and I smelled the rich scent of wet earth. And I gave thanks."

The rains began soon after the prayer session.[6]

COMBINING ANCIENT AND MODERN KNOWLEDGE

During the Renaissance, before the rise of rationalism and the industrial revolution, the line between mystery and science wasn't as defined. Today renewed interest in "green" building, feng shui, and quantum physics is giving birth to a new renaissance, enabling us to once again reach beyond apparent polarities to achieve a more profound integration in our environmental designs and in our lives. Centering his designs on the vital patterns of life was a key to da Vinci's genius. Centuries later, we are still uncovering the many layers of meaning in his inventions and theories. Vitruvius, sixteen centuries before da Vinci, and the early Greeks before him suggested that we can bring life and longevity to our designs by paying attention to proportion, pattern, and shape, thus incorporating the intangible mystery of life along with science and the humanities in our built environments.

In the next chapter, we will look at the placement of specific elements and furnishings in the home with an awareness of the body metaphor and the energy columns. Then we will look at specific solutions for many common—and several uncommon—situations you may face in your existing home or office.

7

RESTORING BALANCE AND VITALITY

Building with integrity, wisdom and strength is done with receptivity to the earth's powers.
Receptivity allows you to set aside your thinking . . . Contrary to seeing with our external
eyes, following a line between subject and contemplated object, inner vision is holistic, total
perception. It requires that we become a part of what we wish to accomplish.

—Marko Pogačnik

AFTER FOLLOWING THE energy web down to finer and finer levels, from the outer grounds into the home, we will now focus on how the web plays out in day-to-day human life. Body radar plays a role in this. There is as great a need to develop and use our sensitivity in our human environments—our buildings, neighborhoods, and cities—as in the natural settings described in part 1. Modern life poses significant challenges to using the very sensitivity needed to navigate it successfully.

By addressing both the tangible and the intangible aspects of energy flow, the suggestions in this chapter can help you to create sustainable indoor environments filled with nature's life force, which will restore energy, concentration, mood, and mental acuity. Once created, environments with a healthy, balanced circulation of life force are easier to maintain.

Machaelle Small Wright describes this self-balancing quality of living systems, or biospheres, in the *Perelandra Microbial Balancing Program Manual*: "When a biosphere is balanced, it maintains appropriate activity and interaction among its parts. It naturally and automatically repels anything that does not correspond with or enhance the balance of all that is in the biosphere. When a biosphere is out of balance, it weakens and becomes vulnerable to, and even serves as a magnet for, outside elements that support the imbalance."[2]

In this book, I use clutter as an everyday example of balance. In my classes on clutter, I discuss how, for example, a jumble of boxes and papers in a corner tends to grow and expand, as if on its own. Groans and nods of agreement circulate throughout the room as many relate to how easy it can get out of hand; a clutter pile is a magnet for more disorder. Restore balance in the house body by eliminating clutter and restore vitality.

While our homes and offices are no substitute for time spent walking in the woods or sitting by a stream, we can create a truly restorative environment with the breath of life, one with a more consistent circulation of vitality than many modern environments offer.

THE SHAPE OF THE STRUCTURE: KEEP IT SIMPLE

In the midst of rapid, often chaotic change, architectural designs that are in harmony with natural laws strike a soothing, grounding chord. Thomas Gordon Smith, a professor at the School of Architecture at the University of Notre Dame, author, and practicing classical architect, has spearheaded a revival of the classical style based on these principles, and it is once more gaining popularity. The *New York Times* covered the modern design trend toward classic simplicity in architecture, praising the "fresh and free" feeling of Smith's work and noting that design classes at the Classical Institute in New York are "attracting more and more real estate agents and developers whose clients crave something more authentic than faux colonials and poorly proportioned McMansions." The classical style based on Vitruvian principles is as relevant today as it was in ancient times. In the Greek and Roman classical principles set forth by Vitruvius, Smith sees a "stability, balance, and harmony" that modern design has generally lacked.[3] Christine Franck, an international designer and teacher honored in 2002 by the Prince of Wales with a Prince's Foundation Award for "outstanding contribution to the study of architecture and design," speaks eloquently about the urban need for architecture that celebrates order instead of chaos so that it helps you make sense of and relate to the world around you.[4]

These classical shapes feel better for solid reasons. A simple, balanced shape brings good circulation to a building, allowing the breath of life to flow easily through it. The patterns and proportions of classical architecture echo the natural pattern and proportion of earth. So instead of creating a dissonance that we must then remedy, when we build in this way, we create a pattern that resonates with the surrounding patterns of nature, including the cells and structure of our own bodies. This facilitates a reciprocal exchange of life force in which both humans and the earth can flourish.

The basic building shapes that fit this bill are also the basic building block shapes in nature: rectangles, squares, circles, and octagons. Some oddly shaped buildings, while startling and exciting in their unusualness, are sometimes at odds with the natural patterns around them, and may lack one or more energy columns, further contributing to the lack of balance for the structure and those who inhabit it. Note that this book focuses on basic shapes; if you have a more complicated building shape, the Resources section lists some books that can help you restore balance. All buildings, regardless of shape, can be brought to balance through intangible steps.

A STRONG ENTRANCE

As mentioned in chapter 6, in feng shui tradition, the front door is considered "the mouth of chi," the entrance for vitality. The importance of the front door's relationship to a design has been echoed in the West by Vitruvius and his followers. Vasari, architect of the famed Uffizi Gallery in Florence, Italy, noted that the main door for an ideal sixteenth-century palace, such as the Palazzo Barbarigo situated on the Grand Canal in Venice, could be seen as the mouth to the structural body.[5]

A strong front door attracts healthy chi into a structure. The breath of life enters and exits through this mouth, so a lively, unobstructed entrance is a key to good circulation of vital energy throughout a building. Even if you primarily use a side or back door, the front entrance or door design is usually larger and grander in some way, naturally claiming more attention.

COMPONENTS OF A STRONG ENTRANCE

The following are some important design aspects to consider:

- ✦ *Large and welcoming:* The main entry door should be larger with more design elements than other exterior and interior doors.

- ✦ *Good view going in as well as coming out:* The view on entering should reflect the occupants' highest intentions, hopes, and dreams, reflected by a lovely vase against a beautiful wall, attractive closet doors, and a handsome rug. The view on exiting should also be uplifting. Plants and garden art can be used to achieve this effect.

- ✦ *Visible from street:* Obstructive shrubbery or clutter should be cleared away.

- ✦ *Opens easily:* Hinges and door knobs must function well; furniture or other clutter should not limit its opening.

THE IMPACT OF ENTRANCES: TWO STORIES

Sam had been out of work for six months with chronic head pain that a string of specialists had been unable to diagnose or cure. Upon visiting his house, I went straight to the entrance, the head area, and found that while the rest of the shrubbery around the house had been pruned, here it was overgrown and there was not a clear and easy path to the door. I suggested that he prune and de-clutter his entrance area while holding a clear intention of bringing clarity and order to his problem.

Several weeks later, a very surprised Sam called to tell me that just days after carrying out my recommendation, he had suddenly found a specialist who had diagnosed his problem and provided the cure, a new medication and a change in diet. "I was so skeptical," he said, "and I still don't understand how it worked, but it certainly did work. I'm amazed at the speed of the solution!"

In the Midwest, a cooperatively owned community grocery store was struggling financially, with a lot of competition from other local stores. One member, a builder who had studied intuitive environmental living, suggested changing the entrance to attract and allow more life force into the store. The entrance was not obvious from the street, which made it a challenge to attract customers, and in turn contributed to the business's stagnation. "The Board laughed when I first brought it up," Eric said, "but after the logical efforts—more publicity, more diversity in our merchandise, etc.—failed to improve business enough, they went for it."

Using the building-as-a-body model, they moved the front entrance to a more central position, bringing more balance to the structure. They added attractive plants and paint to further enhance the entrance, and saw a satisfying increase in revenue. Within several months they were stunned when their biggest competitor decided to move to another location. At its annual meeting, the Board acknowledged that the biggest change in the store's fortunes came after moving and improving the entrance.

WELCOMING LIFE AT THE ENTRANCE

In West African tradition, echoed in Bali and around the world, a welcoming shrine is placed at the entrances of villages and individual homes. It declares the inhabitants' intentions, hopes, and dreams for their village or household and screens out energies that do not support those intentions. Welcoming elements can be as simple as a single statue, tree, or art piece, or a tiny, lovingly and deliberately placed garden. The intention behind the object is what makes the difference; its function resembles that of an invisible air filter, circulating clean and clear energy around the entrance.

This intention needs to be refreshed or awakened regularly and given attention, a loving touch, or appreciative thoughts and actions by bringing flowers or stones, watering plants, or pausing for a contemplative moment. Such actions reconnect us with what is important to us, increasing vitality in ourselves and in our surroundings and bringing our dreams to life.

Once an intentional area has been created it is important not to neglect it or it can cause a breakdown in vitality. Just as your attention and intention draw in the kind of energy (and therefore results) that you visualize, neglect or abandonment attracts a neglectful kind of energy. Neglect slows down the flow of energy and begins to collect energetic grime, similar to the way that clothes or papers dropped on the floor tend to attract more clutter. Christopher Hansard put it this way in his book *The*

Tibetan Art of Living: "Matter is slow moving energy and your consciousness can make any matter relax, open and become pliable. You can make it speed up or slow down. The energy in your surroundings is like a golden cup covered with grime, which your mind can clean so that it shines with love and positivity."[6]

A CALM CENTER

As noted in chapter 6, the center of a building should be a still point in the structure, maximizing the potential of the central energy column. A high-use area such as a bathroom, kitchen, laundry room, fireplace, or stairway can be a source of stress and disturbance when located at the center of your structure because of the way it affects this energy column. Furthermore, the water flow in a bathroom, kitchen, or laundry room adds a vertical motion that distracts from or disperses the Center's rhythmic horizontal cycling. Similarly, the vertical action of a stairway and the excitable quality of a fireplace introduce opposing movement that impinges on the Center's ability to optimally recycle a structure's energy.

Even if you are not fortunate enough to have a courtyard, lobby, or sitting nook located in the Center, you can enhance its function by toning down overactive qualities and allowing a more balanced energy for the building and its occupants. Remedies for balancing an overactive Center are in part 4.

Again, when choosing remedies it's important to remember that there is no one solution, and the more of your own attention, emotion, and creative energy you invest in your solutions, the more effective they will be. For example, one client and his family had their living room in the center of the house. This is usually not problematic, but this living room had many doors and was a busy traffic area in their home. The continuous coming and going in the central energy column area was adding a hectic quality to their family life and interfering with the restorative function of the Center in their home. Since Jim loved to make furniture as a hobby, I recommended that he make a round table for the center of the room and place it with a conscious intention to create a quality of centering, stillness, and focus, even in the midst of activity. A round area rug under the table would further anchor these qualities. It was a solution that he could really pour his creative energy into, and he reported that the new arrangement did result in increased peacefulness with their children and a more harmonious feeling in the home.

THE BIG THREE

Feng shui tradition gives great attention to the stove, desk, and bed, which I call the Big Three, because we spend most of our time in rooms with these furnishings; where and how they are placed in the home have a strong influence on its occupants' well-being. Symbolically, the three significant areas represent body, mind, and spirit, and life tends to run more smoothly when you place them well.

On the physical level, the positioning of these areas has subtle influences on our nervous system and other mental and physical functions. On the intangible level, it's an extension of the building-as-a-body perspective. The stove represents and affects the body or physical energy. To bring together a home-cooked meal is symbolic of physical nurturing through food and the love and goodwill that goes into it. Our digestion, strength, and health are affected by the mood and intentions that go into our food. The desk represents and affects the mind or mental energy. To use a desk stimulates and gives expression to our cognitive and creative expression. The bed represents and affects spirit. Sleep and dreams connect us with the nonphysical, nonlinear side of life, which ideally refreshes and inspires us.

OUR SELF-PRESERVING INSTINCTS

Our physical nervous system is disturbed by movement behind us or out of the range of our primary focus. It triggers a prey instinct of wariness that affects us even when we are not consciously aware of it and sets off chemical responses in our blood and brain, disrupting our concentration and affecting our blood pressure, respiration, and breathing. An article in the *Economist's* publication *Intelligent Life* points out that noise, similar to half-sensed movement, "affects our health, by disturbing our sleep, making daytime concentration

more difficult and prompting unwelcome reminders of the 'startle' response
...The last thing anyone needs during a busy working day is a sudden noise
prompting their body to get ready to outrun a saber-toothed tiger."[7] Our
nervous system registers what's going on around us, and sensing movement
without seeing it not only diminishes our focus and relaxation, but also
causes us to ignore subtle energies we might otherwise sense.

Placing the Big Three in commanding positions helps us develop a finer
sensitivity. It frees us to accomplish more as we are not constantly distracted
on subtle—and not so subtle—levels.

Here are more guidelines for Big Three placement:

STOVE

*Ideally place the stove on an island facing toward (but not actually vis-
ible from) the front door.* If the stove does not face the door,
place a mirror behind it to strengthen its position. The mirror should be the width of the stove and as high as the
height of the cook. This allows the relaxing of vigilance, so
more of the cook's focus and energy goes into the task of
cooking. Also, mirrors increase the subliminal experience
of space and opportunity by creating the illusion of a stove
being twice its size.

The stove should have ample counter space around it. This gives a
sense of spaciousness and of having enough, and a feeling
that tasks are easy to accomplish because you have enough
room to work in.

The stove should not be next to the sink. The stove is associated with
the fire element while the sink is aligned with the water element. As in the physical world, fire and water will cancel
each other, so these potentially incompatible energies will
have a tendency to break down their opposing energy unless
they have enough space to operate or there is a mediating
influence. Green plants and the color green represent the

wood element, which can mediate between fire and water. Wood feeds fire and is fed by water, so it completes a cycle, keeping the life force flowing and renewing itself rather than being flattened. If you have a stove near a sink, place plants or plant accessories, or use green paint in that area.

DESK

This refers to the most-used desk in the house, the one used to conduct the business of the home.

Place the chair so that the occupant's back is not to the door.

Make sure the desk is roomy and fits the scale of the room. This creates a sense of stability and balance, ensuring a better circulation of vitality, bringing objects into scale, and allowing the body a sense of space. Sitting at a small desk often makes extra work and demands more concentration, as it requires awkwardly shuffling papers and taking care to prevent objects from falling off. This constriction can cause you to pay too much attention to physical details instead of your actual work.

When possible, place your home office, library, or study in the front half of the home. Stimulation from the street can facilitate the brain waves. In larger office settings, the office of the CEO or manager should be located behind the central meridian for better concentration and fewer distractions, with a better overview of all the activities. This can contribute to a better mood for the manager.

BED

I consider the bedroom the most important room in the house, and often go there first to check for any possible improvements.

The bed should rest against a wall and have a headboard for security and strength.

Ideal placement is diagonally across from the door with a view of the door. If this above placement is not possible, put a mirror in a spot where you can see the door in it.

The master bedroom is traditionally located in the back half of the home, in the corner opposite the front door. This position offers the most calm, security, and peace for those with the greatest responsibility of running the household and setting the energetic patterns for the home. Its position behind the central meridian affords more protection from the street and the energetic patterns of the larger world, and hopefully provides more support for remembering and acting from deeper intentions.

Attending to positioning supports us in developing finer sensitivity, helping minimize the way that the hectic environments of modern life train us to ignore subtle awareness.

8

EVERYDAY SOLUTIONS WHEN THINGS DON'T FEEL RIGHT

Traditionalist Mayan healers ... know the earth-made world that feeds [us] with all its plants, weathers, soils, animals, oceans, mountains, rivers ... as a wild flowering house they call "Nim Hai." Because the human body is also the earth, our bodies are houses, or "Nim Hai," as well. Therefore, whenever a villager or an entire tribe, place or country is made ill or ... exports its illness to the rest of the world, all the doctors and priests under-stand this to mean ... that the House of the World needs to be re-plastered, re-thatched, somehow renewed ...

—Martin Prechtel

TROUBLESHOOTING TIPS

NO MATTER WHAT difficulties you encounter in your home or office environment, you can cocreate unique solutions with the earth energies around you, using the principles and skills described throughout this book. In general, remember that a healthy relationship with the earth is similar to a healthy relationship with another human, and the same rules apply:

> *Listen.* Take time to tune in and feel the energies present. Use your body radar. Sense what's going on. Trust yourself. The answer will come; nature *will* respond to your respectful, attentive attitude and your intention to create a solution together.

Respond. If there is pain, acknowledge what has happened with respect and compassion. Express your own regret or sadness and your intention to create something different, something beneficial for both earth and humans. If—as often happens—you feel an immediate generosity and wisdom flowing toward you, respond genuinely to them, expressing your own relief, joy, gratitude, and hope.

Listen again. Notice nature's response. Trust your subtle intuitions and imagination. Notice rustling leaves, animals that appear or pass by, and any feeling, image, or knowing that arises in you. Even when using ceremonies or exercises, trust the spontaneous gestures, words, or ideas that come from your heart and instincts. Be yourself in whichever format you use. Let your emotions flow, and stay open to the inspirations and impulses that arise.

Act. Choose at least one idea or insight that you will follow through and make a physical gesture that honors the interchange. For example, when walking on our land, I am constantly aware of the curves and swirls in nature. On one early spring walk, a idea popped into my head to create a small circle in the garden by the house. I have come to trust these sudden bursts of inspiration as messages from nature, so I created the garden to honor the insight to imitate nature's curves and in turn received a bumper crop of tomatoes, herbs, and lettuce. It's important to take the interaction out of the internal world and put it in the physical. Just as in human relationships, it's a way to build trust, which will elicit more communication and teamwork.

Persevere. If the problem is large or long-standing, it may take some time to create the outcome you desire. Don't give up on your partner, the earth, or your dreams for your desired outcome. Express your discouragement, if that's what you're feeling, but also express your hope and determination. Ask what's missing and what more can be done. Call in more help.

COMMON CHALLENGES

NOISY OR TROUBLESOME NEIGHBORS

With neighbors, the Golden Rule goes a long way: greeting and interacting with them in a friendly and respectful way often results in a positive response. So much is created by our expectations and ideas about others. People who are treated well eventually tend to respond in the same way, though it can take some time. Meanwhile, it helps to create "white noise" by placing wind chimes outside or playing your own music. Always use the intention to bring harmony, not to antagonize. Approaching the situation from anger, with a hazy idea of getting even, can make it worse. Those intentions tend to bring a response in kind.

Communicating with the neighbors about their loud music failed, so on his deck George played a CD of Tibetan monks playing drums and chanting ancient prayers for compassion for anger, fear, greed, and mistrust, with the monks' intention of transforming these feelings into harmony.[2] When the neighbors realized that the chants would start when their music began, they moved their music system. Music acted as a boundary. It took patience and repetition, but quiet has descended on the neighborhood, and George's relationship with his neighbors is more civil.

When dealing with problematic neighbors, another technique is to place rocks or plants along a boundary, inside an apartment, or along a fence line, asking these elements to function as an energetic barrier. Walking the boundary can help boost the barrier function, particularly if you walk the lines with a conscious openness to the energies of your own land. This works in the area you inhabit, the area you call home, whether you own it or not. Webster's dictionary defines boundary as "the point at which something ends and beyond which it becomes something else." Walking boundaries can help you tune in to and align with the natural energy present, and help define it rather than have it defined by the loudest energies around. The Exterior Chi ceremony in part 4 is also quite helpful in these cases.

Madeleine's neighbor, who had torn down a modest home on his lot and built a two-story house, began to peer out his second-floor window and comment or complain about a loud water feature and the way she pruned her shrubbery in her fenced backyard. Distressed by the invasion of her privacy and his harassment, she was ready to move, but decided to first try my suggestion of placing a colorful wind sock in a tree closest to his upstairs window with the intention that the sock's movement would create a visual and energetic screen. Some months after this simple action, Madeleine was delighted to see a For Sale sign on the neighbor's yard and was surprised to hear many neighbors express their relief.

Do not underestimate the power of your intention, especially when coupled with nature's willingness to assist. Willing allies surround you, and as you consciously shift the energy in your own world, each of your efforts will be met with a response, and you are likely to see a ripple effect on the people and land around you.

CREATE FRIENDLIER, MORE COOPERATIVE NEIGHBORHOODS

A broader layer of the "troublesome neighbors" solution is to help create the kind of neighborhood you enjoy living in. The City Repair Project (www.cityrepair.org) offers guidelines and support for creating neighborhood gathering places. This project has helped transform a number of neighborhoods with delightful results.

An exciting project in New York City has reclaimed the High Line, a twenty-two-block elevated rail line that runs through Manhattan's West Side and was slated for demolition in 2001. Neighborhood activists formed Friends of the High Line and eventually managed to block the demolition and win over the city government. With solid financial and popular support, the ambitiously innovative park, which includes trees, wetlands, and floating ponds with pedestrian walkways, is expected to be completed in 2007.

CLUTTER

Most people recognize the accumulated trash and treasures clogging their garage or living room as clutter, but another source of clutter that people may not recognize is abandoned or stalled projects outside. When you introduce a new pattern and then fail to maintain it, the stall plays havoc with the natural patterns in the area. It tends to attract chaotic, scattered energy. Neglected gardens or stone patterns such as spirals, circles, and labyrinths created on the land and then abandoned are two examples of stalls that affect natural patterns.

With nature, as in any other relationship, attention, intention, and communication play a big role. Imagine a pile of your personal papers scattered on the family kitchen table. Just as you would communicate to the other family members about your intention to clear and organize the table by a certain time, it helps to communicate to nature that you haven't forgotten or abandoned it, and that you intend to complete it by a certain time. The announcement and intention begins the process energetically and draws the support needed to complete or tidy up a project.

Abandoned cars and piles of junk metal particularly seem to take on a life of their own, often accumulating a concentrated chaotic energy that is quite disruptive to the flow of life force. It is important to either remove them or give them a new role. For example, an old piece of machinery is potential clutter, but if you clean it up and use it for decoration, perhaps with flowers planted in it, it is no longer detrimental; it becomes part of a new, vibrant pattern reflecting your intention of cheerfulness and beauty.

FREEWAY AND INDUSTRIAL NOISE

Josie lived right by a major interstate, so she placed a variety of wind chimes with beautiful tones along that side of her lot with the intention of creating melodic sound to cover the freeway noise. "I feel like I have a wind and brass ensemble playing every day now," she said. "I barely hear the freeway anymore."

If you live in an apartment, try hanging a chime or two outside the windows that face busy roads or industrial sites. Select them carefully for sounds that feel soothing and uplifting to you and that make you happy when you hear them. Indoors, place a soothing miniature water feature on that side of your home to slow down the rushing loud energy and reconnect it to the moderate rhythms of the earth.

Living by a major train yard felt intolerable to Angelo until he began to take walks and connect with different trees in the neighborhood. He enjoyed the feeling of peace and strength they radiated. "I felt like water running down between the stones, finding my way down to my roots," he said. "Listening to the birds, connecting with plants, rocks, and sky, I settled down into a level that drew my attention away from the noisy, nerve-racking city buzz and into something more profound and nourishing for me." Connecting with the devas and wildlife around your place, even just by saying hello and extending your appreciation for their life force, will help both you and them.

LAND SCRAPED AWAY OR FILLED IN TO CREATE LEVEL GROUND

As discussed in part 1, change to the natural contours of the land can create disruptions that may still be felt years later if it happens without communicating with the earth energies there and giving them a chance to adjust. It can result in a feeling of dullness or stagnation in the area because the flow of life force is diminished by the confusion created by that kind of unconscious change.

When this happens, sit down with the earth there, greet the soil devas and other nature energies, and acknowledge the abrupt change that has happened. Let them know that you wish to help restore the original vitality of the land and even bring it into a new level. Give a gift that expresses your intention.

Offering a miniature version of the old contours of the land in your landscaping on the site can be a strong remedy. For example, if a hill was flattened, make a mound with small (or large) rocks that represents what was there before. If you don't know how the land was before, look for old photos and topographical maps or talk to people who remember.

Pay attention to hunches or quick flashes as you do intuitive environmental work, as these are nature's way of sharing helpful information. Take time to formally present the completed offering to the beings and energies there, restating your intention to work with them on reweaving the energetic pathways for that land. Continue to notice what comes back to you; along with good feelings, you may receive more impressions of what else you need to do to restore the full vibrancy of the area.

WATERCOURSES CULVERTED, FILLED IN, OR DIVERTED

When we disturb natural waterways, it can affect the vitality of the area and its livability. In an article for the U.S. Environmental Protection Agency,

Richard Pinkham, Senior Research Institute Associate at the Rocky Mountain Institute, noted that "policy makers, engineers, and builders increasingly recognize the value of maintaining natural drainage patterns and stream channels in new development."

Recognition has expanded to daylighting, a trend of "retrofitting" previously buried waterways. Daylighting brings a previously culverted or piped stream, creek, or storm water drain back to the surface, reestablishing it in its old channels, or creating a new channel as close to the original one as possible. Wetlands and ponds are also restored wherever feasible.

While daylighting can be a complex, expensive process with many variables, individuals and local governments have discovered that it is worthwhile for the economic revitalization it stimulates. Neighborhood property values increase, quality of life improves, and new business is attracted to reenergized areas. As we have discussed, anytime you increase the vitality of an area, everything improves; it's a positive domino effect.

A number of projects have also found creative ways to minimize expense, using volunteer labor, alliance with other agencies and nonprofits, and a host of matching grants. When a two-hundred-foot culvert in Longdale Park, Georgia, fell victim to sinkholes and kudzu vine overgrowth, DeKalb County, with no funds to replace it, had to just fence off the hazardous area, leaving an eyesore—not to mention an energetic snarl—in the middle of this neighborhood park. Parks Department employee Ginna Tiernan, who was in charge of streamside restoration projects, convinced her department they could daylight the creek for less money than it would take to replace the culvert. With Ginna's design time covered by an EPA grant, county crews excavated the culvert and stabilized the banks with rocks and weirs created by trees and sod. The trees have flourished and have been joined by native grasses, shrubs, and more trees to the delight of neighbors, scientists, and county auditors.[3]

LAND ALTERED BY INDUSTRIAL POLLUTION

Occasionally in larger developments, a builder will bury the construction debris on one lot instead of hauling it away. This fill often contains toxic elements that can create both physical and energetic problems. Betsy's husband and son were plagued by respiratory problems after they moved into their new East Coast home. Doctors were unable to locate the cause, so she called me. Betsy felt restless and was unable to settle into the house or sleep well. She tried moving her bedroom to a different room, but that one didn't feel right either. She wondered what it was about the new location that might be causing all these problems.

Walking around her site I found it hard to breathe or to feel my feet. There was a feeling of standing on shaky ground; it reminded me of walking in a park in California that was built over an old dump. When I asked to work with the spot's deva, I had a hard time getting a sense of the being. Its energy felt scattered and incoherent. I got the sense of buried debris under Betsy's house and that there was a disruptive influence that was causing problems for the nature beings and the human occupants.

Betsy was planning to get her yard landscaped anyway, so she had a landscaper dig in with a backhoe. Without going very deep, the landscaper struck construction debris from her subdivision. Fortunately for her, the majority of the debris was in the yard, and she was able to get compensation from the developer to get the site cleaned up. The bit of debris that was actually under the house stayed, and we worked to reweave the energy web there with lots of green indoor plants to infuse the house with the life force of the earth.

Many people who live in industrially polluted areas lack the funds for physical cleanup measures, which can be extremely costly. There are some cutting-edge intuitive technologies being used to heal pollution in water, which is more malleable than earth. In addition to the startling success of Masaru Emoto and other healers using prayer and intention to clear up polluted water, several dowsing projects, working only with the invisible energies, have returned toxic wells to clean, healthy water. This type of cleansing may not be possible when the problem involves heavy metals and other toxic chemicals in the earth. I would caution you about living on a heavily toxic site.

WATER LEAKS IN PIPES AND IRRIGATION SYSTEMS

Energetically, it is important to quickly repair leaks and other unpatterned water flows, such as floods or a break in an irrigation ditch. These problems have the effect of weeping across the earth and of bleeding away energy. When it occurs near a dwelling, it can impact the abundance flow of the humans residing there. Generally, it makes it harder to focus or concentrate. Having to use more effort to be productive is stressful on the body and can impact the immune system and dilute success. Leaks also have a tendency to attract chaos or stagnation to the land and to the home. Strengthening the healthy patterns of the water by fixing the leak also restores the healthy flow of other energies to the human lives nearby.

Judy lived in an older ranch home in a quiet suburb and ran her own public relations business from a home office. While the big yard had been wonderful for her children, they were grown now, and Judy was looking forward to trading her suburban home for a smaller, more convenient condo and replacing the headaches of self-employment with the stimulation of working for a larger firm. But for months nothing was happening. The flow in her life was very sluggish. Her home had been on the market for months with very little action, and her job search, despite her many qualifications and vigorous networking, was not producing results.

Aware of subtle influences, she implemented environmental remedies such as placing a few small water fountains in the house to stimulate growth and movement, yet her life still seemed stalled. As I walked through her home, I had a strong sense of standing water under the house. "I already thought of that," she said. "I've had the plumber out and all the pipes for the house were fine."

She really had done a lot already, and yet I could still feel a water problem. As we continued to explore, she remembered that the city had repaired some leaking pipes. I felt a tingle on my skin. "I strongly suspect they didn't finish the job," I told her. "Try to get them back out here, and meanwhile bring more green plants into the house to symbolically draw up and stimulate the water and life force under the house until they come back and fix the leak." She called the city again, and when another neighbor complained about water under his home as well, the city came back, found more water leaks, and finally fixed the problem. Several weeks later Judy received an offer for a great job and shortly afterward, her house sold as well.

NOT-SO-COMMON ISSUES

POWER POINTS, LEY LINES, AND VORTEXES

If you suspect that you have power points, ley lines, or vortexes on your site, you may want to contact an experienced intuitive environmental consultant (see the tips in chapter 10). While it is preferable to leave these strong, energetically active areas undisturbed, it is not always possible. In these cases it is important to act wisely, in partnership with Earth, to find mutually beneficial solutions. Just as we rewire a house to accommodate a remodel, we rewire the energetic web on the site by adjusting the energy flow around a building or reconnecting it, and cooperating with nature to reweave the patterns there.

POWER POINTS

If you suspect that you have a power point on or around your property, don't ignore it. Historical records of the area may confirm your suspicion. Did indigenous people recognize the site as a sacred or healing area? Is it a spot where noble deeds were done or where people have gathered for inspiration?

If you cannot leave the area intact and undisturbed, look for ways to honor the energy on the site and to help it accomplish its role. Listen patiently and often, and use all your senses and intuition to recognize the type of energy present and what purpose it may be serving. The exercises in part 4 can help; you may also want to use the services of an experienced intuitive environmental consultant (see chapter 10), but I recommend that you use your own sensitivity first. Environmental work is not an exact science; the more information you have the better.

LEY LINE NEAR A BUILDING

A ley line is a very active masculine element. When it is close to an existing building, introduce softer feminine design elements to help balance the intense energy around the house. Look for ways to stretch or reroute the flow of energy so that it can serve its function well and humans can thrive there. Placing stones or heavy elements on the landscape can also help ground or counterbalance a ley line's buzzy, highly concentrated energy.

When Tom and Meredith first moved to their new home in a rural valley, they were amazed at the wildlife, both big and small, that seemed to stop by in greeting, giving them a hint of the big energy on their land. Some of the larger wildlife representatives—bears, coyotes, and beavers—were a bit unsettling, and they were glad that the visits seemed to be a one-time event. They were pleased by the heightened life force on their new land, but they consulted me when they continued to have less-welcome experiences—strong, restless dreams and an unusual amount of illness and confusion.

Walking outside their home by the side closest to the bedroom, I felt a disruption in the energy. My body radar registered discomfort, an achy feeling, and a difficulty in breathing. I felt unsettled, a bit dizzy, and fluttery inside. It was challenging to remain centered or to feel my feet while standing in that area. Focusing my attention on my body radar by breathing deeply and setting a strong intention to be shown the best solution, I felt a watery heaviness, like something was buried in the ground. I learned that an old oil drum was buried there, but this alone did not explain the problem. I examined the hills behind the property and noticed a dip between the hills, which is a normal route for a smaller ley line connecting to smaller power points such as hills and mountains. I realized that the ley line was ricocheting off the oil drum and destabilizing their home.

It would have been best to take the oil drum out of the ground, but since that was too expensive, I recommended placing lots of stones on the landscape to balance the disruptive energy. Tom and Meredith created a lovely stone-lined path, a granite bench, and a small grove of hardy native plants, ending up with an enchanting area that has become a peaceful, private retreat. They have slept better since, and the feelings of dizziness and confusion have abated.

RECONNECTING A SEVERED LEY LINE

Because ley lines stretch a long way across the landscape in more industrialized cultures, they are often cut by the construction of roads and cities. It is not surprising that a split line has a disturbing effect on humans and other beings in the area and on the earth itself. It's both possible and necessary to reconnect that line so that it can do its important work of energy distribution. Reconnecting large ley lines is particularly important because, like large power lines, they serve a broad area.

Robert, one of my students, lived in a condo next to a freeway. He called me for a consultation because he was experiencing an unusually high number of delays and frustrations in his remodeling process, and kept having a feeling of disturbed energy, a static electricity type of feeling, like a cat having its fur rubbed the wrong way.

Walking the complex's extensive grounds, I found that while much of it felt peaceful, near Robert's condo I felt the unsettled feeling he had described. I sensed a powerful masculine, active flow through the area, which seemed backed up at one point near his apartment, like a dammed stream. We realized that the road had cut right through a major, wide ley line coming from the nearby mountain.

A cut ley line can be compared to a cut electrical power line. The line is hot and gives off wild sparks of energy. Living or working in or near such a disturbed pattern makes it very difficult to focus or organize your life. The energetic chaos can be reflected in chaotic, cluttered surroundings or a chaotic relationship among those who live there. In Robert's case, the effect was amplified by the fact that the boundary of his complex paralleled the freeway. Replicating the line that had sliced the ley line was increasing the disturbance.

Robert was game to try energetically reconnecting the ley line and removing the invisible accumulation, so on a day when the road was closed because of snow, he gathered some friends and trooped out to the interstate. They began by extending greetings and respect to the beings and energies involved, communicating an intention to reconnect the severed energy flow and requesting guidance and cooperation from the devas involved. At my suggestion, they placed a piece of iron rebar and a crystal on each side of the freeway and in the center island along the original ley line. Metal or clear quartz crystals both have the ability to gather and direct energy. The rebar acts like an acupuncture needle and is almost electromagnetic in its function, drawing the current of energy along from spot to spot to restore the flow. The crystal acts like a tuning fork, attuning to the energy of the ley line and carrying out the intention programmed into it—in this case restoring the flow of energy.

Robert wrote to me that the remodel did get considerably easier after the exercise. "I see now the advantage of following intuitive suggestions and will consider them just as important as all the architectural plans."

REDIRECTING A SEVERED LEY LINE

Martha and Tom had a similar problem when they moved into their small suburban house. Even after extensive redecorating, Martha still felt agitated and uncomfortable in their bedroom, and both of them were experiencing interrupted sleep. I didn't recognize anything indoors that would cause a problem, but when I walked outside, my body radar registered a familiar buzzy feeling, a higher magnetic energy, and an image of a cut electrical line. I realized that the fence cut through the ley line, causing a backup of energy that was now spreading to their bedroom—the room nearest the site of the cut line.

Since the line was so close to their house and the neighbor's, our solution involved connecting the line, stretching it a bit, and coaxing it to soften and curve around the buildings. We announced our intention and asked for nature's cooperation, and then shaped sections of wooden lattice and fastened them along the top of the fence to create a line of rolling curves.

Because we are dealing with energy when working with ley lines, it is often easier to instigate new patterns than you might imagine. In the same way that ripples form when you drop a stone into water, your thoughts, emotions, and intentions, as well as your actions, have a strong and immediate energetic effect on the world around you. You don't need to use nearly the amount of effort you might think you need, because you are not alone. You are working with invisible partners. You can gain cooperation by working with the patterns, which are quite powerful, or you can create resistance and disturbance by disregarding them. Life on earth operates according to patterns and responds well to that language.

Because of this cooperation, we didn't even need to move the fence; it was enough to simply create the suggestion of soft curves along the top of the fence line, and invite the energy flow to reroute around the house. Soon Martha and Tom began sleeping well and enjoying their new bedroom.

VORTEX IN A STRUCTURE OR ON A SITE

Vortexes, as described earlier, are powerful and somewhat unpredictable, and there are different types with different functions. Ella called me when she had been recently diagnosed with breast cancer and wanted to see how her environment could be improved to support her healing process. As I walked into her living room, my body radar registered distress; I could barely breathe and had a sense of being pushed out of the room by a repelling energy that seemed to spin in a circle. I was not surprised to hear that she did not spend very much time there at all.

Upon walking around outside, I found a similar swirling energy in a circle of trees. This circle felt more welcoming; I could breathe and stand more easily. The energies were a common configuration for vortexes: a case of two paired vortexes. The repelling experience from her living room occurred because the vortex movement there was counterclockwise. The more welcoming vortex outside was moving in a clockwise motion. If one were not part of a building site, the two vortexes would have a balancing effect on the area; however, since one of the vortexes was now part of a house, the balance was off. By assisting nature in reinstating the balance between these vortexes, larger problems can be averted, just as tending an infection in your own body could avert bigger problems for the body in the future.

Ella is a professional photographer, so these swirls of energy were great for her creativity and inspiration, but living with such concentrated energy on a daily basis was having a negative impact on her health. To begin the balancing, I placed quartz crystals in the living room to diffuse the energetic movement. The crystals kept the health of the vortex intact but softened its effect by spreading it over a larger area. We then performed the Tracing the Nine Stars Ceremony (see page 211), pulling the energy of the room throughout the house to broaden it even further. As part of the ceremony, we placed a plant at each of the nine energy columns in the house to keep the vortex stretched and grounded in the newly enlarged pattern of movement. This gesture works much like an acupuncture needle that distributes overactive energy in a certain organ or area. The work, which is quite delicate, needs to be reinforced periodically by repeating the ceremony and maintaining the health of the plants. By doing this, Ella's health stabilized, and seven years later, all is well.

While it is relatively rare to encounter a vortex in your home or office, as humans continue to expand their presence on the planet, it will probably happen more frequently. It is possible to work with the energy but be aware that vortex energy is quite strong. It is important to have a strong, clear intention and to be vigilant about maintaining and reinforcing the newer pattern. Also note that the intention is not to get rid of the vortex or diminish it in any way. Vortexes have extremely important roles in the energy web of our plane. They act as regulators, balancers, and distributors of life force. The goal of intervention is to soften their intensity by expanding the shape and size of the pattern, lessening their impact on nearby humans but allowing them to still function.

BUILDINGS OVER NATURAL WATER SPRINGS

Water closest to its source usually has more potency or a more concentrated life force. Therefore, a home placed over a water spring can be disruptive to sleep, health, and money flow. Sometimes placing plants in the rooms and painting the walls in a shade of green can help balance the energy and ease the disturbance.

Shirley, a longtime student of feng shui and earth energies, and her family moved to a new home with an incredible view near a nature reserve, but she and her husband were not sleeping well. Her husband, a real estate broker, noticed that his prospects had suddenly dwindled alarmingly. She used several of the approaches in chapter 4 to balance the energies in their home, but they were still plagued with sleepless nights, his business remained stagnant, and her health began to suffer.

Shirley recognized that a water problem must be involved, since money and health were both impacted. With her body radar, she sensed a water flow under the house, but thorough inspections did not find any leaks. One day, while hiking by several of the abundant springs in the nearby park, Shirley realized that the water flow she sensed under their bedroom might be an underground spring. I consulted with her on the phone to confirm her evaluation, and when I centered myself and checked the floor plan she had sent me, it was as though I was on the site and could *see* a spring there and feel the disgruntled energy of its nature beings.

The case was unique because the house was not actually blocking the water or disturbing it in a physical way. Only the energetic pattern was disturbed because the house was placed within the energy field of the underground water, and yet the discord was enough to create a disturbance in the water, which in turn rippled disturbance into the home above it. Earth artist Marko Pogačnik explains that when humans make changes in the natural world, "a huge crowd of elemental beings must take action, for within each split second each must make sure that the dynamic shaping of the world remains in unison with its cosmic blueprint."[4] The nature beings involved with this spring, it seemed, were not able to shape the pattern well here and were struggling with the drastic change imposed on them by the house construction and then the presence of the family.

To calm the disturbance and reweave a new pattern, Shirley made an offering to the deva of the water spring, acknowledging the situation and setting forth her family's intention to remedy the disturbance to the best of their ability. I suggested that she create a water feature near the house, a miniature version of the rushing spring underneath her house, using great boulders and a pond to symbolically draw the water flow away from the house and anchor it in a new pattern. Her family pitched in and built it, and they soon began to enjoy a good night's sleep as peace returned for both nature and humans. Her husband's business took off so precipitously that Shirley got her license to help him handle the torrent of business flowing their way.

BALANCING BUILDINGS OVER A CAPPED WELL OR BURIED OIL TANKS

Properties that were occupied around the turn of the century are most likely to contain the buried hazards of wells and oil tanks, both of which can have a constricting effect on living and health.

One client who lived in an 1840s Victorian house called because family members were all suffering from low energy and immune system problems. Feeling a tightness in my chest when I entered the family room, I asked some questions and realized that an old capped well lay beneath that room. The stagnant unmoving water in the well was a major source of the energetic disturbance that was affecting them.

I suggested placing plants in the family room and using lively shades of green for walls and furnishings to support circulation and movement. Using the Tracing the Nine Stars ceremony (see page 211) can also supplement and diffuse the congestion and reintroduce healthy circulation of vitality in the family room and throughout the house; even without it, the family did feel better, and the resident teenagers' grades improved.

Sophia was suffering severe insomnia in her new home and experiencing a lot of conflict with her husband. They had argued before in a normal way, but the arguments had become more intense since their move. The most bitter battles always seemed to erupt in the bedroom, Walking into that room, I felt the same constricted, hard-to-breathe feeling I had felt with the capped well. It seemed centered in one area of her bedroom but it did not seem to feel like water; it felt heavier, more viscous. I asked her if there was anything buried in the vicinity. Sophia thought for a moment and then realized, "Well, yes, there's a buried oil tank left over from the old heating system on this side of the house!" Once they dug it up and removed it, her health improved and the arguments simmered back down to a normal level.

NATURE BEINGS AND COMPUTERS

Computers can be affected by invisible energies. The problem is universal. In Iceland, a land bristling with cell phones and laptops, it is generally accepted that elves or other hidden beings can create computer problems.[5] On our land we had computer problems that I sensed were due to elves who had moved into our wires because they resembled a nest. This affected the electronic circuitry, causing the computer to break down. I thanked the elves for their friendship and invited them to move into some nests I had created for them on the deck out of old pieces of roots and odd whirly pieces of wood. I also placed crystals on the computer to make it less attractive for them, since the crystal rock energy is too busy for them.

After one last visit to the repair shop, the computer has been fine.

HONORING LAND SACRED TO INDIGENOUS PEOPLES

Inhabiting or owning traditionally sacred land brings a certain level of responsibility to appreciate the centuries of prayer and respect that have accumulated there, as well as the strong earth energies that probably caused it to be used as a sacred site in the first place. Ceremonies or symbolic gestures and words honoring these intangible realities help us bring our own energetic fields into a more compatible alignment with the surrounding force field.

A large landmark hotel in a picturesque and popular Western tourist town had a puzzling history of failure for decades, with lots of turnover as successive owners fell into financial difficulties. Guest complained of doors slamming, ghosts appearing, and a creepy discomfort. Old-timers reported that the hotel was built on the site of a Native American burial ground. One wise owner contacted local tribal elders and hosted a ceremony to honor the past, express regret and respect, and clear the unfinished business. The hotel is now flourishing.

CURING LONG-TERM PROBLEMS IN THE HOME

In the next chapter we will cover what to do with sites that have a negative history of their own; however, if you have a persistent problem or dissatisfaction in your home, consider looking into your own past, especially if the same problems have followed you from one dwelling to another. Clare Cooper Marcus is a true pioneer in looking at home spaces and their effect on our lives. Inspired by her landmark book, *House as a Mirror of Self*, I occasionally have clients draw a diagram of their childhood homes. Exploring these early living patterns can give tremendous insights into present, persistent challenges with living arrangements.

Recognizing patterns from the past can bring more harmony to the present and allow you to consciously release those patterns. Many people find it effective to create a small ritual to say good-bye to old habits, memories, or beliefs that no longer serve them. You might write down or draw what you are leaving behind and burn it or bury it. You might find a stick or leaf to represent an old thought or pattern and toss it into a river. Whatever action you choose to symbolize letting go of a painful or limiting past, remember to end by welcoming the images and feelings you want in its place. If you are near the river, face downriver as you release what no longer serves you; then turn and face upriver to welcome a brighter future.

EVERY PROBLEM HAS A SOLUTION

When you increase the level of harmony and vitality by solving the dilemmas such as those described in this chapter, some of the noticeable first surprises are the synchronicities, the remarkable coincidences that often occur. In the beginning especially, your mind may try to explain these away by looking for logical explanations. But if you persist, you may conclude that we are not alone, as quantum physicists Amit Goswami, PhD, a pioneer of the new science "Science within Consciousness," or John Hagelin, PhD, a leading scientist and longtime investigator into the foundations of human consciousness have, that the world is filled with consciousness, and that there are no accidents.[6] A mysterious, benevolent consciousness seems to meet, match, and support our creative efforts. The more we recognize it, the more cooperation becomes possible.

Is it always a smooth road? Of course not—what would be the fun of that? But by retaining your curiosity and continuing to experiment and observe the results over time, you will discover what doesn't work and what does, and you'll continue to expand the boundaries of what you believe is possible.

PART THREE

Moving, Remodeling, and Building: Bringing Ease to Every Stage

9

CHOOSING AND DEVELOPING A SITE

*Start by doing what's necessary; then do what's possible;
and suddenly you are doing the impossible.*
— St. Francis of Assisi

CHOOSING A SITE

THE INFORMATION IN this chapter can help take away some of the guess-work in choosing a new apartment or office to rent, a house to buy, or land to invest in by helping you discern types of invisible energy patterns around the property and recognize nature's signals to make the best choices.

Linda called me from Colorado, where she was looking for her dream house. She had found a place she loved, with a glorious view of the mountains, but there was no obvious boundary on one side of the lot. The boundary seemed to run down the middle of an open irrigation channel and was not clearly delineated. Since she had battled a nasty boundary issue at her old home, she wanted to make sure she wasn't buying a similar headache. When she called, she had just a few hours to decide whether to make a bid before going back to the East Coast.

I suggested that she walk the boundaries and ask for signals from the land and nature spirits, trusting her intuition and body radar to let her know whether the place was a good fit for her. As she walked the property boundary

139

with that intention, the neighbor on the line in question came up to say hello and was friendly and welcoming. That synchronicity was her signal. She submitted her bid, got the property, and found it easy to clarify the boundary with her neighbor. She is now living happily on her Colorado acreage.

LOCATION, LOCATION, LOCATION

The old real estate saying holds true but in an even deeper sense. It's important to look past the specific building, apartment unit, lot, or parcel you're considering and take in the context, the whole territory on which it is located. Traditionally you would look at the surrounding property values and the proximity of schools, parks, stores, and other amenities. With an awareness of earth energies, you simply look a bit further, using your intuition and body radar as well as your logical mind.

If you are designing or building for others, subtle influences will affect your buyers, thus affecting your customers' level of satisfaction with your work. For landlords, these energies affect your tenants. Locations with unhealthy or unbalanced energetic patterns will tend to result in ill health, clutter, family strife, money troubles, and less creativity for those who live or work there. These factors can be changed, but it is important to be aware of the hidden pros and cons of each location before you buy or rent. Physical factors may also influence your decision (for instance, you may be limited to a certain location or price range), but the intuitive information will help you to make the best decision from the options that fit your criteria.

FIRST IMPRESSIONS

When visiting a location for the first time, create a quiet listening space in yourself and pay attention to your emotional and physical responses and your intuitive hunches. It's best to begin before you physically set out for the visit. With each new site, track any sensory information such as that described in the next two sections and make note of feelings or hunches.

Before you leave to look at properties, take a moment to do the Attuning to Nature Beings exercise in part 4, or say your own a prayer for guidance and grounding. Take a moment to ask for signals from the natural creative forces at each site.

As you approach a site, pay particular attention to your first impressions. Jot them down, along with any fleeting thoughts that cross your mind as you approach or enter the property. Remember that your perceptions tend to be most accurate when your body radar has not yet taken in too much data. After touring the site for a bit, your mind gets active and the more subtle intuitive information can get buried or tossed aside. Be sure to gather as much data as possible on the energetic level before adding left-brain data. Many times a property is chosen in the first five minutes just by standing and taking in first impressions.

Once you have registered the initial impressions, take a moment to register some of the other information that nature is providing. Walking the boundaries can be a good way to get a feel for the character of a particular area. If you are looking at an apartment or office, walk the halls and around the building.

RECOGNIZING BALANCED AND IMBALANCED ENERGY

Life will respond to your request for signals. Some signals may come in the form of physical responses—your stomach tightens, your skin crawls, your heart leaps, or you breathe a sigh of relief—so be sure to notice how your body feels. Then consider signs from nature. Here are some common signals:

Green Light: Indications of Balanced Earth Energy Patterns

- Easy-to-find site: Good directions, light traffic, clear entrance
- Pleasant birdsong
- Hearing a favorite song or music you like while approaching or on the site
- Lush green landscape, including trees and shrubbery
- Wonderful smells
- Friendly dogs or cats
- A wedding party goes by as you arrive
- Parents pushing a newborn baby in a carriage

- A rainbow

- Wind—if it feels good or refreshing to you (Note: This may signal energy that can help you move and evolve more easily at the site.)

- Clouds that appear in friendly or auspicious shapes, or that give you a good feeling when you look at them (Note: A dragon in the sky is considered a particularly good omen. According to Professor Lin, "If you see a dragon, you can be a leader in your field. Turn around and face outward and visualize that you become this auspicious symbol while living at this site.")

- Deer standing nearby

- Peacock with the tail feathers spread out

These types of signals can indicate that a site has a lot of life force and will make a good place to rent or buy. A balanced site will radiate beauty, generate good events, and feel fresh and clean, celebrating new life coming toward you. I remember looking for our first home with my husband. As we walked into one potential house, a bride and groom went by in an open carriage. The house felt right to us, the rent was within our budget, and the happy event passing by was a strong confirmation, so we moved in. While we lived there, Ray received a promotion, my practice took off, and we settled into a harmonious pattern with each other.

Yellow-Red Light: Indications of Earth Energy Imbalance

- Hard-to-reach site: Poor directions, or the way is obstructed by traffic or other impediments

- Squawking birds such as crows

- Dead bird or rodent on the lot

- Spindly landscape; dying or dead plants on the site

- Unpleasant smells, such as stale food or a musty odor

- Barking dogs or fighting cats

- Neighbors arguing as you arrive
- Broken windows
- A front door that is difficult to open or close
- Burnt-out light bulbs
- Leaking toilet
- Wind—if it feels harsh, unpleasant, or aggressive
- A personal event that happens as you arrive or while touring the site (For example, while you are at the site your brother calls your cell phone to tell you that your mother's birthday party has been canceled. The event may be unrelated, but the timing is no accident.)
- Tripping or hurting yourself while inspecting the site

SQUAWKING BIRDS SIGNAL TROUBLE

Paying attention to these types of signals paid off for Selena and her commercial investment properties. She had been having a lot of trouble with one of her real estate sites where there was an unusual amount of property damage, a fire in one office, and a sharply increased tenant turnover rate. Just as we walked onto the site, a flurry of squawking crows landed on the roof of her building and on surrounding telephone wires and trees.

Walking the site with an extra level of alertness, we noticed two cars full of young people in the parking lot, and something about the scene felt off to both of us, not to mention that the activity was unusual behavior for the time of day and for this business location. We began to wonder about drug dealing, although there was no previous history of it in this part of the city. Selena asked specific questions of neighbors and tenants, and discovered that they had observed a number of drug-related incidents on her site.

The squawking birds were the first indicators, causing me to be more alert to a potential problem and thus probably more receptive to the unease we felt with the parked cars. While it may seem like a lucky coincidence that the cars were present during the short time we were visiting the site, I had seen this kind of coincidence so many times in my practice that I no longer consider it as such. I now expect it when I ask for signals from the environment about the condition of a site. Selena had walked her property many times in her years of owning it and had never seen indications of a problem before. Our intention to receive signals from the life around us was answered in the form of the squawking birds and the car showing up in the short time we were there.

Once Selena had this clarity, she was able to take action. On a physical level, she gave more attention to cleaning and beautifying the property. She was encouraged to hear that the fire in the office was a blessing, a cleansing and loosening up of the site's lingering energetic habit of misfortune. We performed the Exterior Chi Ceremony (see page 214) on the site to clear the sluggish energies associated with the drug dealing and to stimulate a new, more vibrant flow of life force there. It would take time and persistence, but within the first month Selena reported that a neighborhood-watch program had been initiated, several arrests had been made, and she had attracted some encouraging new tenants. A few months later, she reported that the neighborhood was improving and that she felt complete with the property. Plus, she had found a buyer who was a fire restoration contractor who could devote the time and energy needed to help with the upgrades.

PHYSICAL PATTERNS AROUND A BUILDING OR PROPERTY

In the same way that ley lines and power points are often reflected in physical features on the land, the invisible patterns of energy flow on or near a site are often reflected in physical patterns that we see. While you are in an especially receptive state and noticing subtler clues from nature, allow yourself to notice visible patterns—first in the surrounding neighborhood and then on the site.

For an exercise to hone your ability to read your surroundings, see the Choosing a House to Rent or Buy exercise on page 227. When you arrive at a potential site, begin by looking around with a relaxed gaze and taking in overall impressions before you begin the exercise.

After registering your first impressions, pay attention to the following specific aspects with regard to the whole building (it can be helpful to consider the position of the individual unit as well):

SHAPE OF THE BUILDING AND SHAPE OF THE LOT

Look for shapes that are balanced, with few protrusions, recesses, or indentations (see page 109 for a list of ideal shapes).

LOT OR BUILDING SIZE IN RELATION TO SURROUNDINGS

A lot or building that is much smaller than surrounding ones can create a sense of diminishment or constriction if no steps are taken to improve it and bring out its own strength and beauty. Some people have compensated for a small house with extensive, strong landscaping around it. Sometimes these improvements have included a water feature.

RELATIONSHIP TO NEARBY BUILDINGS

The orientation of surrounding buildings has an energetic effect on your home or business. Buildings, trees, telephone poles, and other vertical elements create patterns or channels that direct the movement of life force, which swirls around them like a stream around rocks.

A NOTE ABOUT CORNERS

It is not ideal to have your home or business located where the corner of another building "points" at you, because energy flows fairly quickly along the straight sides of a building, creating an eddy at the corner as the two streams collide. The eddy is unsettling to your body radar, like a whirlwind might be. The chi is more insistent than gentle. While you may not visually notice the effect, most people will be uneasy with the configuration and feel as if an invisible arrow or barrage of life force is coming at them. People tend to be less relaxed, successful, or creative in that space than where buildings are parallel and the flow is more optimally measured. Furthermore, since it gives the other building a stronger position, your attitude toward the people in that house or building may be affected by the "knife edge" pointed at you.

Remedies for the corner configuration, where it cannot be avoided, include screening the energy with landscaping or other attenuating elements like wind socks or wind chimes.

ACCESSIBILITY

A site that is difficult to access often has an energetic obstruction as well. A winding access road symbolically reflects a constricted amount of life force coming through. It takes more effort for it to get there. It also takes more effort for guests to reach you. Challenging access may create irritability and off-balanced energy when they arrive. One important compensation for this is to provide clear, easy-to-follow directions for anyone coming to your place. If the site is the best choice for other reasons, it is important to do some work to correct the energetic pattern. One remedy is to place landscape elements such as trees, shrubs, or signs at the edge of each turn, in the center of the curve. The repetition of a fir tree or a distinctive shrub at each turn can be a visual cue that guides visitors along the road to your place.

NEARBY ROADS

The roads around a home or business are also life force pathways or conductors. Pay attention to angles, curves, and connections to get an indication of the chi path and how vitality flows to or near your potential site. Note that there is a difference between what is good for a business and what is good for a residence. The rushing energy of a busy street may be great for attracting business and keeping things brisk and lively, but is not conducive to the rest and rejuvenation necessary in a home environment.

There are detailed analyses of the impact of different kinds of roads in some of the feng shui books listed in the Resources section, but I encourage you to use your own body radar to pay attention to the various aspects of each site. Use outside information mainly as a way to help you become more aware of the information you are picking up with your senses and intuition.

In Figures 15a and 15b, the road "hugs" the house, figuratively and literally, as the building is literally embraced by life force. Vitality tends to flow gently in these configurations. In Figure 15c, the houses are not directly across the street from one another. This placement allows more energetic privacy between structures. There are always cures if you find yourself directly across the street from a neighbor. For instance, a well-placed tree in the front yard can create the privacy screen for you.

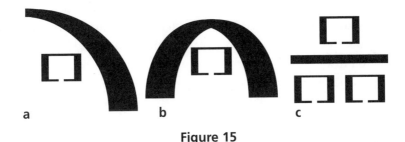

Figure 15

Figure 16 a shows some potentially challenging or detrimental arrangements for a dwelling. Generally any roads curving away from the structure draw life force away from the home, as illustrated in Figures 16a and 16b. Dead-end roads are well named, since the energy tends to stop or dwindle there. I once noticed a house in my old neighborhood that directly faced the end of the road (Fig. 16c); its porch was constantly falling apart and being repaired. To cure this kind of arrangement, place lots of lively plants on the site to enliven the life force.

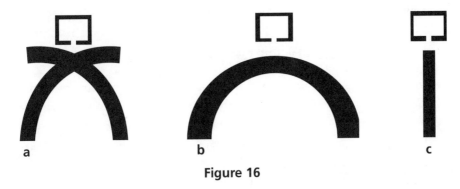

Figure 16

NEARBY BRIDGES

Bridges as a rule have a lot of strong life force around them and tend not to be very grounded, which makes it challenging to anchor and prosper in a home close to one. Suspended in air, across water, and especially with an arching shape that pulls in heaven, larger bridges that funnel commercial traffic and commuters generally have a very busy, bustling energy. Many businesses may thrive in the active environment near a bridge or large road.

For residences, most people will do better in a quieter, more earth-connected environment. One residential situation that might work well near a bridge would be a condo or high-rise apartment building, where units are well-insulated from the noise and impact of the constant movement of traffic. The upper floors, especially those higher than the bridge, would be best for most people. The lower floors could be an ideal environment for retail and other businesses.

NEIGHBORHOODS

Along with the usual pros and cons of a residential neighborhood, the continuity and repetition of homes on streets and the lack of stimulation and distraction found in more fast-moving areas energetically creates feelings of peace and security. In neighborhoods, quiet normally descends at night.

Conversely, if you are looking to locate an office, the same location will probably not be the most supportive environment for high productivity or commerce since high traffic, people walking and talking, and the interactions that result from this stimuli are vital for a thriving business.

UNUSUALLY STRONG EARTH ENERGIES

The presence of power points, ley lines, or vortexes does not rule out a property for consideration, but remember that for the well-being of humans and all other life forms it is best not to build in close proximity to these concentrated energies.

TREE CONFIGURATION

In chapter 4, we looked at the roles that trees play in the landscape. Trees also act as an anchoring force for intentions and as support for projects inside the house.

In addition to considering the character and role of individual trees on a potential site, look at the placement of the nearby trees; it gives an indication of potential energy patterns and signals for certain life experiences of residents in that location. Here are some possible configurations and their traditional meanings:

- *Trees growing to the left of the structure when you are outside facing the front door or encircling the structure (Fig. 17a):* Occupants should benefit from long-preserved wealth because these trees anchor a strong and stable energy near the Flow energy column of the building, making it easier to concentrate and to direct creative energy into monetarily successful ventures.

- *Trees planted or pruned in a curve to embrace the structure (Fig. 17b):* Life can flow easily here and is likely to bring good fortune. The chi is drawn toward the structure in gentle curves, thus creating circulation and health for both land and humans.

- *Trees growing in a line facing the gate:* Security and stability are likely here, as these trees act as sentinels protecting the property.

- *Dense stand of trees at the rear of the structure (Fig. 17c):* Occupants have the potential to be outstanding and to achieve fame and/or success in their chosen field. Located close to the Reputation energy column, a group of trees growing at the rear of the building provides a constant reinforcement for that sector of the occupants' life. It's like having the right people at your back, the same way that successful people look back and say, "These people were always there for me. I always felt supported, knowing they were rooting for me no matter what." Trees, with their gift of grounding and anchoring, give the constancy and support that inspires confidence of success. It's not an accident that there are many old trees on college campuses.

- *Trees that allow the sun to filter through are especially good:* Shade creates a more reflective environment, stimulating more inward feelings that nurture the body, while sunlight is more active or outward, nurturing the brain. The diversity and complexity of the life force is shown in the interplay of sunshine and shadow, which stimulates the brain; the leaf and branch "sparkle" is similar to light dancing on water.

149

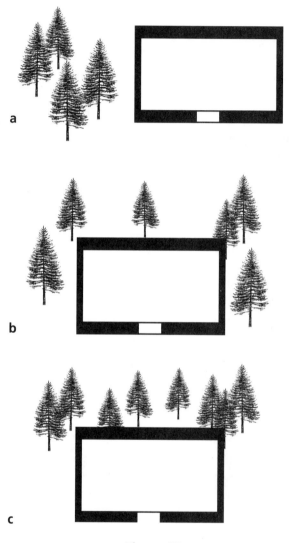

Figure 17

THE QUALITY OF SURROUNDING WATER

Water is a particularly good indicator of the level of vitality in an area, so observe it carefully:

    ✧   *Is the water flowing or stagnant? Clear or murky?*

✦ *If there is a pond or stream, are the plants healthy or is the vegetation dying or absent? Are there a lot of native plants or do invasive colonizers predominate?*

✦ *Are there bugs, ducks, frogs, lizards, or a lack of life?*

✦ *Sound: Is it gurgling over stones, lapping, or swishing against the borders? Or is the sound absent or agitated?*

✦ *Motion: Rippling, flowing light glinting off the surface is a good sign of life force.* Dull-looking water often reflects a dampened vitality in the water and the surrounding area. Moving water has more oxygen and generates negative ions that uplift mood, boost immune function, and increase concentration.

✦ *Location of waterways near the site:* A location near the starting point of a river, a stream, or even a sewer carries a potential for progress. Water just emerging or beginning its flow has the energy of birth. It communicates a joyful energy of possibility and of transition from one state to another. A location near a sewage treatment plant or where a waterway dries up or ends usually means a drop in energy and carries a sense of ending rather than ongoingness or progress.

ROCKY SITES

While a rocky site can be harder to build on, rocks carry a strong energy, and the combination of earth and stone gives a basis of real stability and strength. It can withstand not only weather but energetic turbulence. The stone energy imparts a deep, unconscious sense of relaxation and security, which may give occupants more energy for creative thought and problem solving.

SITE HISTORY

As Deepak Chopra and many other teachers have explained, when we focus our attention on one thought, emotion, or action, it affects our reality.[1] As we continue to revisit a particular thought, we are actually feeding it with our attention and emotion. With repetition, the thought form continues to grow stronger, gathering energy that is, like itself, in a process of magnetic attraction. With enough attention, it can actually manifest in the physical world.

Biologist and researcher Rupert Sheldrake explains the concept from another angle. Sheldrake, along with a number of developmental biologists since the 1920s, recognized that while genes play an essential part in the development of all living cells, they do not explain the sort of memory on cell patterns that passes from generation to generation. The memory happens, they propose, due to organizing fields of information, which pass on patterns or habits to other cells. These fields extend beyond the physical cells in the same way that magnetic fields extend beyond the surfaces of magnets, and the way that the earth's gravitational field extends far beyond the surface of the earth, keeping the moon in its orbit.

Sheldrake calls these morphic fields, after the Greek word for form. When a natural event like the mutation of a plant cell occurs, it creates a morphic field, and, through a process he calls morphic resonance, it increases the likelihood that the event will recur. In lay terms, when something happens once, it is likely to happen again, and it becomes more likely to do so the more times it happens.[2]

Events such as a long illness or a happy family life act like energy stamps on a site. They leave a lingering energetic signature that can continue to influence all life in that area, causing the same type of events or conditions to recur there. You have probably noticed places in your town where restaurants or stores fail repeatedly. Sudden death, long illness, or a history of violent conflict leaves a site with low vitality and a tendency to attract more of the same energy. Likewise, a happy domestic life and joyful events leave a lingering vitality and a tendency to attract similar energy.

The Black Sect Tantric Buddhist feng shui tradition holds that human patterns occurring on a site tend to repeat within three years. For example, if a family sells because of a sickness or death in the family, the occurrence of sickness has a tendency to repeat in three years for whoever occupies it at the time. The same is true for happy or auspicious patterns.

When considering whether to purchase such a property, in some cases you may choose to steer clear, especially if the site has multiple problems, since changing these patterns may take a long-term diligent effort. Intention and ceremony can foster the evolution, growth, or development of both the human inhabitants and the place itself. And since humans and land coexist, these changes ripple out, supporting a broader evolution.

Here are some questions to ask the seller, agent, and neighbors when investigating a site's history:

- ⊕ Why is the property being sold?

- ⊕ What types of events have happened in the neighborhood?

- ⊕ What is the seller's history with the property and why is he or she selling now?

HEALTHY OR UNHEALTHY HISTORY

Expansive, upbeat circumstances tend to leave a positive energy stamp on a site. Healthy patterns of living for the new owner of a place are present if previous occupants left because of promotion, the need for a larger home due to welcome birth, the need for larger home office due to a successful business, or downsizing for a simpler life. Negative circumstances such as the previous owner's divorce, illness, death, and bankruptcy call for further consideration before purchasing a place.

As these life events are so common, at some point you may end up choosing or inheriting a place where negative events occurred. Use the Sure-Fire Cleanse (see page 209) and Exchanging the Chi Ceremony (see page 210) to clear the old energy and bring in more life force and vitality.

A real estate agent called me because her client's home had been sitting on the market for a year. She was puzzled because it was in a prime area, where neighboring homes sold briskly, but only a handful of potential buyers had even walked through the house in many months.

In questioning the history of the site, I learned that someone had been ill in the home for quite some time, which had evidently left a strong energy imprint that had dulled its healthy patterns; the site was dusty with history. I recommended the Sure-Fire Cleanse. The simple action had a powerful and immediate effect and polished up the energetic field. Ten minutes after the cleanse, the owner was amazed when he stepped outside and a passing car slowed down so the passenger could lean out and ask, "Is this house for sale?"

Dispersing the imprint from the past had opened up new possibilities for the site, and the house sold soon thereafter. Because we in modern cultures are used to linear time and geared to a world of physical action, such speedy results challenge our notions of reality. But in the world of intangibles, of thought and energy, instant change is possible and does occur with more frequency than most of our belief systems generally recognize.

Sarah asked me to check out a potential site for her new house. It was in a new development and larger than her current lot, had a good view, and was at the right price. It all looked good, but as we walked around the site, my body radar felt a large disturbance in the natural patterns on the land. I sensed fear and anger and a dense feeling in the air.

I told Sarah my concerns and suggested that she check the history of the area. She decided to buy the lot without checking. Since everything seemed so right from a rational standpoint, she felt the invisible side would work itself out. But a few months later Sarah told me that she was having construction problems. The new foundation kept cracking, supplies were delayed, and schedules were snagged. Homes around her were almost finished while hers languished with delay after delay.

Remembering my suggestion, she had checked into the history and found that her lot had been a Pony Express stop, and that there had been an incident of violence and murder there in that era. At her request, I went back and helped her with the Exterior Chi Ceremony to clear the contrary energy stamp from long ago and to restore harmony. Dispersing old energy patterns with our intentions and actions, we invited the creation of new patterns of vitality and balance. Construction resumed, the house foundations were successfully installed, and the building process proceeded uneventfully from then on.

CEMETERIES, HOSPITALS, AND OTHER INFLUENCES

In the feng shui tradition, cemeteries and hospitals are considered inauspicious neighbors for residences and businesses because of their slow-moving life energy. I teach classes in a wonderful bookshop on a street full of colorful, bustling shops. The street is always busy, except for one block where a hospital sits. The shops across from the hospital are neither as busy nor as bright, and tend to turn over more quickly. The atmosphere around the hospital is incompatible with the faster, sparkling ambience conducive for successful retail business.

A young mother who was living by a cemetery called me because her young son was not sleeping well in their new home. Upon arriving, I noticed that there was an unusual stillness and heaviness in her son's room, like the feeling in an unused closet stuffed with clutter. Talking with his mother, I discovered that the small churchyard next to his room held a few old, unmarked gravesites. This explained the stagnant energy in his room; we resolved the problem easily by moving his bed to a new room, where he began sleeping normally again.

Take time to explore areas in your city to look for signs of history and the effect it has had on the neighborhood. Also look at the types of structures and businesses around hospitals. Are they well kept and thriving? How is the turnover rate? If a house has been for sale for a long time, how does the property feel to you? Use your body radar to get a sense, and then check around to see if you were right.

Finally, pay attention to noise, toxic materials, the type of industry in the area, traffic flow, and any other nearby circumstances that might have an impact on the site. Get a feel for the neighborhood by visiting at different times (weekday and weekend, evening and daytime, and rush hour) to see if your impressions change.

BENEFITS OF EVALUATING A SITE WITH BODY RADAR

By adding more intuitive data, evaluating a site can help you make your choice with less stress and less agony over the options. It can help you choose the area that will give you the most satisfying experience, and it can save money by bringing to light hidden problems or potential problems even when the seller fails to disclose them.

Mike and Aimee were excited about their first home in a large suburban subdivision. After living in a small apartment, the backyard was a source of delight for their toddler and for them. But they were a bit frustrated by continued construction behind them and asked me to see why this area of the subdivision was lagging so far behind the rest, with a string of accidents, equipment failure, and other delays.

Outside, I sensed irritation or toxicity in the ground and asked about the site's history. They said it had been a part of a large nursery, and I guessed that there were pesticides and other landscaping chemicals buried in the ground that were affecting their attempts to lay down a new pattern. They would have to clear up the toxicity before they could proceed effectively.

A few months later, Aimee told me that they had indeed found chemicals and that the work had been stalled because the developers had been scrambling to come up with the money for a cleanup effort. Once the cleanup had happened, building progressed more smoothly, and the houses behind Aimee and Mike's were completed without further delay.

Because the nursery owners did not disclose the problem when they sold the property to the developers, it pushed the developers over budget to remove the chemicals and cost them valuable time to raise that cash before they could complete the homes and recoup their investment. That would be enough to put some firms out of business, which is a good reason for even developers to use these skills. The buyers could have moved on to find a better site or they could have at least paid a lower price that reflected the problem, leaving themselves enough money to correct the problem in the beginning.

Once you have chosen your place or it has chosen you, it is time to deepen your relationship with it. Great things happen on both sides when humans come into conscious relationship with the world around them. The next section explains methods of conversing with the earth spirit while laying out a site in nature.

DEVELOPING A SITE

Before creating a site plan or signing the rental agreement, take time to let the elements in your new environment speak to you. Including intuitive and sensory data along with the logical, rational elements of site planning will lead to a site plan that maximizes hidden assets, and corrects or compensates for hidden liabilities. Some people find that their alliance with a place speeds up the process or even helps a seemingly impossible deal suddenly work out.

CHOOSING WHERE TO BUILD

In classic feng shui terms, the best location for a home is in the midst of a wonderful medley of elevations—ideally a hill with a large mound or grouping of trees located behind the structure with two smaller hills, man-made berms (mounds), or groves of trees on either side; a slightly lower hill, berm, or small trees in front of the structure should complete the scene. The arrangement can serve as a natural earth shelter from the elements. Lacking the ideal terrain, it is good whenever possible to position your home in the center of your lot, a position of strength in lieu of natural protections, with the door facing the street. Also a few trees planted close together or even just one behind the building or on the sides of the structure can substitute for natural berms.

The exercises in part 4 will help you get to know the energies in the area so that you are properly connected when developing a site plan. On our site, my husband and I actually took four months to decide where to place our wooden yurt. We had time, since it was an auxiliary structure that would serve as a sanctuary and classroom. We began by choosing potential sites. We picked a few areas that were hidden and some that were more exposed or open. We also picked sites that matched the purpose of the structure with the energies nearby.

The next step was to narrow down the choices. We waited for a few days before we went back and retraced our steps to see if impressions were the same. A different perspective and day can give a more definitive perception, strengthening some impressions or fine-tuning them. We let more time go by. We looked and listened for signs of nature's approval or disapproval on each site. We found a feather when we came back to one area, which seemed like a gift and an affirmation of our choice. Also, two different times when we went back to look at that particular site, a gentle rain began that felt a bit like hands caressing us, which we interpreted as an affirmation or benediction.

I asked some of my students to visit and give their feedback on our potential building sites. Hearing other words and descriptions of the different areas gave me a clearer picture.

One day after going through all the steps, the location for our sanctuary became clear to us. Nature's symbolic communications had provided us with clear direction, and now we felt a strong inner knowing. We had done our part and the earth and nature energies had done theirs. The construction process flowed easily because the pattern was clear. It was like slowly finding all the pieces of a puzzle. Taking our time with the process allowed a real interweaving between humans and nature.

Our building has been in place for some years now, and it feels wonderful. It's a peaceful and inspiring place to work and dream. Others who have used it for meetings or classes have had a similar experience there. Nature seems pleased as well, with an increasing diversity of plant life and more birdsong echoing around the land. A sense of joy rises up to meet us as we come home every day.

There are three equal partners on our land: Ray, nature, and me. As a team we have created more than Ray and I had thought possible.

REMINDERS TO HELP YOU MAINTAIN A SITE'S VITALITY

In previous chapters, we discussed the importance of not building in areas of strong earth energy. Similarly, for the well-being of the land and its occupants, some important considerations regarding water and trees should be thought through before you begin to build or landscape. By making your changes to the land in harmony with the energy of existing patterns, you ensure positive effects on the health and creativity of the new occupants.

The following checklist will help you maintain or enhance the original, authentic qualities of your site's earth energy. These are reminders of details to pay attention to, but the ultimate guide is your own intuition and body radar and the rapport you develop with your land.

> *Retain natural patterns (or reproduce in miniature):* When you need to make extensive changes on your site, in addition to giving nature adequate notice and tuning in to harmoniously ways to do it, use your landscaping to reflect miniature versions of the patterns originally present on the land, such as rocks and native plants. If drastic changes were made before you came along, increase the vitality of the land by using old photos, maps, and stories to help you re-create a miniature version of how the land looked when it was thriving.

⊛ *Observe the original lines:* Pay close attention to any unusual plant groupings as you walk the site. Notice naturally occurring curves and circles in rock configurations and trees and the pattern of meandering water. Echoing these lines in your landscapes and structures creates a resonance that strengthens the patterns on the land.

⊛ *Whenever possible, leave an area of trees completely wild and uncultivated:* Trees left in their natural pattern have their own method of self-propagating. The ideal arrangement for circulating a property's chi is leaving an intact, unaltered pattern of trees. These configurations allow the subtle helpers to do their work of weaving and circulating life force undisturbed, thus creating strong patterns of vitality that need time to take hold. "Preparation for Tree Cutting" in the next chapter gives suggestions to ease the impact when leaving tree patterns unaltered is not an option.

We decided to leave most of the tree patterns on our land intact and untouched by construction. At one point I noticed a density of color in one grove of trees. As I spent time there, my body radar sensed a brightness where there was no sun, a concentrated magnetic energy, an overwhelming sense of joy, and eventually an internal image of a playful gnome. When I realized he was there, I asked for more signs or symbols to verify his presence. To acknowledge him, I began leaving offerings at the place I felt him most strongly. I became aware of a web of supportive nature energy he was reinforcing around the trees that we had left to nature. Such webs strengthen emotional stability for humans and support the experience of more peace and a sense of continuity. This relationship developed because of our agreement to leave that group of trees wild and mostly untouched.

⊛ *Work around trees with strong earth energies:* Spend time getting to know your trees, and discover whether you have any that have taken root around strong earth energies. When growing around strong earth energy, trees' role as anchor is amplified and should not be disturbed by cutting. One client wanted to make sure he did not disturb any major energy centers when building on his land. I suggested that he preserve a circle of trees that gave off a strong restorative feeling. The circle of trees helped contain and sustain the life force. He later reported that his young son loves to play there, and that both he and his wife feel recharged by sitting quietly in that spot.

Powerful tree patterns are sometimes indicated by the following:

- *A symmetrical or geometric grouping of trees:* Earth energies often generate in a circle or a spiral. If you find more than three trees growing in a circle, it can be an indication of a very strong spiral of earth energy that holds a restorative quality for both humans and the land. Five trees grew together in a circle on our land; we called them the five sisters. The trees were a major energy factory for our place. Trees with special earth energy jobs should be protected so that they can do their work without interference. If you cannot preserve such an area, invite the energies to transfer to the remaining trees and shrubs, and the life force can transfer as you are cutting the trees (see page 233).
- *Trees with unusual curves or "faces" in the branches or trunk:* Unusual shapes such as faces are usually an indication that nature beings have made a home in these trees, so it would be better for nature if you kept the tree. It's a power spot, an important link for generating or distributing the chi on your land. A tree that is more lush or greener than the rest can also be a sign of more chi. It is good to leave those generators in place.
- *An old tree with unusual features:* An old tree can be a refuge, a threshold for humans and nature to meet, or

a healing presence in which to rest. One day, my friend Judith took me to her favorite woods. Although it was a city park, it had been left quite wild in parts and thus anchored a strong, supportive energy for the city. The paths were well worn and popular, as many people were drawn to replenish their energy in this oasis of healing.

Judith and I were both longing for a quiet moment to savor the cathedral feeling of the towering forest around us. She motioned me over to a huge old tree. A lightning strike had hollowed out this beautiful giant many years earlier. The tree had adapted to the change, creating a hidden refuge. We climbed into it, and time seemed to stop as we drank in the delicious experience, feeling one with nature in the magical inner space provided by the special tree.

Municipalities often protect large old trees for the history that they carry and the meaning and feeling they have for people. Look for unusual trees in your area.

Rerouting water: When you plan water flow coming through culverts, pipes, water features, French drains, or sceptic systems on your land or in your neighborhood, there are two principles in particular to keep in mind. First, listen to the water itself. Then communicate your needs and plans clearly, and listen to what comes back to you. Communicating your plans includes staking out the new route you're proposing and taking a day or two to spend time there, noting the feelings that come, along with any new ideas.

Water table and well placement: Before purchasing rural land, pay close attention to water tables in the area. Find out how deep neighbors had to drill to find water. Old-timers in any dry area would not consider digging a well without having a dowser come out and find the location. A good dowser can tell you not only the location but the depth and often the flow rate of the water there.

◈ *Water feature:* Water, with its movement, sounds, and reflected light, is a major component in an environment. Bring a portable water fountain system inside and place it in a favorite spot. Whenever possible, place a water feature outside at the Flow column of your lot or subdivision.

When a building is reflected in a nearby body of water, movement in the water both reflects and creates movement or progress for the building, such as work on a favorable addition. If your property lacks a stabilizing mountain behind it, placing three vertical stones in a reflecting pond can represent one. In the Portland Classical Chinese Garden in Oregon, tall jagged rocks resemble the symbolic mountain in its large water feature. The effect is striking: one feels transported to an ancient waterway in the wilds of China even in the middle of a busy urban block (see part 4 for a list of guidelines for constructing an ideal outdoor water feature).

With our strong intentions and actions, we contributed to the sense of joy and beauty in the valley around Fir Haven. Using the guidelines provided in this chapter, you will be able to make the same contributions to your site and in the land around it.

10

BUILDING DESIGN, CONSTRUCTION, AND REMODELING

Whether people are fully conscious of this or not, they actually derive countenance and suste-nance from the "atmosphere" of the things they live in or with. They are rooted in them just as a plant is in the soil in which it is planted.

—Frank Lloyd Wright

ALWAYS OUTSPOKEN ABOUT the influence of nature on his work, the great American architect Frank Lloyd Wright counseled his apprentices to "study nature, love nature, stay close to nature," adding, "It will never fail you." Wright's enduring legacy of buildings that "grow naturally from their sur-roundings" bears impressive witness to the wisdom of his advice.

This chapter will help you attune to nature during the design and construc-tion phases of a new building or a remodel. Homeowners and apartment dwellers can also apply these tips even when making smaller changes such as painting, adding new furniture, pruning trees, or welcoming a new member to the home. A change in the environment still creates an impact no matter how small.

NATURE'S VOICE IN THE BUILDING DESIGN PROCESS

Any new structure is a big change to the local energy web; even remodeling can have a significant effect. It is important to communicate the intended change before it happens, to give nature time to loosen the old pattern and adjust to the new addition or change. In turn, it's important to listen so that the change is smoothly introduced into the environment.

Communication with nature can be informal, like a chat with a friendly neighbor, or be a bit more formal with the use of ceremony. Most people use a bit of both. In any case, begin by going to the area that will be affected and talk with the plants, rocks, water, soil, and whatever energetic beings you sense there. Speak—silently or aloud—as you would to any neighbor, telling them what you have in mind, what your purpose is, and what outcome you hope to create. Then take time to listen and take note of any impressions that come in response.

Sometimes you will just have a peaceful feeling as you would after a satisfying conversation with a pleasant neighbor. If you are unaccustomed to interacting consciously with the energies around you, you may not recognize the emotional tone coming from the environment. You may suddenly find yourself feeling angry about something someone said to you earlier, the traffic sounds, or the trash someone has left on the ground. Context is the key here. If a feeling comes spurting up when you're intending to communicate with nature, it's probably at least partly coming from the energies you are reaching out to. Remember, this is symbolic, right-brained communication.

A distressed reaction such as anger or fear from the environment tends to happen in areas where nature has been affected by unconscious changes in the past, but that doesn't mean you will always feel the same in those areas. You are equally likely to find nature pleased to be greeted by you and eager to cooperate. If you do find distress, clearly repeat your intention to create a mutually agreeable solution and listen for more information. What do you sense is the problem? Perhaps the energies on your site have been impacted by thoughtless interventions in the past and need a little time to trust you are coming in with a different approach. Take time-outs in nature and practice recognizing thoughts and emotions around you to deepen trust and communication.

Many times, nature energies will respond to your overtures immediately with enthusiastic cooperation. You'll often experience its response as an idea coming into your head, such as a better way to do what you are planning, an angle that hadn't occurred to you before, or a sudden certainty that all will work well.

Communicating with nature is generally simpler and more effortless than you imagine. The trick is to turn off the mind-chatter, especially doubts or worries about what others might think. Remember, there's no question of whether nature will communicate with you. Nature, or the intangible side of life, is *always* communicating. The question is: can you allow yourself to hear it?

CONSTRUCTION AND REMODELING

PREPARATION FOR TREE CUTTING

Cutting trees is often a big change that has a complex effect on the area's energetic web, other nature energies, humans, and animals. When tree cutting is unavoidable, the important thing—for both humans and nature—is to approach the task with awareness and a sense of connection. Tree cutting undertaken with attention and respect can actually be a boon to the land's physical and spiritual energy. While not as drastic as cutting down trees, pruning also has a distinct impact and should also be undertaken with care and communication.

Cutting one tree or even a group of trees does not necessarily affect the general earth energy. Trees filling important roles in the energetic web of the landscape are exceptions and should be approached with extra care (see page 233).

Many indigenous people traditionally thank and honor trees or animals they harvest, celebrating and expressing appreciation for the being's life force and willingness to give its life on behalf of the tribe or village. As these people know, acknowledging and expressing gratitude to neighboring life forms strengthens your relationship and increases vitality for all involved.

EASING THE IMPACT ON HUMANS

Humans often react to tree cutting with shock or grief, especially when large trees are cut. The recommended steps are often as important for us as they are for trees and the rest of the environment. Amy, a schoolteacher, often took her students outside to hold class under a large tree. Lessons under the gentle giant were the children's favorite part of the week. Arriving at school one sunny May morning, she was stunned to find that their favorite tree had been cut down over the weekend.

The children had a similar reaction and kept asking about the tree throughout the day. They were so distressed that they couldn't really focus on lessons, so Amy finally decided to take them outside. They sat around the stump of their old friend and talked about the tree. Each child had a chance to say his or her favorite things about the tree and share whatever feelings he or she was having. Amy gave them time to say good-bye and to ask for a blessing for the tree.

"I was amazed by what a difference it made for me and for the children," she told me later. Taking the time to feel and express their feelings and to honor the connection they had felt with the life force of the tree allowed them to go on with their day with a sense of peace.

Like the rest of nature, humans connect in energetic patterns. We do best when our patterns and habits with life are consciously acknowledged and honored, and when we take the time to allow nature and ourselves to adjust to a change in any pattern.

AN EXAMPLE OF CONSCIOUS CUTTING

A group of friends living down the road were planning to turn an overgrown blackberry thicket into a large vegetable and herb garden, which would make use of the rare sunny area on their forest property. To do this, a giant cottonwood tree had to come down.

In preparation, they visited the tree and announced their intention, along with their appreciation and respect for the tree's beauty and all that the tree had contributed over the years. They explained their need to cut down the tree now, to provide safety for the building and its occupants (since the tree was old and rot had set in) and to open up a sunny garden space, and they invited the tree to transfer the life force to the remaining trees in the area and be a part of the new pattern on the land being created with the garden. They then staked out the garden beds with sticks and yarn, allowing the nature of the place to open and blend energetically with the new patterns proposed.

Several weeks after staking out the garden, the time came to cut down the tree. They performed a ceremony, using sage smudge and again thanking and appreciating the tree and requesting her to bring her spirit into the garden and be part of the new life emerging there. They also invited her to guide the humans in cutting her down (see Preparation for Tree Cutting on page 233).

When it finally happened, the huge tree dropped smoothly and quietly into the forest behind her, nestling in as if it had been there for years. The space felt undisturbed and peaceful, so much so that onlookers were amazed. My neighbors were convinced that communicating with nature and allowing time for the old web to loosen and the energy to flow into the new pattern had made a tremendous difference. "I had expected to feel traumatized, but when it happened, it was so fast, so smooth and natural," one of my neighbors told me. "One minute we were standing there, braced, and the next minute we were blinking at each other wondering if we had imagined it. It felt like nothing had happened, like it had always been this way. Everything was so peaceful. And the garden has been spectacular this year! It really feels like the tree's strength and spirit is there."

A WHOLE NEW SIDE OF CONSTRUCTION

Building with an eye to the earth's energies is not new. It is only new to us in the developed parts of the world. Indigenous folks around the globe still consider all sorts of intangible factors when they construct their buildings. Many will not build in an area where there has been death, at least not without ritual cleansing and prayer. And many use some form of discussion with nature and offer respect to the elements and energies in the area, though these energies may be perceived in different ways.

Building is essentially the art of cocreating patterns with nature. Construction becomes so much more interesting when we pay attention to energetic patterns and interactions. In situations that seem random or out of our control, we can begin to see subtle cause and effect. Actions undertaken without awareness or concern for the environment bring repercussions that are seemingly out of the blue in the same way that it does when people walk through a construction site without an awareness of others working on scaffolding above them or someone swinging a hammer nearby.

It's helpful but not necessary for everyone on a construction crew to understand this. As an owner, designer, carpenter, plumber, or electrician, you can affect the way the job goes and the finished result. The following tips

167

will give you some ways to bring earth spirit living into the process for your construction, remodel, or other change.

ACT FROM VISION AND A SENSE OF PURPOSE

Poetically speaking, houses are vessels holding the central fire, the home fires, for humans and for the earth. In a sense, buildings connect the energies of heaven and earth. They surround us with much more than just protection from the elements. Ideally, they reflect our idea of beauty, nourishing our spirit with a reflection of our dreams. The buildings in which we spend so much time—homes and offices—are instrumental in our interface with the natural world around us.

Builders and owners traditionally use dedication ceremonies before starting construction to symbolically take the important step of stating the project's intention. By announcing your intentions in good faith, you invite nature, which opens the way for cooperation from all sorts of energetic sources (see part 4 for ground-breaking and other dedication ceremonies). Use one of these traditional ceremonies, make your own, or simply take some time to think about your essential purpose behind each building project you are involved in.

FORMULATE AN INVOCATION

The statement can be formal or informal when beginning the building, designing, or change process. Once created, repeat the statement daily. Here are some invocation examples:

- May we work as cocreative partners with the visible and invisible elements and energies here, interweaving with existing patterns, enhancing both old and new.
- May we create beauty, harmony, order, and balance in form.
- May we open to what we need to know, respecting the original will of the place.
- May we create a building filled with vitality, a blending of spirit and matter and heaven and earth.
- May all those involved work smoothly and joyfully together as a team, with respect, compassion, clarity, and the joy of shared creativity.

CONSIDER THE USE OF CEREMONY

It is useful—and fun—to mark each new stage of design, construction, and simple change with a ceremony. Staking out a house foundation or a proposed landscaping change, for example, is a way of communicating with the environment and gives the nature beings and energies of the place an opportunity to shift the patterns and integrating the new design. A ceremony helps the construction process flow more smoothly and allows nature to thrive on and around the site. Noting an addition of a new member to a household through ceremony also gives the less substantial members, the nature beings, time to adjust and welcome the new member.

Depending on your schedule and inclination, ceremonies can be as elaborate or as simple as you wish. A moment of deep attention and sincere appreciation can be every bit as powerful as an extended ceremony to bring order together again. (See part 4 for traditional ceremonies for different phases of construction.)

HONOR THE WAYS OF WORKING AS WELL AS THE WORK ITSELF

Creating a building, painting a room, and rearranging furniture is sacred labor. Workers on the job site, installing plumbing, studs, or wiring, implementing design ideas, welding girders, or hanging drywall, are implementing the vision of owners and planners. Heaven and earth combine on the site through the hands of the physical laborers. Thus the level of intention and the emotional and energetic tone on the job site affects the energy of the finished product. A home built or worked on by people who enjoy their work and feel respected and appreciated has a very different feeling from one built or worked with a lot of anger and tension.

Imagine if, each morning, everyone came together in a circle on the job site and attuned to the project, picturing it completed in its ideal state and opening up to support and guidance for the day.

There are two potential versions to create the effect on the job. The first is informal, down-to-earth, and very effective. Tom is foreman of the maintenance and construction department for a large nonprofit that owns five large residential properties for battered women and their families. A tall, sturdy man with curly brown hair and the strong, calloused handshake of a construction worker, Tom starts the day with the whole crew in a casual circle at the maintenance office. They usually begin with a bit of personal news: whose son made a soccer goal, how many fish someone caught over the weekend, or whose back is acting up. Then they look at the day's work orders and decide together who will do what, taking into account who's good at what, who wants to learn what, who works well together, and the projects that are most urgent.

The work gets done effectively, the workers enjoy it, and clients are satisfied with the job. Without talking about it, Tom has modeled respect and clarity of intention. His morning circles and his attitude throughout the day have helped his staff members respect themselves, each other, the nonprofit staff, and their clients. He inspires his crew members with gentle reminders of the underlying purpose of the nonprofit and the clientele they serve.

A more individual attunement was practiced by an owner who, in the morning before workers arrived or in the evening after they left, would stop by the job site for her new home and stand quietly, picturing her home complete and beautiful, with nature thriving all around it. She called on the invisible helpers on the project, including what she called the guardian angels of the land and the house, to guide and support the crew that week. She would also stop by with coffee in the morning or lunch treats at noon when she could, thanking the crew and appreciating its work. "I was careful not to bug them and to stay out of their way when they were working, but it was important to me to appreciate their contribution to my dream," she said. "And the funny thing is, the general contractor told me he had never seen scheduling so smooth. Even when one crew would get behind, the other would be able to adjust its schedule so that things just cranked along. He told me he wished he could bottle whatever it was that made this job so smooth and fast. He joked about what was in the coffee and sandwiches, and I never had the guts to tell him about the invisible crew I'd been calling in."

MAKE SURE THAT DAILY OPERATIONS REFLECT YOUR DEEPER PURPOSE

Pay attention to the ordinary, repetitive aspects of building. It's important to keep the site clean and orderly while building. Clutter can encourage confusion, while a relatively orderly site will attract an easier, more accident-free construction and a more settled, peaceful energy in the completed building. Renew your intention to maintain order daily—not in a stern, martial-law way, but by focusing on what feels good to you. Create from joy and vision, not from an attempt to control.

Whenever possible, recycle the trash that generates quickly during construction. Burying trash on the site is *not* a good idea from an energetic or feng shui perspective.

Finally, make sure that any clearing of nature's plantings on the site is really necessary, not just easier and more convenient to the building process.

KNOW THAT THE EARTH APPRECIATES YOUR INTENT

Know that your intention to create your project in partnership with the earth is met with willingness and delight by the earth. Carolyn loved her island property and spent summers there for several years before she was ready to build. When the time came, she was determined to build her home on the spot she loved the most. It seemed to have a special magic; she could bask for hours on the granite boulders, enjoying the view of distant trees and harbor. But after soliciting input from nature, she realized it was a power point, and nature was giving her clear indications it was not a good building site. Sitting there one day, she had a feeling, as clear as if she had heard a voice in her mind, that the integrity of the powerful place would be compromised if she placed a building there. She kept getting an image of these rocks, unchanged and undisturbed, with a feeling of peace and power. When she started planning her house there, she noticed a pinched feeling inside, a feeling of weakness quite different from what she had felt with the other image.

She chose to go with a different location, one that her architect recommended. Once the house was built, he pointed out how much money she had saved by not going with her preferred location on the rocks. But the real thrill came as she prepared breakfast on the first day in her new home. Looking up, she discovered that her favorite spot was perfectly framed in her kitchen window, as undisturbed and lovely as it had been in the image that had kept recurring in her mind. Gazing at it, she felt the same quiet joy she had felt for years sitting on those rocks, and realized that her sweet exchange with nature would be a part of her daily experience whenever she worked in the kitchen. Every day she feels the wonder and the great gift that came from honoring nature's invisible needs.

EARTH-SAVVY DESIGN AND CONSTRUCTION

"Treat nature as a model and mentor, not an inconvenience to be evaded or controlled." These wise words epitomize the work of William McDonough, internationally renowned designer, professor, and former dean of University of Virginia's School of Architecture. His firm's earth-friendly designs saved Ford Motor Company a reported $35,000 in environmental cleanup at its Dearborn, Michigan, Rouge Center and won tremendous goodwill for the company by boosting local efforts to reclaim the Rouge River for recreational use. In addition to a grassy ten-acre roof where birds nest, the huge plant now channels all storm-water runoff into newly constructed wetlands where native plants filter contamination from years of steel manufacturing before discharging clean water into the river. McDonough's book *Cradle to Cradle: Remaking the Way We Make Things*, coauthored with German chemist Dr. Michael Braungart, has been adopted by the Chinese government and spurred an invitation to design seven new cities in China. The BBC reported that planned cities look and function like gardens of Eden but "meet the usual requirements for cost, performance, and function."

With his work and his words, McDonough consistently makes the point that building and manufacturing in harmony with nature makes sense from a business standpoint, as well as for planetary survival. Inspired by the story of how New College in Oxford, England, replaced its dry-rotted beams in the 1600s with wood from trees planted by the builders 350 years earlier for that very purpose, McDonough often uses tree planting to offset environmental impacts of construction. His team's prize-winning high-rise design for Warsaw, Poland, stipulated that the client plant 6,400 acres of new forest to offset the building's effect on climate change. After an initial check, the client cheerfully complied, noting that it cost only a small amount of its advertising budget and was paid back many times over in positive press.[2]

A growing number of design and building professionals are tuned in to nature and reaping the benefits for their clients by working in alignment with her.

QUALITIES TO LOOK FOR IN AN INTUITIVE ENVIRONMENTAL DESIGNER OR BUILDER

In looking for a professional to support you in designing or building in ways that are healthy for you and the earth, look for training and experience, of course, but there are other logical factors to consider as well, such as their awareness of energy and ecological costs associated with the built environment that can prove to impact long-term investment.

Many architects, developers, and lenders in the real estate industry are aware of the new trend in sustainable buildings. The U.S. Green Building Council (USGBC) creates strategies to implement energy conservation.[3] Its most effective strategy, the LEED (Leadership in Energy and Environmental Design) Green Building Rating System® measures the effect construction has on energy use, ecosystems, and other social-environmental impact by offering a certification system for owners where points are earned in areas such as energy conservation, indoor air quality, reduction in water use, and daylighting. Demonstrating both the economic advantages and less quantifiable benefits, the LEED rating is now sought by more and more players in the building process. Most professional groups and schools have some committees, departments, or councils geared toward sustainability, and popular Green Building Conferences are scheduled regularly in the United States and in many countries.

This is good news, but attuning to nature is not so conducive to rational measurement. Schooling and LEED accreditation certainly can help, but it is neither a guarantee nor a measurement of people's ability to sense energy or their ability to partner with the vital force on your site. How, then, do you choose consultants for your project?

The list below is a starting point, but beyond these factors rely on your instincts. Attending talks or classes at bookstores, community colleges, holistic health centers, or builders guild meetings is a great way to get a feel for different consultants' approaches and personalities as well as factual information about their area of expertise. Does the builder or architect feel like someone you'd enjoy working with? Do you trust him or her? Your own in-person conversations and recommendations from friends and other clients may give you clues, but ultimately, your intuition will let you know who is right for you.

1. *Technical qualifications*

When choosing a builder, architect, planner, or landscape designer, consider his or her training and accreditation. Some schools have particularly exciting programs, so a bit of online research into the philosophy and reputation of your prospect's schools can be helpful. Schooling isn't everything, of course. Many wonderful builders and landscapers have learned their trade on the job, with great mentors, natural skill, or both. But if he or she completed a good program, that gives you a sense of his or her interest and orientation. The websites for organizations like USGBC can be a good starting point for your search. Also, find out what licensing is required in your area and make sure your builder is properly licensed.

Environmental intuitives are wonderful to use in conjunction with builders and architects, just as dowsers are commonly used in conjunction with well drillers. The intuitive consultant can help you identify energetic patterns and issues on your site, which may factor into choosing and designing sites. Look for people who have apprenticed for a long time with a gifted, experienced master teacher. Many dowsers, for instance, learn their craft person-to-person, with the ability passed down in families. I recommend going with an experienced intuitive as it takes about ten years to develop the depth and nuance and the ability to remain grounded and perceive clearly, especially when working with big projects. References are especially important here, along with your own response to the person. Do you know anyone who can vouch for his or her high level of expertise? What is your own gut feeling? Refer to the Resources section at the back of the book for some earth intuitive, dowsing, and builder resources.

2. *Respect for intuition—both yours and their own*

It is good to meet your potential builder on your land or at the place you're remodeling to see how he or she responds to your land and your own intuitive insights and input about the project.

A good builder or designer will probably not bend to your every thought. He or she should balance your vision with the knowledge of materials, cost, procedures, scheduling, local ordinances, and a number of other factors. But if you find yourself feeling defensive, ashamed, or hesitant to discuss what is important to you, it is probably not a good match. Attunement with the land and other intuitive factors is a delicate relationship; good chemistry between the participants is important for it to thrive.

You can also inquire whether he or she is open to using ceremonies and exercises as part of the building process. A negative response may not be a deal breaker as you can do them on your own.

3. *References*

Does your prospective builder have a good track record with clients and projects? It is always important to talk to people who have worked with a builder and to see some of his or her work. Even if the project is different from your own, you can still get a sense of how the person works and his or her attention to detail, reliability, and communication skills with clients and other contractors.

See if your prospective earth intuitive has references for you. Many times, one hears about a builder by word of mouth. This can be a good reference in itself. If he or she has a website, check that out for testimonials as well.

4. *Use of sustainable materials*

What is your builder or architect's training and experience with earth-friendly materials? Is he or she open to using sustainably harvested lumber? Is he or she aware of alternatives to PVC and other toxic flooring materials? Look at some of the resources for builders and remodelers at the back of the book if you are not familiar with the issues and options. Ideally you want a builder and an architect who both have experience in working with the materials you want to use.

5. *Understanding of environmental concerns*

Your builder need not be an expert in an environmental area, but if he or she isn't at all concerned about environmental impact or isn't willing to educate himself or herself, you are likely to be unhappy with both the process and the outcome. You want your architect or planner to be at least as aware as you are and knowledgeable about different approaches and alternatives. And you want a builder who is open to suggestions that will benefit the environment.

6. *Enough time or flexibility in his or her schedule so that you don't feel rushed*
It's great to have your project move along speedily, but sometimes contractors can be trying to squeeze so much in that your project suffers.

Now that you've thought about these factors, let's go back to where we started: your partnership with nature. Don't forget that nature can be your partner even in the contract or selection process. Pay attention to synchronicity; those "random" coincidences are one way that life force communicates with us. Glancing at the list of Green Light/Yellow-Red Light indications on pages 141–143 will help remind you to pay attention to the signs and signals that can take a lot of anxiety out of the process of choosing your teammates. Using the ceremonies and exercises in part 4 will more naturally bring earth energies into alignment with your building and remodeling efforts.

A LAST WORD

Congratulations! You have now learned the essence of intuitive environmental living and the art of cocreating patterns with nature. I hope that this book has given you a broader, deeper grasp of earth intuitive concepts, and that through practice you will enjoy increasing your experiences with the energies themselves. I invite you to apply everything you have learned to deepen your connection with nature in learning in your built environment and expanding your awareness of what can be accomplished together. If these concepts stir you, please share them with family, friends, and colleagues. As the authors of *Presence: An Exploration of Profound Change in People, Organizations and Society* put it, "the possibilities of larger fields for change can come only from many perspectives—from the emerging science of living systems, from the creative arts, from organizational change experiences and from direct contact with the generative capacities of nature. Virtually all indigenous or native cultures have regarded nature or the universe or Mother Earth as the ultimate teacher. At few points in history has the need to rediscover this teacher been greater."[4]

While "direct contact with the generative capacities of nature" is usually associated with natural settings—a hike in the woods, a leisurely day at a warm beach, or a springtime stroll in a city park—you now have the keys to revive or preserve those potent generative capacities right where you live and work. In addition to the wonderful getaway times in nature settings, create an indoor environment that is itself a force of nature: whole, restorative, beautiful, and balanced.

I invite you to create in simple everyday ways such as placing a new mirror at your entrance, coaxing a spring bulb to flower, listening to a small water feature in your living room, or calling in invisible helpers as you remodel your bathroom. Acting from a clear intention and purpose, paying attention to helpful cues from your environment, giving nature time to adapt to changes, recognizing and honoring your connections to all of life—all these activities connect you with nature, your teacher and partner. You are part of a cutting edge in awareness and practice, and I joyfully anticipate the adventures you will have.

Finally, here is an attunement for you, dear reader. I send it out as a wish and a vision as we journey through these challenging and promising times together.

AN ATTUNEMENT FOR THE READER

Stand or sit comfortably and breathe deeply in and out, feeling the ground beneath your feet. Be aware of the earth beneath you, this amazing being, your teacher and partner. Be aware of your body, this wonderfully complex instrument that knows so much. As you breathe, connect with the air and wind around you and feel yourself breathe with the earth.

Call in the great creative forces of this amazing time, bringing balance, order, harmony, and beauty to a central place in our lives again. Feel your gratitude for life's visible and invisible layers, and for the many helpers both known and unknown who are eager to assist and guide you.

Send appreciation to the earth spirit, the great devas of the waters—in the oceans, lakes, creeks, reservoirs, puddles, irrigation canals—and the tree spirits—in great forests, in our backyards, by our freeways, and in all urban areas; to the birds, our messengers, who remind you of life's soaring joy, and the stones, large and small, our ancient wisdom keepers; to fire, with its renewing properties, both in wild nature and in urban areas; to the air and winds circulating a great breath of life force.

Call on the web of life circulating around the earth and ask for its invisible support in weaving the web of a sustainable future. Awaken and call the immortals and angels of your lots, homes, apartments, and high-rises. Know how the ways you live and work in your buildings impacts your future. Be more open to your natural instincts and sense a response from earth and life.

Call for life's help to trust these natural urgings and to notice the opportunities and networks to further develop these skills. Ask for strength and support to overcome any obstacles in order to live in this passionate way with the earth and to live with joy and a vitality or force that knows all will be well.

Eagerly anticipate the ripple effect, the evolving force of balance rolling out to your neighborhood, your town, and your nation from your small but exquisite acts of attunement with your environment. Feel a great exchange and transformation. See the earth and all her inhabitants return to balance now. And so it is.

These times are different.

These times are stirring our hearts.

We are coming together.

Part Four
Attunements, Body Radar Workouts, Cures, Ceremonies, and Conscious Practices

ATTUNEMENTS

AN ATTUNEMENT IS a way of harmonizing with your surroundings or a location you are calling to mind. It is a way of settling into a place, like calling a meeting with a site's tangible and intangible energies. Attunements can be done in any setting: indoors, outdoors, urban, rural, or wilderness. Choose a place and time where you can sit comfortably and will not be interrupted. If you have an outdoor spot, sit near the part of nature you want to make contact with: a pond, a group of plants, a tree, or a mountain. If you are indoors, imagine yourself at such a location or at your favorite spot in nature. Physical proximity is not necessary to communicate with these nonphysical beings. It is useful to bring a pen and paper and write down whatever comes, particularly if the awareness surfaces gradually. Many people discover their answer when they write about the experience directly afterward.

ATTUNING TO NATURE BEINGS

1. Get comfortable. Take some deep breaths. Let go of your thoughts. Continue to breathe deeply. Feel the air and the wind around you. Be conscious of breathing in the air and imagine it circulating throughout your body and relaxing you further. Be aware of your surroundings. Look at and feel what is in front of you, beside you, above you, and below

you. If thoughts make their way in, return your attention to your breath. Feel your feet on the floor or on the ground. Imagine your feet connecting with the earth and with imaginary roots reaching down through the dark, moist soil deep in her core.

2. Allow yourself to feel gratitude to nature for her beauty, her ability to live through changes, and her beautiful colors, shapes, moods, and diversity. Feel gratitude open and relax. Gratitude alone can place you in the heart of nature. From this place of gratitude, be open to whatever feelings and thoughts arise in you. Sense the earth respond to your gesture by sending up her life force through your roots to your feet and the rest of your body. Feel a strength and calm wash over you as you become one with this partner, the earth.

3. Close your eyes and continue to breathe deeply. As you breathe in, imagine a blue sky above you with puffy white clouds multiplying rapidly. As you breathe out, imagine all the puffy clouds dispersing along with all your thoughts. Continue to breathe, letting the thoughts and puffy clouds rush in and letting them continually disappear until the stillness is almost a hum. In this place, ask to be fully protected and ask for any sensory reactions or signals from life. Ask to stay fully grounded. If you notice any confusion, stop and repeat these first three steps.

4. Extend an invitation to the deva in your area. Ask this being a specific question, or just ask for general information about your natural surroundings. Ask to receive impressions or pictures. Notice any doubts and critical thoughts that crop up. Set them aside, breathe in and out, and come back to an open-minded attitude to return yourself to a receptive state.

5. One signal of devic contact is a sudden wave of joy washing over you. Continue to breathe into that space and allow

impressions or solutions or a new level of clarity to enter. Sometimes it's sudden; other times the awareness surfaces more gradually.

6. Our relationship with nature is based on three levels: thought, emotion, and action. Taking action on your insights is important. Whatever solutions, ideas, or inspirations have come to you, choose at least one to act on as soon as possible. Action engages and grounds the insight. It's where the rubber meets the road. Action makes the difference between a lovely passing thought and real change. Nature responds to thought and intention, but actions cement the bond, creating an ongoing working relationship.

MORE CLUES FOR ATTUNING TO NATURE BEINGS

Where to begin your connection

- Areas lush with growth
- A wild area (It may be in the city as well as in a park or national forest, an abandoned lot in your neighborhood, or a weedy hedge between apartment buildings.)
- A corner of your yard or a part of the neighborhood you feel particularly drawn to
- A patch of your garden with well-established trees and plants
- A location in your garden that has blooming plants year-round
- Near a prolific houseplant
- In view of a favorite vision of nature, such as a single tree branch from your window
- Around compost piles or bins
- Next to an indoor water fountain
- A place where you can sit quietly and tune in to what is being communicated

Attitudes conducive to contact

◈ Staying open and alert

◈ Becoming childlike

◈ Singing and dancing

◈ Being spontaneous

◈ Originating from joy

Some possible signs of contact

◈ Smells, sounds, colors, and lights, which are nature's most common ways of communicating

◈ Breezes and winds, which are whispers and murmurs from nature

◈ An experience in which time seems to stop and there is stillness

◈ A sense of camaraderie

◈ An inexplicable change of mood in yourself or in the atmosphere

Best times to sense the presence of nature beings

◈ When you feel drawn into the moment

◈ During dawn or sunset

◈ 11 AM to 1 PM—a transition time in the day when many levels tend to blend and interact more easily

◈ 11 PM to 1 AM—the corresponding transition time in the night

◈ At full moons and new moons

◈ During equinoxes and solstices

◈ February 1, May 1, August 1, November 1—midpoints between the solstice and equinox

◈ Immediately after rain or a thunderstorm

ATTUNING TO WATER AND TREES

Many times you can feel an ancientness or authenticity to certain locations. The feeling can take different forms, but I experience it most often as a feeling of ease, a relief from the more frenetic energy of modern life, a comforting feeling of being held by something vast and powerful. You may have felt this in old cathedrals or a redwood forest or on returning to an old family farm. Many of us who lack an ancestral farm or estate have experienced this feeling when reading favorite childhood books that transport us to wonderful adventures in idyllic scenes.

One place that gives me this feeling is a cave near my home, a hidden place beside a local creek. It is still wild, with an original, authentic pattern around it, undisturbed by human activity or construction. There is a hum of power that feels grounded and peaceful. When I sit there, I have an experience of deep stillness in the powerful field of water and stone present there.

Nature beings associated with water and trees have a great deal of information to share with you about buildings and other structures. Try the following attunements to connect to the water and trees in your area.

EXPERIENCING WATER AS A LIVING ORGANISM

Walk around your area and notice any evidence of vast water history that has shaped the landscape around your home or apartment. Aerial or topographical maps may help you pick out the remnants from this geological past, such as ancient riverbeds, ravines, or a deposit of river rock. Geographical societies, libraries, and the geology department or bookstore of your local college are also good sources for information. When you discover these areas, visit them and notice what you feel there. Does it feel different from the more developed areas around you?

1. Sit comfortably and take a few relaxing deep breaths. Now call to mind a special experience you have had with water in nature. Perhaps it was a walk by a stream, one that gently meanders or rushes vigorously over stones. Perhaps it was a stroll by the ocean, with the sun glinting from waves sighing along the beach, or a stormy gray sky with great foamy breakers roaring

in. It could be a day when you sat inside and watched rain or snow falling and landing on the earth in a rhythm.

2. Imagine that you are in that time and place again. Use your senses fully, extending them further than you normally do: See the air. Feel the water. Listen to the light on or around the water. Watch the movement of the water.

3. Now see yourself stopping and connecting with the water. Let go of "doing" and just be. Allow yourself to open to an exchange with the water, like you are engaging in a conversation. Be aware of the water as teacher and mentor, and see what you can say to the water with this deeper awareness. Give yourself plenty of time to be with this moment.

4. Now visualize stepping into the stream, ocean, snowflake, or raindrop and becoming the essence of the water. Hear what the water has to say to you. This time, as you are seeing and hearing water in a new way, you may find impressions or insights you had missed before. Try writing them down to extend the moment even longer.

5. Realize that you and the water are one; you are a part of one another. Take this experience back to your present, and when you next walk by water, you will probably find that you experience the water differently. When you are ready, stretch and look around the room. You can do this attunement at any time and revisit this place to connect with water's living wisdom.

SENSING THE ENERGY OF TREES

1. Try to find streets with large trees located near streets with no trees. An older neighborhood near a newer neighborhood or a commercial area will often show this contrast. Walk or bicycle down a couple of streets with large trees and see how you feel. Notice your mood and any physical

sensations. Then walk or bike down a few streets without trees, and pay attention to how you feel as you are passing through.

If possible, go back and forth a bit and notice any differences in your own mood, energy, or physical sensations as your own energetic system responds to the different energy fields. If your daily commute takes you through a variety of areas, use this time to notice how each area affects you.

2. Find a park or natural area with an open meadow space (such as a ball field) and large trees (or one particularly large and beautiful tree). Spend some time walking and sitting in each area and notice how you feel in the open space and how you feel near the tree or trees. Write down your impressions in a journal or notebook, as it will help you retrieve your impressions more completely later.

3. As you go about your days, notice the presence—or absence—of trees near the buildings you encounter. How does it affect you when there are trees? When there are no trees? Jot impressions and observations in your notebook.

4. You can connect to one tree. Simply sit and use the process in step 3. Visualize and feel yourself linking to the roots of the tree. Feel the whole tree from the top down to the deepest part of the roots. Be aware of the tree's energy field that extends far down beneath the surface of the earth. When possible, it's great to physically stand or sit near the tree, close to the extended roots. Connecting with a tree in this way is wonderful when you feel depleted, tired, or out of sorts.

Practice these attunements with the water and trees in your area about once a week to establish a regular connection. Remember to act on your inspiration from nature. Practice and taking time-outs will enhance and expand your awareness of your home and nature relationships, opening you to instinctive solutions and ideas for your home or office.

BODY RADAR WORKOUTS

HAVING ATTUNED TO nature beings and asked for information in the previous section, you may suddenly have the thought that a large stone would be great in a certain area of your property. Or you may suddenly have a cozy feeling as you imagine a yellow wall in your kitchen. You may even stray off into a daydream of happy family conversations there. Experiences like these can be messages from nature. Imagination is the medium, not the originator, of many creative solutions.

In order to recognize nature's messages, it's important to get a feel for how you experience them. Since the thoughts and feelings of other humans can be easier to recognize than the messages from nature, we will start there. Try the following workouts as often as possible for a week or two and you will begin to get more in touch with nature.

RECOGNIZING THOUGHT FIELDS AND EMOTIONAL FIELDS

We tend to think our feelings and thoughts originate from ourselves, but we are actually influenced by thoughts and feelings around us. Thoughts and feelings, especially when strongly held or repeatedly experienced in a given location, create a field of energy called a thought field or an emotional field. Being in contact with one of these fields tends to activate or intensify our own similar thoughts or feelings in the way that a guitar string will begin to vibrate and sound when a resonating frequency is sounded near it. In the presence of an angry emotional field we often find ourselves feeling irritable or angry. Our logical mind will supply reasons from our own experience of current or historical situations, but with practice, you will be able to recognize when the thought or feeling is originating outside yourself.

1. Prepare to take a walk in your neighborhood. Before leaving, get out your journal and jot down your current mood. Note what you are thinking about along with your feelings.

2. Take your notebook with you and continue to notice your thoughts and feelings as you stroll through your neighborhood. For instance, if you walk by a house where the neighbors tend to argue, you may notice that you feel anger as you walk by. It may come in the form of angry thoughts about a person or situation currently in your life. Just note what you feel without judgment.

3. If possible, do some detective work. If you find yourself frequently having certain thoughts or feelings in a particular area, see what you can discover there. If you feel peaceful and relaxed, are you near a house where people often play beautiful music? What's the history of this spot?

4. If you take public transportation to work, take note of different people sitting near you. Notice any changes in your own mood, new thoughts, or body sensations.

With practice, detective work, and a state of receptivity, you can often get a good idea of where your "inexplicable" reactions are coming from.

TAKING A TIME-OUT IN NATURE

1. Choose a favorite natural area such as the ocean, a lake, forest, wetland, or mountain. It is best if the area's natural patterns are

relatively unchanged by humans. If you are unable to get to such a place, choose an area where you feel happy and peaceful, such as a local park or golf course, or a particularly lovely old neighborhood. Go there early in the morning when few people are around.

2. Take your journal with you and note your feelings and thoughts before you start. Then go for a walk and continue to notice your mood and thoughts. How does this natural area affect you? What influences do you notice?

3. Also watch for nature's response to you: birds flocking around, the sun emerging from behind a cloud, an animal crossing your path, a sudden rain storm, and trees whispering or waving. I'm not suggesting that you expect grandiosity, nor should you be superstitious, but set aside old assumptions about how the world is and see what happens when you play with the idea that nature is communicating with you. Be curious and observant. Notice if birds start singing just as you have a certain thought or if a rainbow appears when you resolve an inner dilemma.

4. In addition to walking, spend some time just sitting quietly. Breathe deeply and slowly. This will further quiet your nervous system and sharpen your senses. Now what feelings, thoughts, or effects do you notice?

5. You may want to note observations in your journal, but give yourself at least fifteen minutes to just pay attention before you begin writing. It is useful to make a few notes to catch shifts or contrasts in your feelings or thoughts, but throughout the session, focus more on paying attention than on writing or commenting.

After spending some time in the area and away from others, you will probably notice a sense of space and clarity. You have just created an energy time-out for yourself. Many people walk by the ocean to restore perspective, find a feeling of peace and expansiveness, or just feel good. This is partly due to negative ions that occur naturally near waterfalls and oceans and during thunderstorms. The negative ions attract positively charged dust and smoke particles. These new, heavier, combined particles then fall, leaving purified air that can uplift and refresh so that we feel the influence of the life force moving through nature.

A time-out in nature can settle, calm, and give a sense of just you, your authentic self. With this clarity, you can more easily recognize influences and communication coming from outside yourself.

PAYING ATTENTION TO FIRST IMPRESSIONS

This is a great workout if you have been feeling overwhelmed at home and don't know where to start. Your body radar can help you become aware of a draining chaotic energy pattern. Sometimes going away and coming back to the site—especially if you've adapted to a level of clutter—will help you to see what to do next. Without thinking about it, you will just know.

1. Take your journal with you when you are away from home for several hours or more.

2. When you return, stop and record your impressions as you approach your house or apartment. What mood are you in? What feelings come up as you approach your home? What do you suddenly find yourself thinking about? Be sure to notice any fleeting thoughts that don't make sense and ones you might normally dismiss without another thought. Do you notice certain smells? Certain sounds? Make a note of these impressions before going farther.

3. Pay attention to your thoughts and feelings as you walk through the door. Where is your attention drawn when you first enter your home? What are you feeling now? What are

you thinking? What smells, sounds, and sights are you aware of? Jot them down.

4. Follow where your attention is drawn. It will point you toward the area that needs your attention or one that nourishes you that perhaps could be expanded or strengthened in your home.

It's a good idea to do this a number of times within a few weeks and compare notes. Look at similarities and differences. Are there certain areas that grab your attention each time? Were you aware of them before? Do the different details you notice from one time to another surprise you?

DETECTING POWER POINTS, LEY LINES, AND VORTEXES

By noting how your body radar responds in known high-energy areas, you will gradually learn to fine-tune your awareness. It's a bit like tuning a piano and educating it to recognize middle C. Once you get a sense of how a power point or ley line feels to you, it will be easier to recognize it when you come across it.

To get a feel for different aspects of the energy web, experiment with these workouts when you visit a new location. Try this workout several times. Be sure to give yourself several opportunities to practice each step.

LIMBERING UP

To begin, find a place in nature to practice. It could be a city park, your backyard, or a landscaped area at your apartment complex. If you are practicing in an urban area, choose a time when there is the least human activity, like early morning. The less activity there is, the easier it will be to focus, but if a busy neighborhood is your only option, don't hesitate to do the exercise there. Earth currents exist everywhere.

1. Bring your journal and a pen. Stand or sit in your chosen area for a few minutes, feeling the earth under your feet and the

air on your skin. Breathe deeply for a few minutes, taking in the surrounding views.

2. Imagine a green cord extending from your belly into the center of the earth. Feel yourself connected to the center with the cord and feel yourself protected and grounded.

3. Begin walking the site, approaching it with curiosity, respect, and alertness. To heighten your awareness of earth energies, visualize that you are walking about six inches below the surface of the ground.

4. Let go of any doubts or other distractions and just trust that you are now sensitive to data from the site.

5. Use all your senses. What do you see, hear, smell, and feel? Notice your emotions, especially mood shifts, however subtle. Pay particular attention to sensations that start after you enter the site and stop after you leave it. Physical sensations can include body aches, a buzzing feeling, or a change in breathing or muscle tension (tightening or relaxing). All these sensations and emotions can help you calibrate the energy around you. Jot down everything you notice in your journal.

Try this workout several times a week for a few weeks. Review your notes each week to look for similarities, differences, and trends.

RECOGNIZING STRONG EARTH ENERGY FIELDS

To help you learn to recognize strong energy patterns, review the information about power points, ley lines, and vortexes in chapter 2; then go to a known earth-energy spot near you. If you don't know of any such spots, find one that you suspect could be one. Look for areas of unusual beauty: large waterfalls or buttes, an especially large tree, caves, springs, mountains, or locations that were sacred to the ancient inhabitants of your area. All these places have strong earth energy, and, depending on their history, they may also have intense emotional fields. Because of their intensity, I do not recommend going to battlefields or other areas with a tragic history when you are just starting to do this particular exercise.

To do the exercise, visit the energy spot, taking with you your journal and pen.

1. Begin with the previous exercise and be sure to record your first impressions.

2. When you have recorded these initial impressions, review the lists on pages 29–30. Did you have any of these sensations or impressions? Write down what you experienced.

3. Repeat this exercise in as many power spots as you can find. Compare your findings to help you determine what the area's energy pattern is.

CURES

IN FENG SHUI, cures are intended to raise consciousness in your environment. More presence in the environment grounds more chi, and therefore, more flow and balance in your life.

LIST OF CURES

Light: Add bright objects

- ◈ Lamps (the brighter the better)
- ◈ Mirrors
- ◈ Faceted round crystal ball

Sound: Add objects that create clear sounds

- ◈ Wind chimes
- ◈ Bells

Life force vitality: Add living beings or symbols of life

- ◈ Fish tanks
- ◈ Bonsai
- ◈ Plants (silk or real)

Weight: Add heavy objects
- Stones
- Statues

Color: Add colorful objects
These colors are associated with each energy column. Use the color from different column areas in design, paint, or accessories.
- Red (Reputation)
- Green (Family)
- Yellow and brown (Health)
- White (Children)
- Black (Career)
- Pink (Joy)
- Blue (Knowledge)
- Purple (Flow)
- Gray (Helpful People)

Mobile objects: Add objects with movement or that encourage movement
- Fountains
- Windmills

Power energy: Add electrical objects
- Computers
- TVs
- Radios

Hydraulic power: Add structures or objects related to water's movement
- Waterfalls
- Fountains

Decorative objects: Add objects that are unique to feng shui
- Bamboo flutes
- Beaded curtains

Fragrance: Add objects with delicious aroma

- Natural potpourri
- Essential oils
- Fragrant fresh flowers

Texture: Add objects that stimulate touch for weight and grounding

- Wall hangings
- Area rugs

Objects of personal significance: Create your own sensory additions that hold special meaning.

REMEDIES FOR AN OVERACTIVE CENTER

Mirrors generally help contain energy, particularly when placed with that intention. Placing mirrors on all four walls of a central bathroom, laundry room, or kitchen will help to contain the active energy within that room, leaving the house's center more available to serve its primary function of renewal. Stones and plants generally help calm an area by settling or grounding the energy. Please note that these ideas and the following ones are just suggestions. I encourage you to create your own unique solutions based on your awareness of this central energy function in your home and your own taste and inclinations (see A Calm Center on page 112).

Bathroom

- Place mirrors on all four walls.
- Place a plant in each of the corners.

Kitchen

- Place mirrors on all four walls.
- Use flooring with a design that radiates from the center of the room.
- Use lots of greens, yellows, and browns in the kitchen's color.

Laundry room

- Place mirrors on all four walls.
- Place a light fixture in the center of the ceiling and hang a leaded round crystal from its center.
- Use yellows and browns.

Fireplace

- Place nine vibrant green plants around the fireplace area.
- If possible, paint the fireplace green.

Stairway

- Hang a crystal from the ceiling at the foot of the stairway. As you do so, hold an intention for this crystal to act as a traffic cop, slowing down the movement of energy in this area.
- Place a mirror at the top of the stairs with the same intention.
- Weave green vines into the railing by the bottom of the stairs to anchor or ground the area.

ASPECTS OF THE PERFECT CURE

The following recommendations can strengthen your cures:

1. *Use new objects:* New objects allow the new chi to make an imprint more easily on an object. A new object is like a fresh clean canvas—ready for the paint and the artist's inspiration.

2. *Use objects of good quality:* Well-made objects will give the cure a strong, solid pattern to hold the intention. The good quality attracts and builds on other good qualities.

3. *Create a cure that has meaning to you:* An original cure using your own personal ideas can be especially strong.

4. *Use the right-sized object:* Make sure the object fits the scale of the cure. People sometimes choose to use a small crystal for a cure that needs powerful energy. Choosing something too small can lessen the cure's effect or even drain the chi flow. The same can be true if you are a "more is better" person who uses three objects for a cure that calls for one. This can also drain the process. Cures require balance for the good intentions to hold on to the new pattern.

5. *Use increments of nine:* Nine, the number of completion or fullness, is used a lot in this tradition. It makes a strong "so be it" or "it is done" statement. When hanging a cure such as a crystal or wind chime on a cord or a string, measure the length in increments of nine.

6. *Use red cords:* Traditionally, cures use red satin ribbons or cords. Red attracts the eye and symbolizes vitality and good luck. Fishing line can be used if you do not want to use color.

7. *Strengthen an object before you use it:* An object to be used as a cure can be strengthened by placing it on your altar for nine days beforehand. Or you can place the object at a church or temple for nine days to absorb its sacred energy. You can also place the object in a special spot in nature to absorb the energies there.

8. *Pick an auspicious time of day:* Choose the hours between 11:00 AM and 1:00 PM or 11:00 PM and 1:00 AM to carry out the cure. They are peak times, when chi is strongest or most concentrated in the daily cycle.

9. *Use the cure within three days:* If you have a list of cures for your space, do at least one of them within three days after your awareness of the need for a cure.

10. *Pick an auspicious day:* Pick an auspicious day to enact a cure. Some auspicious days are a full moon, a new moon (a good

time for new beginnings), a birthday, an anniversary, or a day that is special for you.

11. *Clean:* Ideally, clean the whole home before enacting cures, or the least clean around the area where you will apply the cure. This supports the new order and pattern for the chi.

12. *Strengthen cures that seem weak:* If a cure does not seem to be working, as a one-time exercise, tap the object three times to stimulate the intention and the chi.

THE THREE SECRET REINFORCEMENTS

The Three Secret Reinforcements of body, mind, and sound are the main tools for amplifying and strengthening any cure or adjustment in the Black Sect Tantric Buddhist tradition. It is a means of using the senses in our bodies as grounding rods for our intentions in our design applications. Doing the Body, Mind, and Sound process simultaneously can create the most powerful results.

1. *Body:* Use your body to express what you mean in your heart. This typically involves physical movements with your hands, where there is a lot of energy. Hand arrangements or positions can be used to help anchor intentions. Statues of Buddha and Hindi gods show figures that use a variety of hand positions, each of which represents a function. In the Tibetan tradition, the hand positions are called *mudras.* Two main ones used in the Black Sect Tantric Buddhist tradition are the Heart-Calming Mudra and the Expelling or Ousting Mudra.

   ❀ *The Heart-Calming Mudra*
   This mudra creates a circle or circuit around your heart and is meant to calm, refresh, and renew the heart area. It is meant to prepare you and help you focus.

   Perform the heart mudra by placing your left hand on top of your right hand, with your fingers pointing outward, palms facing, and the tips of your thumbs touching.

Start with the heart mundra before you begin the whole Three Secret Reinforcements process.

◈ *The Expelling or Ousting Mudra*
This one is meant to wake up the area around the region of the cure placement. It works with the energies first and opens up the area for new patterns. It is meant to push away any obstacles.

Perform this mudra by pointing the first and pinky fingers straight up and holding the middle and ring fingers against your palm with your thumb. Women, use the right hand; men, use the left. Then flick the middle and ring fingers out from the palm. Repeat the flicking motion nine times or until the space feels different, opened, or cleared. Use this mudra in the area for the cure right before placing objects there. For example, when placing a mirror on the wall, use these hand motions toward the wall that will hold the mirror. (Note: When making a turning-point decision, do the mudra with both hands.)

2. *Mind:* Take time to visualize your intention for the cure. Calm your mind and see as many details as possible, and create the process from beginning to end. This allows the cure to be more real.

3. *Sound:* Use an ancient chant or prayer to amplify your cure. Repeat the chant or prayer nine times. Chant words of your own choice or the traditional Buddhist chant: *Om mani padme hum.* Loosely translated for this use, the ancient and complex chant means "I now connect to life's deep wisdom from many invisible circles around me and around the environment, and I acknowledge the power to transform and illuminate this building."

RED ENVELOPES

Professor Lin Yun, Grand Master of the Black Sect Tantric Buddhist tradition, has asked us to exchange red envelopes (usually nine red envelopes) every time information from the tradition is shared with someone. As you learn this information, if you choose to share it, please honor the tradition of the red envelope.

Purchase new square or rectangular red envelopes of any size. Place either paper money or coins in each one. While placing the money inside, visualize that good luck, good health, and lots of protection will touch each person involved with this exchange. If you are the receiver, do the Three Secret Reinforcements. You are free to use the money as you wish. However, it is recommended that you treat the red envelopes as sacred objects; reuse them in another feng shui exchange or burn them in a fire. As the envelopes burn, envision that the wishes and prayers from the exchange are offered once more and released to the sky.

1. *Preservation of sacred knowledge:* An ancient Chinese custom, the exchange of red envelopes is used on auspicious occasions such as New Year, weddings, and birthdays and is always associated with good luck. Red, the color of blood, symbolizes vitality. In this exchange we acknowledge the tradition associated with feng shui and ask that the vitality of the shared information be preserved and honored for the current and future recipients. The red envelope is used as a tangible, physical representation of this exchange of ideas and qualities.

2. *Protection:* The envelope's square or rectangular shape is associated with the idea of a shield that protects us from too much information and from inappropriate data. We ask that we be given just what will integrate into our life in a balanced way. When we open up to larger patterns, we wake up more senses in the body, and we want to make sure we can naturally process this new awareness without any unnecessary clutter.

3. *Strengthen the exchange:* Nine red envelopes are used because the number nine represents completion. Money is used because it represents vitality and a reality of buying and selling. The physical act of exchange gives a message to our senses that this is real and certain.

CEREMONIES

THIS SECTION LISTS a selection of building ceremonies utilizing both Eastern Black Sect Tantric Buddhist and Western traditions to mark different stages or events with home life, ranging from starting a building project to cleansing and refreshing a well-loved building. With the feng shui ceremonies, it is suggested to exchange red envelopes with all participants to honor these vital and ancient ways.

INITIATING A CEREMONY

1. Come prepared with your materials. Make sure you are rested and have enough time for the ceremony.

2. Find to your center. Visualize letting go of concerns, worries, or plans for the day. Ask to be truly present to the occasion.

3. Do some grounding. Visualize a green cord going into the center of the earth from the trunk of your body and feel connected to the strength and power of the earth to anchor you to the event at hand.

4. Acknowledge the invisible beings and helpers on your land and invite the nature beings to participate. You might

visualize that your interested family members are present in spirit as well.

CEREMONIAL INGREDIENTS

All good ceremonies have ingredients—some visible, some invisible. The following tangible ingredients are chosen for their significance to the Chinese and used for their symbolic or literal relationship to transformation or change. These physical components strengthen and support the changes to the invisible patterns, which precede and underlie any physical change in your environment or life.

Cinnabar powder

- Cinnabar is a fine red powder composed of mercuric oxide. This powder, used in minute amounts, has been used for centuries in Asia to symbolize transformation.

- There is a Chinese saying that if one were fortunate enough to drink water from a well with cinnabar in the stone, one would be guaranteed longevity. The powder is available at Chinese herb shops. Red food coloring can be substituted.

High-proof liquor

- Preferably 151 proof, usually rum. Liquor represents transformation because of its potency.

Uncooked rice

- Symbolizes new growth and new life

Oranges

- The aroma of oranges is good for cleansing and refreshing, and also for changing one's physical condition or mood. Oranges have an awakening quality, which is perhaps why they are often consumed at breakfast in our culture.

Realagar powder

    ⚜ This yellow powder composed of sulfuric oxide is used for cleansing energy, especially in muddy energy situations. Realagar powder is available at Chinese herb shops.

THE GOLDEN CICADA CEREMONY

The Golden Cicada Ceremony from the Black Sect Tantric Buddhist tradition is performed when you are about to emerge or desire to emerge into something new. Cicadas live underground as nymphs for up to seventeen years before they mature and crawl out to shed their skins and emerge transformed into winged creatures, going from the ground to the air in a completely new form. In ancient China they were a symbol of longevity or immortality, and also of loyalty to one's integrity or authenticity at all costs.

The Golden Cicada Ceremony is usually a personal preparation before other ceremonies. Traditionally it is used the night before your birthday and at New Year, or when encountering bad luck, financial troubles, or health problems. It is ideal to perform this ceremony when you first plan a construction project, move into a new home or office, or launch a creative venture. Because it connects you to your depths by triggering a response in your whole being and engaging both the right and the left side of your brain, it helps your plan emerge from a place of deep connection and integrity.

Materials

    ⚜ 1 egg

    ⚜ Small pan with water

    ⚜ Small bowl

    ⚜ Cold water

    ⚜ ¼ teaspoon cinnabar powder or red food coloring

    ⚜ Unopened bottle of 151 rum or other high-proof liquor

    ⚜ Eyedropper

Procedure

- ◈ Part of the ceremony will be outdoors, so before you begin, identify a location outside your house that is at a higher ground level. This is symbolic for going to a higher, better, newer level in your life; it can be a big city park or in an unpaved area with some plants and earth.

- ◈ Don't let anyone see the egg once you begin to prepare for the ceremony. The ceremony is private and personal; it is just for you.

- ◈ Between 11 AM and 1 PM, cook the egg in the pan until its hard-boiled (about 6 minutes), without breaking or cracking it. Don't talk or let yourself be interrupted, therefore allowing yourself to fully focus on what you're doing.

- ◈ Place the cooked egg gently into a bowl of cold water. When it is cool, set the egg aside and dry the bowl.

- ◈ Place the cinnabar powder on your palm (women place it in the left palm, men in the right).

- ◈ Put rum into the eyedropper. Add 1 to your present age. Add that number of drops of rum to the powder in your hand.

- ◈ Stir the mixture with the middle finger of your other hand.

- ◈ Rub the egg in the mixture until it is completely dyed, then set it aside.

- ◈ Rub your hands together until they are dry. As you do so, imagine your palms being cleansed and sealed with a healing protection.

- ◈ Carrying the egg in the bowl, go to the location you have chosen. Carefully remove the eggshell and place the shell in the bowl while visualizing the Golden Cicada shedding its shell and seeing yourself emerging into the new phase you desire.

- ◈ Eat the egg while visualizing yourself being reborn and emerging radiantly into your new home, the new year, or your new project. (If you prefer not to eat the egg, break up the egg and scatter it around you, preferably in a natural area where it can go back to the earth.)

⊕ Walk one hundred steps in a direction away from your home and scatter the eggshell in another natural area. As you throw it away, imagine you are throwing away all the outdated habits of the past, negative energy, or unlucky chi.

⊕ If you wish, use the Three Secret Reinforcements to strengthen the ceremony.

SURE-FIRE CLEANSE

This cleanse has a powerful and immediate effect. It polishes up the energetic field and often leaves a fresh feeling behind. It is a good way to clear any disturbing emotional or mental imprints from the past in a room and is especially appropriate when first moving into a building or after a death, sickness, or a strong argument in a room. You can utilize it in one room or the whole building. Use the following cleanse one room at a time.

Materials

⊕ 2 tablespoons Epsom salts

⊕ 1 tablespoon rubbing alcohol

⊕ Glass dish

⊕ Hot pad

⊕ Match or lighter

Procedure

⊕ Place the dish with the salts and alcohol on a hot pad on the floor in the center of the problem room.

⊕ Close the door and all windows in the room, and light the mixture in the glass dish. A smokeless blue fire will result, lasting two to three minutes. Stay with the fire.

- After the fire has gone out, keep the door closed for a few minutes, allowing the room to absorb the energetic changes.
- Repeat the procedure in each room of the house for a more thorough cleanse.

How does this work? According to the Epsom Salt Council, Epsom salt (magnesium sulfate) baths help flush toxins and heavy metals from the bather's cells and eliminate them from the body. They also allow the absorption of sulfates. In burning these salts, the detoxifying benefits are released into the air, eliminating emotional or mental toxins in the area.

EXCHANGING THE CHI CEREMONY

The purpose of this ceremony, which comes from the Black Sect Tantric Buddhist tradition, is to clear out stale or stuck energy and to renew the life force in a home or business. It is traditionally performed on New Year's Day to clean out the old energies and patterns and to bring in fresh energy for the year ahead.

I recently performed this ceremony for a client whose house had been on the market for eighteen months. It had been vacant for over a year, and the energy in the house felt stale and dead. Two weeks after the ceremony, the house sold for full price.

Materials

- 9 oranges
- 2 bowls or baskets
- Knife

Procedure

- Gather the oranges in a bowl or basket.
- Between 11 PM and 1 AM or 11 AM and 1 PM, open all the doors and windows of the building. (It is important to open every single opening. Leaving any opening closed can create an insistent energy, much like an angry dog, trying to get out.)

As you open them, visualize bad luck and potential for misfortune, disaster, sickness, or evil exiting and visualize the building filled with positive energy, light, warmth, joy, abundance, and the energy of the highest deity you know.

- Traditionally, Buddhists repeat the chant *Om mani padme hum* nine times. Loosely translated for this use, the chant means "I now connect to life's deep wisdom from many invisible circles around myself and around the environment, and I acknowledge the power to transform and illuminate this building." Substitute another prayer or intention if you prefer and repeat it nine times.

- Go to the front door and, in this calm and positive frame of mind, cut nine round pieces of peel from each orange. You will then have 81 pieces. If your building is very large, use more oranges, going up in multiples of nine until you have several pieces for each room.

- Now break the rounds into small pieces and carry them in a bowl or basket, scattering one handful in every room of the building, beginning at the front door. While scattering the orange peels, visualize beautiful golden light filling every corner and closet. The light or vibrant life force will assist in removing any bad luck, sickness, or unpleasantness—anything unlike itself—from the house. Some people like to sing or have someone play music during the ceremony.

- After fifteen minutes, close all the doors and windows and return to the front door. Feel yourself and your surroundings refreshed and renewed. Repeat *Om mani padme hum* or your favorite prayer nine times to end the ceremony.

- Leave the orange peels in place for at least three days; preferably, just let them decompose naturally.

TRACING THE NINE STARS CEREMONY

Tracing the Nine Stars is a blessing and purification ceremony from the Black Sect Tantric Buddhist tradition that traces and connects a building's nine energy columns in a prescribed pattern. It strengthens the energy columns in a building and keeps the circulation of life force active, balanced, and current. The pattern is the same route that the planet Saturn traces in the sky. Saturn is symbolically often associated with bringing things into form.

There are two ways to perform this ceremony:

1. Walk through the house doing the visualizations and asking for and accepting a blessing in each column area, or

2. Superimpose the column areas over a blueprint or sketch of the building. Trace the pattern with your finger and send your own life force to each of the points as you do the visualizations. Finish by asking for and accepting a blessing in each area.

Beginning with the Family energy column, walk or imagine your way through the nine areas in the order listed below, with a specific visualization in each spot. We start with Family, suggesting that when we can harmonize the family, all life can evolve from that foundation. As you move from one area to the next, visualize each area building upon another. When you feel the cumulated support in an area, proceed to the next column.

1. *Family:* Imagine your family unit together in harmony. If you live alone, include close friends, church, support groups, or even co-workers who feel like family. The feeling of connection, respect, kindness, and cooperation is important. Begin with the immediate family relationships in your household and extend from there to a wider family of relatives and friends. When you feel and imagine a cooperative warmth, proceed to the next column.

2. *Flow:* Here, with a family foundation, concentrate on manifestation. Feel yourself with abundant time, energy, and money for all your needs. As you sense flow increasing, proceed to the next column.

3. *Health:* Feel yourself settle into a deeply centered place, and see the column taking in energy from the other eight energy columns, regenerating and sending it back to each one and easily doing its job of optimizing health and restoring life force for the building. From a deeply centered place, move on to the next column.

4. *Helpful People:* See yourself developing in the world, blessed with great mentors showing you the ropes and giving you great contacts in areas that carry you forward. Visualize yourself meeting people more easily through travel, even if it's during your commute to work or trips to the grocery store. When you feel yourself held by family and friends and blessed by many invisible helpers, proceed to the next column.

5. *Children:* Visualize yourself supporting children—your own or any children you love or teach—in ways that help them thrive, creating a stronger world for generations to come. When you feel full of nurturing love for the children in your life, proceed to the next column.

6. *Knowledge:* See yourself evolving and deepening your knowledge and self-cultivation. When you feel you have more attention and commitment to developing your knowledge, proceed to the next column.

7. *Reputation:* Visualize yourself being well-known for your gifts or work or being promoted at work. You might imagine that it is now easier to attract a prominent person in your field of interest, someone who can help you advance in your knowledge, practice, or business. With reputation strengthened, move on to the next column.

8. *Career:* Imagine maintaining a more satisfying, successful career, even if you are already happy at work. When you

feel clarity surrounding a successful career, move to the next area.

9. *Joy:* Imagine a joyful, satisfying partner. Visualize the ease with which you maintain a marriage and that your inner union or inner development flowers easily.

10. *Completion:* Finish the ceremony by imagining all nine areas together, energized and circulating with life force, balance, and new growth in each and supporting the land and the neighborhood.

GIVEAWAY CEREMONY

The Giveaway Ceremony, a Native American custom, is traditionally used for marking personal transitions such as a coming of age, a marriage ceremony, or a move. I suggest adapting the ceremony to support opening to a new form or pattern of living as you change your environment.

In a giveaway, collect objects that were important to you in your old way of living but may not fit you in your new stage. Gather your dearest friends and family together and give these items to them in some ritual or ceremonial way. Make the event as formal or as informal as you want, but be sure to visualize that as you give away what was in your life, you are passing abundance on to loved ones and opening yourself to the new and wonderful abundance of this next phase of your life.

This ceremony allows you to let go of the old ways and open to possibilities you may not have imagined while still surrounded by your old, familiar objects. A garage sale is another way of letting go. As you sell an item, visualize the same wish of abundance for the new owner as well as for you and your family.

THE EXTERIOR CHI CEREMONY

Use the Exterior Chi Ceremony, a traditional Black Sect Tantric Buddhist ceremony, to celebrate the first step of your new building project. The version below opens the way for successful new construction.

This lovely, ancient ceremony expresses a wish for fertility or bounty for both land and humans. Rice, the main ingredient, has been used in various parts of the world, from ancient to modern times, as a symbol of fertility. In the West, we toss rice at weddings as a wish for a full pantry.

Before you start, it is traditional to repeat the Tibetan Buddhism chant *Om mani padme hum* nine times. If you have a prayer that is special to you, feel free to use it instead. The intention is to create mindfulness in yourself, a state of attention, and openness to life, so use what is most effective for you and those involved.

The Exterior Chi Ceremony is best performed between the hours of 11 AM and 1 PM, a peak time in the day.

Materials

- Large bowl that can be easily carried around the site
- Uncooked rice (9 to 12 handfuls per participant)
- ¼ teaspoon cinnabar powder or red food coloring
- Shallow bowl
- Unopened bottle of 151 rum or other high-proof liquor
- Eyedropper

Procedure

- Decide who will lead the ceremony; usually it will be the owner or someone designated by the owner. (Unless otherwise noted, the leader is designated to perform the steps in this ceremony.)

- Bring the ingredients and gather with participants or well-wishers at the entrance to the lot or property. If you want participants to join the leader in throwing rice, be sure you have enough for everyone.

- Before beginning, determine the age of the oldest person who will live or work on the site. If that's not possible, use the age of the owner. Adding 1 to that number determines how many drops of liquor you will use in the ceremony.

❖ While a participant holds the large bowl, pour the rice and cinnabar into it.

❖ Open the bottle of liquor, pour some of the liquid into the shallow bowl, and use the eyedropper to place the specified number of drops into the bowl of rice.

❖ Mix the ingredients, using the middle finger to stir. Meanwhile, have participants meditate on their intention for transformation. Imagine the new life and vitality for the project entering the bowl like fresh air. See many helpers, visible and invisible, coming to support the endeavor.

❖ Stand at the entrance, facing away from the future building site.

❖ Announce the group's intention that this land's energetic web will remain intact and undamaged by the building process, greet the deva for this land and the resident nature spirits, and announce the desire to work in cooperation with them. Ask for their support and guidance so that the earth energy in the area is actually improved with your building process. Repeat the intention to feed and enhance the site and not to disturb or diminish it. Let them know that you are using this ceremony to sow seeds of blessing and grace for this land.

• Toss the first handful of rice in an *outward* fashion, visualizing that you are feeding the past, filling it up so that it is complete and ready to give way to a new time. Voice your desire for harmonious relationships on this land between humans and the invisible inhabitants and humans and nature, creating a place of beauty and order: "May every person who lives here, as well as every person who visits, feel safety and peace. May the earth here experience peace."

- Toss the second handful of rice *downward*, as if you are sowing seeds. Visualize that you are planting seeds of blessing. Invite the invisible helpers, the energies of Earth, to help plant the seeds for good fortune: "May the earth here experience peace and good health, and may the neighborhood, the city, and the country benefit as this project thrives."

- Toss the third handful *upward* as you visualize the project elevating and strengthening the vitality of the land. Invite the heavenly or intangible cosmic energies to join you. Wish good health and prosperity to all present, and voice your desire for all mankind and the planet to benefit as well: "May the sunshine surround the land, and may the many invisible helpers shine their light on the property."

  For best results, recite *Om mani padme hum* (or the prayer or affirmation of your choice) each time you throw the rice. As you toss the rice, it is good to share the wishes or blessings out loud to include the other participants.

- Walk around the perimeter of the property in whichever direction feels appropriate to you. Stop at regular intervals and throw the three handfuls of rice as you did the first time. Continue around the site until you return to the starting point, making sure to save a little of the rice mixture.

- When you get back to the beginning point, divide the remaining rice mixture among the participants by placing a small amount in red envelopes for each person to take home. Suggest that they put the envelope in a special place to remind them of the day. Whenever they see it, it will prompt them to add their intentions to reinforce the good intentions and prayers for the project.

The rice mixture should stay on the land for at least twenty-four hours, but it can be swept off sidewalks and walkways if necessary.

GROUND-BREAKING CEREMONY

The Ground-Breaking Ceremony from the Black Sect Tantric Buddhist tradition is done before laying the foundation. It is one way to begin bringing the new pattern into form and to begin planting the seeds for it in a way that honors your dreams and intentions for your building.

While it is normally performed at the corners of the lot or property, if your property is very large, just do the ceremony at the corners of the future building instead. Performing it at both sets of corners can have a stronger effect, but it is not necessary. If you are doing both sets, start with the corners of the lot. If you are doing only the corners of the building, set a clear intention for the ceremony to radiate out to the whole lot.

Materials

- ✤ Shovel

- ✤ Uncooked grains, rice, or beans in five different colors—enough for a pinch or a handful of each type at each corner of the lot and/or building

- ✤ Bowl that comfortably carries the grain or beans

- ✤ 4 or 8 coins, one for each corner of the lot and/or building The coins are symbolic of planting the roots of wealth for you and for the land. (I like using old Chinese coins because in addition to symbolizing abundance, their shape—round with a square cutout in the middle—represents the energies of earth and heaven.) You can also use a coin from your own country for a personal connection.

Procedure

- ✤ Pick an auspicious or favorite day, preferably one that falls a few days after staking out the perimeter of the building so that nature has had time to absorb and adjust to the coming change.

- ✤ If possible, do the ceremony between 11 AM and 1 PM.

❀ Begin by digging a small 1–2-foot-deep hole at each corner of the property or building or both. Holes only need to be wide enough to hold the grains. It is all right if the grains are dug up later with the building process or landscaping; it's the symbolic act that counts.

❀ Dig quietly with a feeling of love and appreciation for the earth you are digging into, the many ways it supports you, and the dream you are bringing into being with your new structure. Turning the soil is a symbolic gesture. You are saying hello to the earth and alerting it to the change that's coming and awakening the new pattern by moving the soil.

❀ When the holes are ready, stand facing the front of the property or building and walk with the bowl of grains or beans to the hole at the corner to your right.

❀ Place a few grains or beans and one coin into the hole. Announce your desire to bring blessings to the land, the occupants, and the builders. The grains symbolize seeds and new beginnings. The diversity of grains and color suggests abundance, vitality, and the possibility for many opportunities.

❀ Repeat *Om mani padme hum* or another prayer or song 108 times as you sprinkle the grains and the coin into the hole. Visualize that you are planting seeds of growth and a good means for wealth. See peace, safety, and good financial support surrounding both the occupants and the land. When you are finished, fill the dirt back in and tamp it down.

❀ Move counterclockwise to the next corner and repeat the previous two steps. Continue these steps at each hole, making sure you have enough grains for each corner.

❀ When the last hole has been filled, return to your starting point. Sing a song, give a little bow, or do what helps you feel complete.

If possible, wait three days before placing the foundation. The pause allows the pattern and the energy web to adjust on the intangible level by opening up the pattern and making the building process easier.

BLESSING FEAST TO RAISE THE FIRST BEAM

Placing the vertical supports in the house is another transition in the building process. Pausing to acknowledge the transition can help with establishing the emerging pattern, including the energy columns for the structure. Consciously welcoming the new energy gives it a firmer foundation in the physical structure. The event is a good transition to mark, since the complexity of the project increases from here on, with new elements being added, such as people, materials, activities, and times of coming and going.

The Blessing Feast Ceremony is from the Black Sect Tantric Buddhist tradition, but barn raisings are a part of European and American culture. It may be easier to gather the people you want to participate if you use a more casual or familiar framework and incorporate symbolic elements and intention without the formality.

1. In the tradition of the old barn raisings, hold a feast and invite the people who are involved or will be involved with the project, including designers, builders, contractors, landscape designers, architects, plumbers, electricians, friends, and family members.

2. If possible, hold the feast between 11 AM and 1 PM.

3. Prepare five different meat dishes and five different vegetarian dishes. The variety of dishes is symbolic of diversity, abundance, and many opportunities.

4. Before eating, silently acknowledge the bounty available to all, as symbolized by the meal. Also, visualize the people placing the beam on the house doing a good job. See them enjoying the work and consciously creating a link between

heaven and earth by doing your project. Voice your hope
that everyone will benefit from participating in the project.

LITTLE BUDDHA DOOR PROTECTION

The Little Buddha Door Protection is a subtle protection to strengthen the
door or mouth of the structure, where new energy enters. The practice
comes from the Black Sect Tantric Buddhist tradition, but many cultures
create some form of protection for their dwellings, often by placing a sacred
object or special symbol at the entrance.

1. Several weeks before the walls are finished near the front
    door of the new structure, get a small (3-inch or so), new
    statue of your favorite spiritual symbol (for example, Bud-
    dha, Christ, Quan Yin, a special stone, a favorite saint, a
    god, a goddess, or a quality). We use these symbols not
    because of superstition but with recognition that material
    images remind us of a transcendent reality; when treated
    with intention, the symbol can carry and focus energy in the
    material world.

2. If you would like to strengthen the object, place it in a
    favorite spot in your house or yard where you will see it but it
    won't be disturbed. Or you can take the symbol to a church,
    temple, or special place in the wilderness where it will not be
    disturbed. Leave the object there for nine days and visualize it
    absorbing the available life force from the earth or the good-
    ness from the church or temple.

3. When the door is framed in, just before the wall is finished,
    place the symbol on top of the doorframe. (Let the construc-
    tion crew know beforehand that you are doing this so that
    you can create a time in the schedule with them.) If you are
    using a statue, place it so that it is facing out of the house
    and use sticky putty to secure it so that the hammering won't

knock it down. Once inside the wall, the symbol remains out of sight, functioning undisturbed.

4. Visualize the life energy of the house vibrant and intact, with the symbol representing another layer of protection or good chi for the house, especially at the main entrance.

COMPLETION CEREMONY

Also known as a tree-topping ceremony, the Completion Ceremony has origins in Europe from 700 AD. When forests were vast in Europe, most people lived with the awareness of life energy in the trees. As humans began to build shelter with wood, they would formally address the trees as partners in the project, expressing gratitude to the tree spirit for its beauty, strength, and gift of shelter. Announcing their intention to cut some of the trees for the shelter, they would ask the tree spirit to transfer its life energy to the remaining trees to keep the life force strong in the forest.

When a building was complete, the topmost leafy branch of one tree would be set atop the roof as a symbol of respect for nature's contribution and as a wish for fertility for the land and all who would inhabit the building. In the United States the custom began with the arrival of immigrants from Europe, and now the ceremony is especially associated with skyscrapers, where iron and metal have replaced wood as the main supports.

Today, in fact, the tree-topping ceremony is most often conducted by the ironworkers. According to the Ironworker Association Web site, "It is ironworkers and their skills that make them the first to reach the pinnacle of a structure, and it is around this group of workers that topping out revolves."

The ceremony occurs when the last important beam is cabled and welded into place. At that point, a small evergreen tree is often anchored on top by an ironworker. The gesture symbolizes a peak moment in the construction process and expresses gratitude for the safety of all involved in the project thus far. For the architect, contractor, builder, and owner, it's also a celebration of their shared visions becoming a reality. And it is a moment to pause and acknowledge the new shape rising in the skyline.

The ceremony is another good opportunity to recognize and welcome another level of the intangible side of the creation. With these vertical supports in place, it's a great time to visualize the energy columns of the building being activated. See the columns and framework grounded, connecting with the building's foundation and the earth beneath it, and becoming more solid and secure. The effort also facilitates safety and ease in the completion of the structure.

EARTH STEWARD TRANSFER CEREMONY

During a real estate transaction, there are meetings to cover a myriad of details and good-bye parties to honor the transition for people. Here is a ceremony to mark the moment and acknowledge the change in partnership for the land.

1. Invite friends, neighbors, and, if possible, the new land stewards and ask all to bring offerings for the land. Examples of offerings are natural objects such as a rock, a stone, or a feather.

2. Begin the ceremony with the attunement process at the beginning of the beginning of part 4. Call in the nature beings of the land and invite them to participate. (At our ceremony when we left Fir Haven, many felt the room was crowded with invisible helpers.)

3. Ask the participants to share a story or insight about their experience on the land.

4. Place all the offerings on a cloth and tie the ends together to create a bundle. Give the bundle to the new stewards.

5. Complete the ceremony with drumming, singing, or chanting to weave heaven, nature, and humans into a new pattern of gratitude and joy.

CONSCIOUS PRACTICES

THESE EARTH SPIRIT LIVING practices are everyday applications and ideas for you to apply to your built environment, incorporating the principles and steps to include nature in your home or office life.

FINDING YOUR NATURAL WATER SOURCES

1. Locate the water sources in your neighborhood, county, and region. They may be springs or the beginning of a river or creek. Maps and the other sources of information listed in the previous exercises will help you find them. You may also want to play detective and track a local river or creek to its source. What creeks are near you? Where are the rivers? Are you close to the ocean? Are there any natural springs on your site or in your area?

2. Pay attention to how local rainfall patterns affect the water near you. Even in the city or suburbs you will become aware of ponds, small creeks, or drainage ditches after it rains. What happens to these bodies of water as the rainfall changes?

3. When you have located several water sources, spend some time in each place. How natural do they look? Does the water appear to be healthy? How does it feel?

4. Notice what happens around you while you are sitting there. Does the wind pick up? Are you aware of any sounds from the water? Do you hear birdsong? How do you feel sitting by it? Do you notice a sense of wildness even if there is other activity nearby? Nature will communicate through sensory cues like these and give you an indication of the water's health.

5. Be sure to note human activity as well. Humans, like other parts of nature, reflect the energy they encounter. Do many people come by this water area? If so, notice the general energy tone: do people tend to be raucous, irritated, joyful, or peaceful?

Sometimes it is the lack of sensory cues that informs you of the water's quality. I sat by a creek on one client's land and noticed an unusual stillness—no rocks, no bugs, and little movement of air or water. Instead of healthy waterside vegetation such as native grasses and shrubs to prevent erosion, there was just a thin, thorny, overgrown tangle. Standing there, I also felt tightness in my chest, and it became challenging to breathe, a signal from my body radar denoting a general lethargy for the land. These clues alerted me to the lack of vital force in the creek and its surrounding area and the need for restoration.

When I asked my client about the water flow on the land, she mentioned that before her family bought the land, the creek's flow had been abruptly rerouted through a deep, two-hundred-foot trench some hundred yards away from the natural creek shore to accommodate cattle. Meddling with nature's ways resulted in little vitality for the surrounding area and in the client's life there. The nature spirits needed assistance from humans to repair this blueprint. The client has extensive plans to restore the water to its rightful place, thanks to a grant from the local watershed group.

CHOOSING A HOUSE TO RENT OR BUY

The search for a new home benefits from intuitive, sensory input from nature. Here are some steps to take as you look at different sites. Create a quiet time when you will not be interrupted for several minutes.

1. *Breathe deeply a few times through both your nose and mouth and ask to let go of thoughts:* Sometimes thoughts are tenacious, like class clowns who won't give up center stage. Keep breathing and see the thoughts floating away. With every breath you will feel energized and refreshed with life force. Filled with the breath of life, you are on the same wavelength as the earth and your body radar will be able to do its work more easily.

2. *Set your intention to open to sensory data from your body radar:* Setting an intention allows you to symbolically dive into and part the two sides of the brain, giving each side space to participate equally.

3. *Ask a question of the land and wait for your body radar to scan the environment for an answer:* By asking a question, you use the cognitive process to initiate the process. Then the intuitive process begins to send the body radar out to pull palpable clues from the environment to find an answer. Dizziness, a sudden burst of joy, a choked up feeling, goose bumps, a rush of movement—all are cues from your body radar.
   Some questions to consider on sites:
   ❀ What is in the ground? Are there buried streams or springs? Leaking pipes? Metal debris or toxic waste?
   ❀ What is above the ground? Has clutter accumulated? Have trees or bushes been cut without communication? Has earth been moved or streams rerouted?
   ❀ What kinds of energies are influencing the site? How do the nature beings feel? Are there particularly strong or backed-up electromagnetic energies?

⬧ How is the layout of your home or office? What is located in the energy column areas, especially the Center? How balanced is the house "body"? Is the entrance clear and strong?

⬧ What is the history of the site?

4. *Maintain sustained concentration.* Just as a batter going up to bat in a baseball game does not approach home plate until he or she feels ready, your body radar needs time to focus. You need the patience and intensity of a robin waiting for the juicy worm. Resist temptations to command the senses to communicate or it will cause the space for an answer to collapse. Sustained, patient concentration is a rhythmic sequence. The answer will pop up spontaneously.

5. *Walk around the area a few times, allowing levels and layers of input.* Walking around a site, preferably walking in and out of the earth energy field, allows you to step away and come back for more clarity about your insights each time.

6. *Put all the clues together and come up with an answer.* The clues from your body radar weave images, feelings, and body reactions around the question, and, like a discerning private detective, you put all the clues together and come up with an answer.

LISTENING TO NATURE ON A NEW SITE

Renters and new homeowners can use this practice to become more acquainted with the land and her living patterns.

1. Take a vigorous walk before starting your analysis. Rational thinking plays only a minor part in the process. Your mind's main job here is to pay attention to the input from your senses and intuition. Your body is the main instrument for registering subtle data, and walking encourages several actions: The movement and breathing are ways to strengthen

and attune your instrument. It helps you switch your brain's operating mode from thinking to sensing-feeling-registering-whole-patterns mode. Circulation of fluids and air allows insight to flow.

2. Walking the perimeter of your lot or land is a good way to begin making contact with the pattern there. Renters, walk the perimeter of your apartment complex, office building, or yard, and the block where it is located.

   Even if you walked the land during the selection process, it's important to walk it again. By purchasing or renting this unique part of the world, you have initiated a new relationship with it. You are entering into a partnership with the energies and beings that share your site. This time when you walk the boundaries, it will be with a different emphasis: you will be listening for more detailed information about the land, getting a feel for the natural rhythms and energy flows there, and noting any areas that need attention.

   Keep your mind and senses alert to any flashes of insight about the best locations for structures and water features. Walking with this kind of awareness is a type of physical message for the earth, an energetic exchange that the land loves. Walking the perimeter of the entire site is a symbolic statement that you are taking the needs of the whole into account.

   If you have someone else laying out and designing your building or remodel, have him or her also walk the boundaries while listening and feeling, and consider his or her intuitive insights in the site design as well as your own.

3. For an added level of receptivity and connection, try the Earth Mother Walk. Imagine yourself breathing through your heart as you walk. Walk in a regular rhythm, repeating the word *earth* as you place one foot on the ground and *mother* as you place the other. This creates an experience of walking with the heartbeat of the land.

4. After you have walked the boundaries, spend time in various areas. Wander a bit, talking time to sit for a while in any areas that draw your interest. Sitting and staying observant gives time for layers of information to unfold around you. Notice how your body feels. Do you feel more comfortable and more at ease here? Or do you feel unsettled or restless? Your feelings give you important information about the energy of the location.

5. Leave offerings. Nature responds to symbolic communication. By giving the land a gift, you convey the message that you will add to the land rather than take something away. Leave gifts as you walk the boundaries, symbolizing your appreciation and your mutually supportive intention toward the land that will shelter and sustain you. Your gift-giving signals your goal of partnership with the nature energies and beings that inhabit "your" land.

   Nature energies tend to ignore humans at first, because humans so often ignore them. Offering gifts to these helpers suggests that you honor and value their presence. It is also respectful to offer a token of appreciation after asking for their assistance. Your offering can be material that comes from the earth, such as tobacco, a bowl of water, a flower, or some food. Sweets like a cookie, bread, or cake are traditional faery offerings, according to R. J. Stewart.

Don't worry too much about "doing it right." Offer what has meaning and what feels good to you. Use your spontaneous creativity, follow your intuition, and let yourself have fun. It's a relationship; just be your authentic self.

LAYING OUT A NEW SITE

Utilize this practice as you decide where to place a new structure.

1. Walk the boundaries *again* when you are ready to begin laying out your site. You'll find that you learn more each time

you walk the perimeter, just as you would in successive meetings with a new acquaintance. As you walk, ask nature for input on where to establish the best place for the structure or structures. Make it clear that you are open to hearing how to help meet the needs of the land as well, and that you are aware that the insights will ultimately allow humans to thrive here too. Invite any helpers and allies on the land to make their presence known.

2. Spend time in various areas. Notice the spots you feel drawn to when you are specifically looking for potential building sites. You may sense the same places as before, or you may sense new ones. If a site makes logical sense, spend time there and in other locations, and pay attention to responses from nature. Spending time in potential places for the structure can connect you to wider levels of input. You may want to review the Green Light and Yellow-Red Light signals from nature on pages 141–143.

    Don't spend more than fifteen-minute to half-hour sessions per location at this stage. First impressions are the strongest pieces of data. When we linger too long, our minds can get in the way and start to disqualify the information coming in. Pause at intervals to turn around and take in the view from different perspectives. Pay attention to smells, breezes, sights, and sounds that come by. Does the wind pick up as you are there?

    Place gifts at the potential building sites to communicate with nature. This signals your intentions and solicits feedback. Notice what has happened with these gifts when you return.

3. Feelings or impressions as you walk or sit can be fleeting and easily forgotten, so take a pen and journal with you to jot them down. This will allow you to experience and recall subtler communications.

4. Sing or play an instrument. Nature responds to sound, especially celebratory sound. Many cultures consider drumming as a means of connecting to the earth's heartbeat, and many use it as a way to connect more intimately with nature. Being on the same heartbeat allows ease in communication and insight. The earth's heartbeat resonates with your own. In the regular, rhythmic vibrations of the beat you may be able to sense what the earth is reflecting back to you.

   Any kind of music can initiate the blending of energies, which is another way of connecting to nature's wavelength. It can be a way to experience the language of nature and a great way to open the door for these exchanges.

5. After choosing possible areas for building, walk around those areas six times and imagine your feet six inches beneath the soil as you walk. Visualize that you are connecting to nature by walking into the earth in that area. The "in-depth" walking will allow you to deepen your ties to the spot, to sink in and become acquainted with your new neighbors. See yourself walking in between worlds, between the physical and the spiritual, the tangible and intangible.

   Look from both perspectives. Remind yourself that being aware of the subtle levels around us is normal; we have just forgotten about them. Notice impressions and feelings that come to you from these invisible new neighbors on each of your potential building sites. Ask for nature's feedback on the different choices. Remember to write the responses in your journal.

6. Wait at least a few days for a final decision. A different perspective and day can give a more definitive perception and strengthen and fine-tune impressions.

7. Consider input from trusted, objective friends. Hearing other words and descriptions of the different areas can give you a clearer picture.

PREPARATION FOR TREE CUTTING

1. *Reflect and release:* Go to the area of the tree or trees you are considering cutting, and take some time to sit quietly. Notice if you are having any feelings of guilt, regret, or sadness about cutting these trees. Notice if you feel a bond with the tree or trees. Just breathe and allow yourself to feel. When you are ready, let the feelings go. Imagine yourself exhaling them along with any physical tension. Make sure the change is best for the land and the humans before you make it.

2. *Connect:* When you are open and relaxed, take some moments to sit on the roots of the tree (preferably in silence) and feel or visualize linking with the essence or deva of the tree and communicating your respect and appreciation. Give thanks to the tree for its beauty, shelter, and spirit. Acknowledge and celebrate its contribution to the land. This step doesn't have to be fussy or formal—be as expressive as you want. Notice how the tree affects you and what you love and enjoy about it, and express it through words, thoughts, or gestures. If you want, leave a little gift. The form doesn't matter; it's the exchange of consciousness and of energy that matters.

3. *Communicate:* Announce the change and explain why you are cutting the tree and what you are planning to create in the new space. Invite the essence or deva of the tree to transfer the life force to the remaining trees or shrubs on the land to guarantee that the tree's life force will not be lost.

4. *Listen and feel:* Take enough time to let yourself get a sense of the tree's response. Release your thoughts so that you will hear what the tree's energy is communicating.

5. *Give the tree or trees some time to adjust before cutting:* After your session with the trees, allow two or three days for the pattern among the trees to shift energetically. With the announce-

ment of the change, the web of life force around the trees begins to loosen and widen in preparation for the change. Tree cutting usually is much easier after this step.

TIPS FOR CONSCIOUS BUILDING

For the full text see pages 168–171.

Act from vision and from a sense of purpose.

Formulate an invocation. Here are some examples of an invocation:

- ❖ May we work as cocreative partners with the visible and invisible elements and energies here, interweaving with existing patterns, enhancing both old and new.
- ❖ May we create beauty, harmony, order, and balance in form.
- ❖ May we open to what we need to know, respecting the original will of the place.
- ❖ May we create a building filled with vitality, a blending of spirit and matter and heaven and earth.
- ❖ May all those involved work smoothly and joyfully together as a team, with respect, compassion, clarity, and the joy of shared creativity.

Consider the use of ceremony.

Honor the ways of working as well as the work itself.

Pay attention to the ordinary, repetitive aspects of building and make sure that daily operations reflect your deeper purpose.

Know that your intention to create your project in partnership with the earth is met with willingness and delight by the earth.

CONNECTING TO THE CENTER

1. Create a physical representation of the "Center" or an overriding purpose of the project on the site. Write down your hopes

or mission statement for the project and leave a copy at the Center. Use the setting to remind yourself of what's important to you whenever the project starts to feel like drudgery.

2. Place a new item, such as a flower or a feather found on the site, at the Center every day to say hello and be reminded of the essence. Use the area to place anything that is inspirational to the day: a new hammer, house plans, or a picture of the site so far. Invite nature to come and add her offerings to open the new patterns of building and land.

3. Honoring the Center can happen anytime, not just when you're building. Place a gift at the Center to reignite your house's purpose and open up nature's participation. In Bali and in many other cultures, offerings are made at doorsteps, windowsills, corners of buildings, and other such ordinary places to keep order going in the world.

CREATING THE IDEAL WATER FEATURE

A waterfall with a pond is the ideal water feature for almost any site. According to a Chinese saying, "Water is precious when it converges and diverges." With its movement, sounds, and light reflection, moving water is literally blending and weaving elements.

AN OUTSIDE WATERFALL

Water is a major component in an ideal landscape design. When a building is next to a body of water, the water's movement reflects movement or progress in the building.

In the pond, place three vertical stones that are larger than others on the site to represent mountains. A good example of this can be seen at the Portland Classical Chinese Garden in Oregon, which is established on a city block. Jagged vertical rocks resemble the symbolic mountain in the large water feature inside. Upon entering, one feels transported to an ancient water site in China.

Here are some tips for the perfect outdoor water feature:

1. Intend to work with nature when installing the feature.

2. Have a celebration: create an event with friends and have them bring gifts for the pond, if they like.

3. Place the water feature in the Flow column on the lot, if possible.

4. Place stones in the pond and around the waterfall to make it seem as natural as possible.

5. Include fish and frogs to enhance the project.

    ❖ To the Chinese, the three-legged toad holding a coin in its mouth is the symbol for attracting great wealth and prosperity. In Chinese mythology it is said that the frog comes from the moon, which it swallows during an eclipse. This signifies attaining the unattainable.

    ❖ Native Americans of the Northwest believe that Komokwa or "wealthy one," guardian of the Great Water underworld, gave Frog the unique privilege of cutting the copper. Copper represents unmistakable wealth. Many carvings of frogs have teeth of copper, which is symbolic of privilege.

6. Include lighting to enhance its effectiveness.

7. Make sure there is a switch to turn off the water flow when desired.

8. If possible, place a mirror inside the home in a room closest to the water feature to enable it to be seen inside.

9. Clean out the pond or fountain regularly with intention to stir up abundance in your life. Rededicate the feature yearly with good wishes.

WATER INSIDE

To create your own simple indoor water feature:

1. Buy a bowl big enough to hold a water pump with three speeds (available at home garden stores), your favorite small stones, water, and special crystals. Try to picture it when it's done to make sure it fits the scale of your living or office environment.

2. Set the water pump in the bowl with the cord hanging over the side.

3. Cover the pump with the stones and rocks.

4. Add water to the bowl until it is almost full.

5. Turn on the pump. If water starts to pour over the side of the bowl, lower the speed of the pump or make sure the rocks are completely covering it.

6. You can also buy an indoor water feature system. Make sure the pump has multiple speeds, as the flow of the water is often too fast.

TIPS FOR AN IDEAL INDOOR WATER FEATURE

1. Use intention as you are creating the feature and especially when you place it in the desired location.

2. Two good areas for placement are the Flow column or the Career column in your house.

3. Add plants and lights around the water feature if desired.

4. If possible, place a mirror behind it or on the side to double its power and strength.

5. Clean the indoor fountain regularly with intention to strengthen the flow of abundance in your life.

6. Rededicate the water feature yearly with intention.

WHAT TO DO WHEN THINGS FEEL STUCK

The hammer falls. You keep losing items. When work projects feel stuck, try taking a break from the task. If you are in the process of remodeling or building, or just wishing to be more comfortable or productive in your current quarters, it can be very helpful to take a time-out. Breaking away from your everyday routine can refresh and relax you and give you more ways to acknowledge your relationship with nature, fueling your next step. Nature is always waiting to connect with you and is always just a sound, a beautiful nature scene, or a fresh smell away. It is helpful and refreshing to physically go somewhere; if you can't, start making changes right in your backyard, on your deck, or in the nature outside your apartment window.

Like the seasons, energy flows in cycles and in phases. Working with vital matter requires patience. Expect times of producing and times of rest. Sometimes it's like giving the dough time to rise. An hour or two of no activity may be necessary to give the new pattern time to settle and anchor.

On these days, it is especially important to know how to handle the intensity of the ebb and flow around us. Learning when it is appropriate to move forward and when it is appropriate to step back can be quite a dance. Try the following checklist when things feel stuck on the job.

1. Keep a positive or at least a neutral attitude. Remind yourself or your co-workers that this stall is part of the process.

2. Take a break. Breathe, stretch, or drink water. You may need to step away from the site, perhaps take a walk. These seemingly simple actions are powerfully effective when used regularly. Crews that take "when-things-get-stuck breaks" are amazed by the overall results in job satisfaction. They feel better at the end of the day, and their days are more harmonious and productive.

3. If a small break is not enough to restore smooth functioning, take a bigger break. Going faster does not catch you up. Step back and reconnect to the big picture once again. Remind

yourself of the purpose or mission statement. For a more power-ful time-out, try the taking a silent at-home retreat.

SILENT AT-HOME RETREAT

Plan on two or three days to dedicate the space and time to discover or renew your relationship with nature and enjoy its restorative aspects. House builders especially should take some time on the lot and land. Or better yet, spend the night on the land if you have privacy there. Regardless, it is most important to not have too much of an agenda.

1. *Consider questions like the following:* How do I connect to nature's bigger patterns and therefore my own bigger patterns? What land-to-house connection am I missing? If building, what connection with Mother Earth am I missing? What is my next step living in this place?

2. *It is best if you can be alone.* Otherwise, announce, if possible, that you are going on a retreat and want to be in a private space. If you feel comfortable doing so, declare your inten-tion to everyone around you. If you plan to practice silence, tell everyone you are not speaking for a certain number of days and ask that they not engage in conversation with you.

3. *Determine the retreat's days and times.*

4. *Finish up as many tasks on your to-do list as you can.* Then nagging thoughts of the list are not with you during retreat time.

5. *Prepare food in advance.* Or have simple meals available to put together. Remember, your main focus is retreat and inner exploration.

6. *Break from your regular routine.* No TV, phone calls, or computer time. Breaking away from your routine disconnects you from your patterns.

7. *Make a conscious dedication to explore your relationship with nature.* Ask to truly connect with nature's sensory messages and life force. Dedication and a heartfelt statement of intent pulses out to the larger web of fibers that are felt and not seen. The deeper the intent, the stronger the push on the fibers that then sing a song on the resonance called life. Try some or all of the following:

   ❀ Take nice, leisurely walks without an agenda.

   ❀ Write phrases or thoughts in a journal, whether they make any sense or not.

   ❀ Be spontaneous. (Remember, you have no regular schedule.)

   ❀ Listen to beautiful music.

   ❀ Draw a sketch or design.

   ❀ Dance and sing.

   ❀ If at home, clean out an area that is in disorder. Announce that by clearing and reordering your surroundings you are reordering a new part of your life.

   ❀ Create an offering place or altar. Set up a candle, a vase of flowers, and any symbols that mean something to you. Activate your offering place or alter by lighting the candle each day and changing the flowers regularly.

8. *Alternate times of meditation and being still.* Sit in a favorite nature spot in your backyard or look at a beautiful view from your apartment window or in a wilderness environment. Being still is most important. Meditation loosens up our chi, our muscles, and our thinking. We breathe, feel, relax, and open to a wider input around us. Set this time of silence as an exquisite treat for yourself. (In speaking about Eskimo traditions, Peter Fruechen reported that "the women and men dress in their finest and most beautiful clothes, and then sit quite still, staring out over

land and sea for hours on end. They believed that during this stillness, they received the wisdom of the ancestors.")

9. *To end the retreat, create a closing ceremony.* This can be reading a passage from your journal, singing a song, or asking nature for inspiration to close your special time. Slowly return to your regular routine.

NOTES

CHAPTER 1

1. BBC Radio 4, "Lecture 6: A Royal View—The Prince of Wales—Highgrove," BBC, http://www.bbc.co.uk/radio4/reith2000/lecture6.shtml.

2. Don Oldenburg, "A Sense of Doom: Animal Instinct for Disaster—Scientists Investigate Wildlife's Possible Warning Systems," *Washington Post,* January 8, 2005.

3. CBS News and Associated Press, "Ancient Tribes Touched by Tsunami," CBS News, January 14, 2005, http://www.cbsnews.com/stories/2005/01/14/world.main667173.shtml.

4. *India Daily,* "During tsunami, remote viewing primitive tribes in Andaman Nicobar Islands of India moved to higher grounds—so did most animals," January 2, 2005.

5. J.L. Read, "Brain Capacity," Enchanted Mind 1998, http:www.enchanted mind.com/html/science/brain_capacity.html.

6. Elizabeth Rauscher, "Working with the Earth's Electromagnetic Fields," in *The Power of Place,* ed. James Swan, chap. 20, 296 (Wheaton, IL: Quest Books, 1991).

7. Thomas Banyacya, "The Hopi Message to the UN General Assembly," http://nativenet.org/archive/nl/9301/0164.html.

8. Looking Horse, Chief Arvol. *White Buffalo Teachings.* (Eagle Butte, SD: Wolakota Foundation, 2001).

9. Barrios, Carlo. "The World Will Not End," www.trans4mind.com/counter point/barrios.shtml.

10. Carol Venolia, *Building with Nature 1*, no. 1 (1991).

CHAPTER 2

1. Richard Feather Anderson, "Geomancy," in *The Power of Place*, ed. James Swan, chap. 13, 191–192 (Wheaton, IL: Quest Books, 1991).

2. John Michell, *The New View over Atlantis* (New York: Harper and Row, 1983), 49.

3. James Swan, "Spots of the Fawn," in *The Power of Place*, ed. James Swan, chap. 5, 63 (Wheaton, IL: Quest Books, 1991).

4. Louis Charpentier, *The Mysteries of Chartres Cathedral* (New York: Avon Books, 1966), 34.

5. James Swan, "Spots of the Fawn" in Swan, *The Power of Place*, chap. 5, 72.

6. Beth Hagens, http: //66.63.115.137/grid.

7. Frederick Lenz, *Surfing The Himalayas: A Spiritual Adventure* (New York: St. Martin's, 1995), 169.

8. Elizabeth Rauscher, "Working with the Earth's Electromagnetic Fields," in Swan, *The Power of Place*, chap. 20, 298.

9. John Michell, *The New View over Atlantis* (New York: Thames & Hudson, 2001), 92–94.

10. James Swan, "Spots of the Fawn," in Swan, *The Power of Place*, 67.

11. *New York Times*, "Dowsers Detect Enemy Tunnels; Coat Hangers Also Used by Marines to Find Mines," October 13, 1967.

12. Shirley MacLaine, *The Camino: A Journey of the Spirit* (New York: Pocket Books, 2000), 59.

CHAPTER 3

1. Henry David Thoreau. Quoted from www.gardendigest.com/earth.htm.

2. Robert John (R. J.) Stewart. The quote is taken from one of his series of Faery healing workshops that I co-sponsored and attended here on our land. www.dreampower.com.

3. Dorothy Maclean, *To Honor the Earth: Reflections on Living in Harmony with Nature* (San Francisco, Calif: HarperCollins, 1991), xiii.

4. William Bloom, *Working with Angels, Fairies and Nature Spirits* (London: Judy Piatkus, 1998), 3.

5. Machaelle Small Wright, *Behaving as If the God in All Things Mattered* (Warrenton, VA: Perelandra, 1997), 130–132.

6. Wikipedia, "Shamanism," Wikimedia Foundation, Inc., http://en.wikipedia.org/wiki/Shaman (accessed October 13, 2006).

CHAPTER 4

1. Gary Snyder, *Practice of the Wild* (San Francisco, Calif: North Point Press, 1990).

2. Victor Schauberger, *The Holy Order of Water* (Great Barrington, MA: Bell Pond Books, 2001), 47.

3. Ibid., 259.

4. Masaru Emoto, *The Hidden Messages in Water* (New York: Atria Books/Beyond Words Publishing, 2004), 64.

5. Dorothy Maclean and Kathleen Thormod Carr, *To Honor the Earth: Reflections on Living in Harmony with Nature* (New York: Harper Collins, 1991), 58.

6. Maclean and Carr, *To Honor the Earth*, 60.

7. Joan S. Davis, quoted in Masaru Emoto, *The Hidden Messages in Water*, 61.

CHAPTER 5

1. Albert Einstein. Quoted from Herbert Spencer's lecture at Oxford, June 1933, "On the Method of Theoretical Physics," http://olympus.het.brown.edu/~danieldf/papels/bonolis2004.pdf.

2. Malcolm Gladwell, "The Statue that Didn't Look Right," in *Blink* (New York: Little, Brown, 2005), 3–17.

3. Ibid., 253.

4. Sangharakshita, *Rituals and Devotion in Buddhism: An Introduction* (Birmingham, UK: Windhorse Publications, 1996), 32.

5. Andrew Newberg, Eugene G. D'Aquili, and Vince Rause, *Why God Won't Go Away: Brain Science and the Biology of Belief* (New York: Ballantine Books, 2001), 84.

6. Victor Turner, *Celebration: Studies in Festivity and Ritual* (Washington, DC: Smithsonian Institution Press, 1982), 11.

CHAPTER 6

1. Winston Churchill. Quoted from http://brainyquote.com/quotes/authors/ w/winston_churchill.html.

2. Marcus Vitruvius Pollio, *De Architectura (Ten Books on Architecture)*, trans. Morris H. Morgan. (New York: Dover Publications, 1960), vol. 3, 72.

3. A. T. Mann, www.atmann.net.caeac.htm.

4. Toyoko Matsuzaki, "The Healing Power of Hado" (April 2004 presentation, Portland, Oregon).

5. Marcus Vitruvius Pollio, *De Architectura (Ten Books on Architecture)*, trans. Morris H. Morgan. (New York: Dover Publications, 1960), vol. 5, 155.

6. Gregg Braden, from a radio interview with Patty Purcell, www.outofthis worldradio.com.

CHAPTER 7

1. Marko Pogačnik, *Healing the Heart of the Earth* (Forres, Scotland: Findhorn Press, 1998), 150.

2. Machaelle Small Wright, *Perelandra Microbial Balancing Program Manual*, www.perelandra ltd.com.

3. Thomas Gordon Smith, *Vitruvius on Architecture* (New York: Monacelli, 2004).

4. Debra Baldwin, "Giving Neo-Classical a Little More Neo," *New York Times*, March 11, 2004.

5. Vasari, a description on this website. http://leonardodavinci.stanford.edu/ submissions/clabaugh/reconstruction.html.

6. Christopher Hansard, *The Tibetan Art of Living: Wise Body, Mind, Life* (New York: Atria 2002).

7. Luke Collins, "The Sound of Silence," *Economist* (Summer 2005): 93.

CHAPTER 8

1. Martín Prechtel, Teachings of the Flowering Mountain, www.flowering mountain.com.

2. Tibetan Buddhist Ritual Music of Himalayan Nepal Sacred Land CR-1001, © 2002 Bona-Fi Recordings.

3. Richard Pinkham, "Daylighting: New Life for Buried Streams," Rocky Mountain Institute, 2000, www.rmi.org/images/other/water/woo-32-daylighting.php. The discussion of the De Kalb County Park project in Georgia comes from this report. A summary of the report is available at: www.forester.net/sw_0111_daylighting.html.

4. Marko Pogačnik, *Nature Spirits and Elemental Beings* (Forres, Scotland: Findhorn Press, 1995).

5. Carl Honore, "Home Sweet Gnome," *The American Way: Trends for the Modern Traveler* (July 1, 2005), 46–47.

6. William Arntz, Betsy Chase, and Mark Vicente, *What the Bleep Do We Know!?* (Lord of the Wind Films, LLC, 2004).

CHAPTER 9

1. Deepak Chopra, "The Magic of Attention," in *Creating Affluence: The A-to-Z Steps to a Richer Life* (Novato, CA: New World Library/Amber-Allen Publishing, 1998), 69–75.

2. Sheldrake, Rupert. *A New Science of Life: The Hypothesis of Morphic Resonance* (Rochester, VT: Park Street Press, 1981).

CHAPTER 10

1. Frank Lloyd Wright Foundation, "Frank Lloyd Wright: The Man," http://www.franklloydwright.org/index.cfm?section=research&action=theman.

2. William McDonough, "A Centennial Sermon: Design, Ecology and Ethics and the Making of Things," www.mcdonough.com.

3. U.S. Green Building Council, www.usgbc.org.

4. Peter Senge, C. Otto Scharmer, Joseph Jaworski, and Betty Sue Flowers, *Presence: An Exploration of Profound Change in People, Organizations, and Society* (New York: Currency Doubleday, 2005), 14.

RESOURCES

BOOKS

Alexander, Christopher, Sara Ishikawa, and Murray Silverstein. *A Pattern Language: Towns, Buildings, Construction.* With Max Jacobson, Ingrid Fiksdahl-King, and Shlomo Angel. New York: Oxford University Press, USA, 1977.

Bloom, William. *Working with Angels, Fairies and Nature Spirits.* London: Judy Piatkus Books, 1998.

Braden, Gregg. *The God Code: The Secret of Our Past, the Promise of Our Future.* Carlsbad, CA: Hay House, 2004.

————. *The Isaiah Effect: Decoding the Lost Science of Prayer and Prophecy.* New York: Harmony, 2000.

Charpentier, Louis. *The Mysteries of Chartres Cathedral.* Translated by Ronald Fraser in collaboration with Janette Jackson. London: Research into Lost Knowledge Organization; Distributed by Thorsons, 1972. (New York: Avon Books, 1966.)

Chopra, Deepak. *Creating Affluence: The A-to-Z Steps to a Richer Life.* Novato, CA: New World Library/Amber-Allen Publishing, 1998.

Emoto, Masaru. *The Hidden Messages in Water.* New York: Atria Books/Beyond Words Publishing, 2004.

The Findhorn Community. *The Findhorn Garden: Pioneering a New Vision of Man and Nature in Cooperation*. New York: Harper & Row, 1975.

———. *The Findhorn Garden: Pioneering a New Vision of Humanity and Nature in Cooperation*. Forres, Scotland: Findhorn Press, 2003.

Freuchen, Peter. *Peter Freuchen's Book of Eskimos*. New York: Fawcett Books, 1989.

Gladwell, Malcolm. *Blink: The Power of Thinking without Thinking*. New York: Little, Brown, 2005.

Hansard, Christopher. *The Tibetan Art of Living: Wise Body, Mind, Life*. New York: Atria Books, 2002.

Ingerman, Sandra. *Medicine for the Earth: How to Transform Personal and Environmental Toxins*. New York: Three Rivers, 2000.

Jung, Carl. *The Earth Has a Soul: The Nature Writings of C. G. Jung*. Edited by Meredith Sabini. Berkeley, CA: North Atlantic Books, 2002.

Lenz, Frederick. *Surfing the Himalayas: A Spiritual Adventure*. New York: St. Martin's, 1995.

McDonough, William, and Michael Braungart. *Cradle to Cradle: Remaking the Way We Make Things*. New York: North Point, 2002.

MacLaine, Shirley. *The Camino: A Journey of the Spirit*. New York: Simon and Schuster, Pocket Books, 2000.

Maclean, Dorothy. *To Hear the Angels Sing: An Odyssey of Co-Creation with the Devic Kingdom*. Great Barrington, MA: Lindisfarne Books, 1994.

Maclean, Dorothy, and Kathleen Thormod Carr. *To Honor the Earth: Reflections on Living in Harmony with Nature*. New York: HarperCollins, 1991.

Marcus, Clare Cooper. *House as a Mirror of Self: Exploring the Deeper Meaning of Home*. Berkeley, CA: Conari, 1995.

Marks, William E. *The Holy Order of Water: Healing Earth's Waters and Ourselves*. Great Barrington, MA: Bell Pond Books, 2001.

Matsuzaki, Toyoko. *The Healing Power of Hado*. With Natsumi Blackwell. New York: Atria Books/Beyond Words Publishing, 2006.

Michell, John. *The New View over Atlantis*. New York: Thames and Hudson, 1995.

Miller, Hamish, and Paul Broadhurst. *Dance of the Dragon*. New York: Pendragon, 2000.

Newberg, Andrew, Eugene d'Aquili, and Vince Rause. *Why God Won't Go Away: Brain Science and the Biology of Belief*. New York: Ballantine Books, 2001.

Pogačnik, Marko. *Healing the Heart of the Earth: Restoring the Subtle Levels of Life*. Forres, Scotland: Findhorn Press, 1998.

———. *Nature Spirits and Elemental Beings: Working with the Intelligence in Nature*. Forres, Scotland: Findhorn Press, 1995

Pollio, Marcus Vitruvius. *De Architectura (Ten Books on Architecture)*. New York: Benjamin Blom, 1968.

Sangharakshita. *Rituals and Devotion in Buddhism: An Introduction*. Birmingham, UK: Windhorse Publications, 1996.

Schwenk, Theodor. *Sensitive Chaos: The Creation of Flowing Forms in Water and Air*. London: Rudolf Steiner, 1990.

Senge, Peter, C. Otto Scharmer, Joseph Jaworski, and Betty Sue Flowers. *Presence: Exploring Profound Change in People, Organizations, and Society*. New York: Currency Doubleday, 2005.

Sheldrake, Rupert. *New Science of Life: The Hypothesis of Morphic Resonance*. Rochester, VT: Park Street, 1981.

Smith, Thomas Gordon. *Vitruvius on Architecture*. New York: Monacelli, 2004.

Swan, James A., ed. *The Power of Place: Sacred Ground in Natural and Human Environments*. Wheaton, IL: Quest Books, 1991.

Turner, Victor. *Celebration: Studies in Festivity and Ritual*. Washington, DC: Smithsonian Institution Press, 1982.

Venolia, Carol. *Healing Environments: Your Guide to Indoor Well-Being*. Berkeley, CA: Celestial Arts, 1988.

Venolia, Carol, and Kelly Lerner. *Natural Remodeling for the Not-So-Green House: Bringing Your Home into Harmony with Nature*. Asheville, NC: Lark Books, 2006.

Wright, Machaelle Small. *Behaving as If the God in All Life Mattered.* 3rd ed. Warrenton, VA: Perelandra, 1997.

———. *Perelandra Microbial Balancing Program Manual: Revised and User-Friendly.* Warrenton, VA: Perelandra, 2004.

WEB

City Repair Project
www.cityrepair.org

Findhorn Foundation
www.findhorn.org

H. H. Grandmaster Professor Lin Yun Rinpoche
www.yunlintemple.org

Portland Chinese Garden
www.portlandchinesegarden.org

Tom Brown, Jr.'s Tracker School
www.trackerschool.com

Sacred Sites and Pilgrimage Traditions of the World
www.sacredsites.com

FENG SHUI BOOKS FROM THE BLACK SECT TANTRIC BUDDHIST TRADITION

Kennedy, David Daniel. *Feng Shui for Dummies.* New York: Hungry Minds, 2001.

Post, Steven. *The Modern Book of Feng Shui: Vitality and Harmony for the Home and Office.* Dell Publishing, 1998.

Rossbach, Sarah. *Interior Design with Feng Shui: New and Expanded.* New York: Penguin/Arkana, 2000.

Rossbach, Sarah, and Master Lin Yun. *Feng Shui Design: From History and Landscape to Modern Gardens and Interiors.* London: Sidgwick & Jackson, 1998.

———. *Living Color: Master Lin Yun's Guide to Feng Shui and the Art of Color.* New York: Kodansha International, 1994.

SantoPietro, Nancy. *Feng Shui and Health: The Anatomy of a Home; Using Feng Shui to Disarm Illness, Accelerate Recovery, and Create Optimal Health.* New York: Three Rivers, 2002.

RESOURCES FOR BUILDERS AND REMODELERS

GreenHomeGuide
www.greenhomeguide.com
This is an informative consumer-oriented site that lists earth-friendly products, services, and building professionals, along with a database of articles from its monthly newsletter. According to the website, GreenHomeGuide has "developed our publication standards and rating systems in consultation with the leading green building professionals, researchers, and scientists who comprise our Advisory Board, Technical Advisory Council, and Scientific Advisory Council."

U.S. Green Building Council (USGBC)
www.usgbc.org
The U.S. Green Building Council (USGBC), a "coalition of leaders from across the building industry working to promote buildings that are environmentally responsible, profitable and healthy places to live and work," has more than 6,000 member organizations. Its internationally recognized LEED Green Building Rating System® is perhaps the most widely used standard for sustainable construction.

Energy & Environmental Building Association (EEBA)
www.eeba.org
An educational and supportive site for builders, EEBA's commendable aim is "to transform the residential design, development and construction industries to profitably deliver energy efficiency and environmentally responsible buildings and communities."

Green Resource Center
www.greenresourcecenter.org
This resource is a creation of the American Institute of Architects (AIA) Committee on the Environment (COTE), which "works to sustain and

improve the environment by advancing and disseminating environmental knowledge and values, and advocating the best design practices to integrate built and natural systems to the profession, industry, and public."

DOWSING RESOURCES

Bird, Christopher. *Divining Hand: The Art of Searching for Water, Oil, Minerals, and Other Natural Resources or Anything Lost, Missing, or Badly Needed*. Atglen, PA: Whitford Press, 1993.

Graves, Tom. *Diviner's Handbook: A Guide to the Timeless Art of Dowsing*. Rochester, VT: Destiny Books, Inner Traditions, 1990.

The British Society of Dowsers
www.britishdowsers.org
This organization is one of the oldest and most venerable of its kind. Its large, informative website lists other dowsing groups around the world. Many local dowsing societies offer books, classes, and other information. Note that performance quality varies widely from group to group and among individuals within each group.

Mid-Atlantic Geomancy
www.geomancy.org
This organization maintains a private, scholarly website packed with information and an extensive well-annotated bibliography.

EARTH INTUITIVES

Earth intuition is a new field for the twenty-first century. Some of these websites can inform you about professionals who are related to earth intuition in your area and who are qualified by their professional standards. Some are individual teachers who have many years of experience in related fields such as shamanism, Celtic music traditions, feng shui, and healing. Many of these earth intuitives offer programs and trainings. Research carefully and follow your own intuition before selecting an earth intuitive to work with.

Lynn V. Andrews, founder of the Lynn Andrews Center for Sacred Arts Training
www.lynnandrews.com

RESOURCES

William Bloom, PhD
www.williambloom.com

Tom Brown, Jr.'s Tracker School
www.trackerschool.com

Feng Shui Directory of Consultants and Schools™
www.fengshuidirectory.com

The Foundation for Shamanic Studies
www.shaminism.org

Healing Light Center Church
www.rosalynbruyere.org

The International Feng Shui Guild
www.fengshuiguild.com

Kahuna Source
www.kahunasource.com

The Lorian Association
http://lorian.bigmindcatalyst.com

Kathleen Welsh Luiten
www.kathleenluiten.com

Perelandra Center for Nature Research
www.perelandra-ltd.com

R. J. Stewart
www.dreampower.com

Ann Marie Holmes offers consultations and training.
Visit her website at www.annmarieholmes.com
for more information or to share any stories
and insights you might have.
She would love to hear from you.